'Putting on a Show'

'PUTTING ON A SHOW'

THE INSIDE STORY OF CHESTERFIELD FC'S
RECORD-BREAKING 2023/24 SEASON

LIAM NORCLIFFE

verticaleditions.com

First published in the United Kingdom in 2024 by Vertical
Editions, Unit 41 Regency Court, Sheffield, S35 9ZQ

VERTICAL
editions
www.verticaleditions.com

Follow us on Twitter:
@VerticalEds
@LiamNorcliffe

Cover images courtesy of Tina Jenner

ISBN 978-191-7117-012

First Edition

A CIP catalogue record for this book
is available from the British Library

Printed and bound by Jellyfish
Print Solutions, Swanmore, Hants

CONTENTS

"Our lads are down, but we've got to feel that pain. That's what football's about; you must feel pain. and we're feeling that at the minute. But hopefully, tomorrow's a better day for our club."

Paul Cook, Wembley Stadium, May 13, 2023

1

97 YEARS

It was a punch to the gut. It did not feel real. Surely not. How had it gone so wrong? Why had things been allowed to get so bad? You wanted it to be a nightmare that you would be woken up from immediately. Any minute now, someone was going to shout your name or give you a nudge and the ordeal would be over. *If only.* The cold truth hurt. And sadly it was just the start of an extremely long road back.

It was Tuesday, April 24, 2018 and Morecambe had just drawn 0-0 at home to Cambridge United. It was a sleepy encounter that got barely even a mention, maybe a couple of lines, in the following day's newspapers. It was a result that mattered so much to Chesterfield, but yet so little, because the damage had been done long before. It was the final nail in the coffin, but a coffin which had been ready to swallow them up for quite some time. That goalless draw, 100 miles away, meant they were relegated to the National League. They were out of the Football League for the first time since 1921. Ninety-seven proud years. After back-to-back relegations, non-league football was calling. They had gone down with a whimper. They had not even played. It was a nothing way to go. But it was one very much appropriate for the way things had been unfolding.

That night, dispirited fans tuned into *Sky Sports News* as the yellow ticker tape moved across the bottom of the screen. "Chesterfield have been relegated from League Two" travelled from left to right and it kept on coming back around. It was a reminder more distressing than a Monday morning alarm clock. Then the league table popped up. There was an "R" next to Chesterfield's name. They were below the dreaded dotted line and there was no way out. They had run out of time.

Morecambe's stalemate meant that the rock-bottom Spireites were 10 points from safety with just three games remaining. They were goners.

While some tortured themselves by following the action in Lancashire, others went to bed without even checking the score. They didn't need telling what they already knew.

Three days earlier, Chesterfield had made the trip down to Gloucestershire to face fellow strugglers Forest Green Rovers. If Town had any chance of avoiding the drop, they had to win. Making the journey south that day was supporter Paul Fisher, now a commentator for *BBC Radio Sheffield*, along with his brother Gareth and dad David. There was a sense of fear and trepidation as they set off for the three-hour trek in Gareth's Vauxhall Astra Estate. But it wasn't the car or their route that they were worried about, but their beloved football team.

As they edged closer to their destination, they stopped off at a real ale pub in Stroud, where other Blues had also gathered, before continuing the last five miles down to Nailsworth. From there, they used the park and ride to The New Lawn Stadium, for Chesterfield's first-ever visit there. It wouldn't be a fond one. A few more drinks in the fan zone at the ground. No amount of alcohol, though, was going to lure them into a false sense of hope, or ease the pain that was to come.

Despite looking like they were going to fall through the trapdoor, the Spireites were backed by a strong following, on what was initially an overcast day. The sun came out in the second half. But make no mistake. This was one of the darkest days in the club's 152-year history. "The atmosphere was subdued and tense," Fisher recalled. "There was an inevitability about it. The writing had been on the wall for a while."

Chesterfield actually played okay on the day, but they conceded soft goals and squandered good chances, which was the story of their season. They eventually lost 4-1, with two goals shipped in during added-time as the visitors threw men forward in a bid to salvage their survival hopes. "It was a microcosm of the season," Fisher said.

When Christian Doidge put Forest Green 2-1 up with 12 minutes remaining, a lone Town fan, wearing dark jeans and a grey polo shirt, ran onto the pitch and headed in the direction of the dugout to express his frustration. He was eventually stopped in his tracks by a steward, who was supported by future Spireites Haydn Hollis and Gavin Gunning. It was a desperate one-man protest from someone who was watching his club drown. It was sad. As the full-time whistle was blown, Laurence Maguire and Drew Talbot both sank to the floor, heads bowed.

Talbot, a two-time title winner and Johnstone's Paint Trophy champion with Chesterfield, had returned to the club earlier in the season in December. "When I came back, I wasn't sure what I was coming back to because I think the club was a little bit different from when I had left it," he later told *Legends of a Spire* podcast. "We played Accrington Stanley in my first game and we got beat 4-0. I remember ringing my wife and saying: 'We'll be alright,' because we had played really well but conceded some really sloppy goals. And then we beat Luton, who were top of the league and I thought we were going to be alright. But we just never got going. We would win a couple and then we would lose so many. It was tough. It was not enjoyable.

"Being relegated is one of the worst things as a footballer. I thought I could come back and lift people and help out, but it just wasn't to be. It was really disappointing and I did not take it well. In that game at Forest Green away, I gave a penalty away and that was pure frustration and anger that we had let people down who had put trust in us. I remember sitting there thinking: 'This is not right.' It bothered me big time."

Over in the open terraced West Stand, a handful of frustrated fans, mainly youngsters, gathered at the front and flung their arms about in anger as the players came over to applaud the away following. Like many others, Fisher, his brother and his dad, sloped away back to Derbyshire with a feeling of emptiness. Chesterfield were nine points from safety with three games to go and with a goal difference of 19 worse than Morecambe, they were as good as down. "That's that, then," they thought as they pushed on back up the motorway. Saying very little, apart from looking at the opponents that were beckoning in the fifth tier.

In the press box that day at Forest Green was journalist Graham Smyth, reporting on the Spireites for the *Derbyshire Times* newspaper. At the end of the game, Smyth looked on as manager and club legend, Jack Lester, trudged his way across the pitch towards them. "He looked like he had the weight of the world on his shoulders," Smyth said. During his post-match discussion with reporters, Lester appeared to know what was around the corner. "Whatever happens at this club, I'm sure they'll come back," he said. "I've been in the driving seat when it's gone down so whatever decision the club makes, we'll wait and see. It's just shocking. I'm so sad about it."

Smyth remembered Lester being emotional and downbeat and one moment has always stuck in his mind. When he finished his interview, he took his headphones off, put the mic down and said: "I'm sorry," before walking back across the pitch. He looked bereft of life. He looked like the life had been drained out of him. It was like he had been kicked in the gut."

Lester, Chesterfield's heroic number 14 as a player, had taken over from Gary Caldwell at the end of September, but had only managed to win nine of his 37 games in charge. Two days after Forest Green, he left by mutual consent. "I'm desperately sorry I've not been able to save the club from relegation," he said in a statement.

Lifelong fan Phil Tooley — who has volunteered at the club since 1977 and who played an instrumental part in helping to save it, along with the Chesterfield Football Supporters Society (CFSS) following Darren Brown's disastrous ownership spell in 2000 — had been reporting for *BBC Radio Sheffield* at Forest Green and had found it really tough. He was in bits. "That day was my worst supporting Chesterfield, by some chalks," Tooley said. "There was no day lower. Forest Green had just come up and they resembled where we were going to. It was a case of: 'Is this what we are in for?' I did not say anything on the way home. It was the quietest of journeys. From a historical perspective, it was a real shock. The club had been on a downward spiral since Paul Cook left, but we didn't think we would be looking at National League fixtures three years later. Like most people, I thought we would sail straight back up."

Smyth and Tooley both attended Chesterfield's pre-season training camp in Portugal and they both recalled coming away feeling positive. Caldwell and the players had said all the right things, they had worked really hard and were trying to implement a certain style of play. But it soon became obvious that they couldn't do it and they won just one of their first 10 matches. The eighth game of the season was a 5-1 defeat at Crewe Alexandra, and Smyth and Tooley specifically remember Caldwell coming out onto the pitch afterwards with chairman Mike Warner and company secretary Ashley Carson. The trio spoke and then shook hands, which gave the impression that Caldwell had just been told he was out of a job. That observation was accurate. But after Caldwell went back into the dressing room to tell the players, the squad got the decision reversed and Caldwell was reinstated. His reprieve only lasted two more matches, though and he was sacked again after a 2-1 home loss to Accrington Stanley. "It absolutely flattened me," said Warner on relegation to the National League. "To lose your Football League status is beyond disappointing, really."

Under Lester, there had been some glimpses of hope, with successive wins against Exeter City and Forest Green Rovers in November and against Luton Town and Yeovil Town in January. But such results were few and far between. A 3-1 home victory against Notts County in March put the Spireites within three points of Grimsby Town with two games in hand and with the next three fixtures against teams down at the bottom with them, it gave everyone some optimism. But they collected just one point against Port Vale, Grimsby Town and Morecambe and from that point, relegation seemed inevitable for a lot of fans. A 1-0 home loss to rivals Mansfield only added to the misery. The defeat at Forest Green was their third in a row, and they had lost five of their last six. But most fans had accepted that Chesterfield were going down weeks before.

The general consensus was that Lester was the right man but at the wrong time. He was a great guy, a club legend, and everyone was willing him to do well. It just didn't work out. He wasn't beyond criticism, but most people understood the problems ran much deeper than him. The poisoned chalice had been poisoned long before. Overall, the mismanagement of the club, wrong managerial appointments at the wrong times and poor recruitment were all to blame. The Spireites were not together as one.

"To play under Jack Lester was a massive honour for me, he made me the captain again, but we probably just let him down," Talbot added. "We were definitely trying our best but it just did not marry up right. I took it personally that I had let him down, because he brought me back to try and revive us."

Apart from for financial reasons, Chesterfield had never really come close to losing their league status. Until 2018, they were the only one of the Division Three North founding members who hadn't resigned, been voted out or relegated from the Football League. But club historian Stuart Basson had predicted that tough times were around the corner, when they were struggling down at the bottom of League One the year before. This was just the start, he felt. "Relegation was absolutely unnecessary but inevitable," he said.

Off the pitch, the club was rotten. The management above playing level was being reflected in performances on the field. There had been a number of embarrassments and scandals, including the controversial signing of Ched Evans, the winner of a raffle being faked, and the club being fined by the Football Association for breaching financial rules relating to two players' wages being paid by a private football academy linked to the Spireites, despite being legally separate. The same academy was later liquidated. All of this was reported by the *Derbyshire Times*, who were temporarily banned. A peaceful protest against the running of the club would later be organised in December 2018. One banner read: "Scandal after scandal. What next?"

"There was a dreadful feeling about the club," Basson said. "It was being run really badly." Tooley described the situation as "awful," adding: "It was a laughing stock." Three years earlier, in May 2015, Chesterfield were in the League One play-offs and had a genuine chance of reaching the Championship. Now, after painful back-to-back relegations, they were facing non-league football for the first time in 97 years. It was grim.

2

0.08

A National League statement dropped into the inbox. The five paragraphs outlined how the 2019/20 season, Chesterfield's second in the fifth-tier, would be decided following the outbreak of Covid-19, which had led to a national lockdown and meant no more matches could be played. Clubs had been voting on how best to end the campaign and they had settled on a points per game (PPG) method. In the press release, chief executive Michael Tattersall congratulated Barrow on their promotion to League Two as champions of the National League, King's Lynn Town for winning the National League North and Wealdstone for claiming the National League South crown. There was no mention of Chesterfield.

If there had been, it would have been headlined: "Survived by the skin of their teeth." To be exact, by 0.08 of a point. That is how close the Spireites came to being relegated to the National League North. From the cusp of the Championship to almost tumbling into regional football. How the mighty had fallen. Had they plummeted, some believe that could have been the end of the Spireites as we know it. It could have been phoenix club territory.

Hopes had been high for a successful campaign after John Sheridan, who had been reappointed as manager after the sacking of Martin Allen, had guided them away from relegation to 15th in their first season at this level. But it was a false dawn. Chesterfield did not win any of their first 10 games and Sheridan was eventually sacked on January 2, 2020, with Town third from bottom. Just one victory in 12 had left them five points from safety. Looking from the outside, they didn't look fit enough, didn't have an identity. It didn't seem like anyone was enjoying their football.

The decision to sack Sheridan was made after it was announced that the community trust was trying to complete a takeover of the club from owner Dave Allen. It would later get over the line that summer, in August. Company secretary, Ashley Carson, said at the time: "The decision was taken after full discussion with majority shareholder Dave Allen and also with Mike Goodwin, chairman of the community trust, who is heading up the potential takeover of the club. Whilst I think we all knew the time was right to make this change, it is important that I work very closely with Mike, as ultimately we look forward to a change of ownership very soon. There will be a joint plan going forward so that any decisions taken regarding the appointment of a new manager will be made in full agreement with the community trust."

John Pemberton, who had been working in the academy, was placed in caretaker charge and he galvanised the squad as Chesterfield won five of his nine matches, losing just twice. They were more organised, looked fitter and were harder to beat. The results included hard-fought victories against Sutton United and Eastleigh, a last-gasp 3-2 win over Wrexham and a 4-0 hammering of Ebbsfleet United, inspired by a second half hat-trick from Nathan Tyson. In doing so, Tyson became the first ever Chesterfield substitute to come on and score a treble. "I am very, very proud of that," Tyson reflected. "People think that when you break a record at a club it is a small thing but it isn't. It is a real honour. I just hope the record stands for some time."

But the biggest win of all came on March 7, at rock-bottom Chorley. All eyes had been on this fixture for a while and there was no underestimating its importance. For all Chesterfield's improved results, they had not been out of the relegation zone for three months — so three points represented a chance to poke their heads above water. It was a huge clash anyway, but it became even more crucial with what was to come.

On a slanted, bobbly pitch, the Spireites could have been three or four up by half-time but only led by a single goal at the break, a close-range Tom Denton header from a corner. Just after the hour, Tyson set-up long throw specialist Jordan Cropper for the second, but they made hard work of it and ended clinging on when the hosts pulled one back. Pemberton went onto the pitch at full-time and punched the air in front of the travelling fans, who breathed a huge sigh of relief.

They didn't know it back then, but Chesterfield could not have timed their escape any better. Had they lost, it could have been the penultimate match the club ever played. "I would suggest that that was the biggest win in Chesterfield's history," die-hard fan Phil Tooley explained. "I remember coming back absolutely relieved. It was a major, major victory."

Tyson said: "Looking back now, it is like: 'Wow.' That was the game that actually saved us from going down." His teammate Denton told us: "We should never have been in that position, so it is a good job we stayed up. Otherwise they would not be in the position they are in now. Looking back now, it was huge."

The following week, all Premier League and Football League matches were suspended until April 3 because of the seriousness of the coronavirus, with several clubs reporting players with symptoms. However, the National League, surprise surprise, decided to continue, although only five fixtures went ahead. Before travelling down to Dover on the Friday, Chesterfield asked the league for advice. Defender Haydn Hollis and a few others had not been feeling well. The squad had been waiting around at the ground for ages before they had to make the long journey south.

"They did not come back to us," Pemberton said. "We were hanging on and on and we just had to make a decision to go to Dover. What I did not want to do was put it on myself to cancel the game and not travel down and the club end up with a fine. I did not know where we stood on it."

Whilst down in Dover, Tyson remembered the game being in the balance even up to the point of arriving at the Crabble Stadium, after hearing that one of Dover's players had fallen ill. He said: "It was a weird time. We didn't know what was going on. We wanted to play the game but we were also like: 'Should we be playing?'"

The match did go ahead and Denton continued his fine form, scoring from the penalty spot in the 80th minute, his fifth goal in eight games, to give Chesterfield the lead. But they conceded a late equaliser and had to settle for a point. That ended up being the last game Spireites fans were allowed to attend for 14 months because two days later, the National League season was halted and, although it was initially scheduled to restart again on April 3, in line with the other leagues, the country later went into lockdown. The final table was decided on PPG in June.

Chesterfield had finished the season with 1.16 points per game. Ebbsfleet United (1.08), AFC Fylde (1.05) and Chorley (0.68) were the three that went down, with Maidenhead United only surviving because of the knock-on effects of League One Bury going bust, which meant that the leagues needed to be balanced out. Had it not been for Pemberton, Tyson's hat-trick, Denton's goals and those four points from Chorley and Dover, Chesterfield would have been relegated for a third season in four years. Maybe they would have come straight back up. Perhaps they would still be down there now. Or maybe the club would no longer exist in its current form.

"My personal opinion is that we would not have gone down anyway," Pemberton said. "I think we had turned a corner. I think we had shown more than enough in the games that we had, that we were strong enough to stay in the division." Tyson agreed. "Had the coronavirus not happened," he said, "I do believe we would have finished higher up."

In years to come, when fans would be asked about important games of the past, "Chorley away" would be on the tip of their tongue. That was Chesterfield's lowest ebb and thankfully there were brighter days to come.

3

TRUST IN THE TRUST

The sun beamed down on 1866 Sheffield Road as a new era beckoned. There were smiles on faces. Everyone had a spring in their step. The dark clouds had made way for fresh optimism. The scarves were out. It is always a good day when the scarves are out.

It was August 7, 2020. The government's Eat Out to Help Out scheme, which offered a 50 per cent discount on food and drinks in restaurants and pubs during the coronavirus pandemic had been introduced. It was welcomed by business owners, but slammed by scientists. Later that month, some lockdown restrictions would be eased further, with indoor theatres, bowling alleys and soft play areas all allowed to open.

On Whittington Moor, the community trust, the club's charitable arm, were about to give their first press conference after completing a takeover of the club from Dave Allen. They had made history by becoming the first of its kind to own a football club. The trust, a registered charity with supporters at the heart of it, was founded in 2009 and does tremendous work with people young and old around sport, education and health. It started out in a Portakabin at the stadium with three or four people, with chief executive John Croot at the forefront of it. After moving into a bigger and more modern base in The Hub in the East Stand in 2013, they are now engaging with thousands of people a year and really making a difference.

They had first registered their interest in buying the club the previous October and had hoped to get the deal over the line much sooner but for delays, with the pandemic not helping the situation. But they got there in the end, with the help of Derbyshire County Council and Chesterfield Borough Council, who had both loaned them £500,000 each. A local consortium with good intentions had tried to get a deal done but they couldn't make it work and so the trust decided it was down to them. Had they not done so, there was a very real possibility that the football club, and the trust itself, may have ceased to exist.

When the idea was first floated, there were lots of question marks and doubts about whether a charitable trust could own a football club. Peter Whiteley, a supporter since 1972 who was working for the trust at the time before being made club company secretary when the takeover was completed, said: "I thought it would not be practical. I wasn't even sure if it would be legal. It had never happened before; there was no precedent. It was a case of: 'Can we do it and should we do it?' I initially thought that it couldn't happen and that it wouldn't happen. It wasn't because I didn't want the model that we ended up with, but more because I just didn't think it would be possible financially. And whether, in governance terms, the charity could be the absolute owner of its own elite sports club."

As time went on and legal advice was sought, it became apparent that there was nothing that said it couldn't be done, as long as the finances were in order. Lots of due diligence was undertaken on the football club itself and the trust's own business plan was scrutinised before they managed to get it over the line. The prospect of a deal was kept secret for a long time, with community trust chairman Mike Goodwin writing to Allen in October 2019, before it was made public two months later. That letter, by the way, is on show in the trophy cabinet in reception for everyone to see along with the Spireites' other silverware. That precious piece of paper represents the day the fans got their club back.

For all his criticism, Allen had always said he wanted to hand the club over to the fans and did so, having taken a significant financial hit personally. Later on, he would receive payment following promotion back to the Football League and the takeover by the Kirk brothers, which was agreed as part of the initial deal with the community trust. It had not been all bad under Allen. He had taken the club into a beautiful new stadium, there had been two League Two titles, a Johnstone's Paint Trophy triumph and they had come close to getting into the Championship. But after losing in the League One play-offs in 2015, he opted to go in a different direction, resulting in manager Paul Cook leaving and the squad being ripped apart. And everything went downhill from there; back-to-back relegations, scandals, fans not attending games and sponsors stepping away. It was toxic.

One person who was on the receiving end of some criticism when the club was on its downward spiral was director Croot, who helped save the club in 2001 along with the Chesterfield Football Supporters' Society (CFSS) and who became chief executive when the trust took over. But rather than disappear into the background when he was under fire, Croot decided that it would be better that he stayed so that someone knew what was going on behind the scenes. The result of that was personal abuse online.

"I stayed simply for the club really," he said. "It would have been easy to have walked away really on a number of occasions. I always felt I had a wealth of experience. It is somewhat ironic that some other clubs would ring and ask me for advice, which happened a lot over the last 10 years, and yet people at your own club who were in positions of power don't take advice or treat you seriously. It was quite clear that the powers-that-be were struggling to get somebody to sell the club and, just like in 2001, somebody, at some point, was going to have to step in."

And it's a good job he did stay because although the trust was made up of highly intelligent and professional people, Croot was the one with the inside knowledge of the football club and was able to quickly identify the areas that needed fixing. "The relationship with supporters was broken because of things that had gone on in the past," he said. "With supporters, you have got to be truthful with them. If mistakes are made, the best thing you can do is hold your hands up."

With Allen wanting out and some murky characters circling like sharks, the club could have fallen into the wrong hands. For the second time in 20 years, the supporters, with the help of the two councils, had rescued it. A new era was beginning. "It was a relief when it happened," Whiteley said. "At the point where the deal was done, and we knew the next day that we were going to walk into the stadium as the owners of it, it was brilliant. And then the hard work started. The amount of goodwill that we got was astonishing, and it has continued."

The role of the two councils should also not be forgotten. Had the town lost its football club then it would have had a detrimental effect on the local area. At the time, Councillor Tricia Gilby, leader of Chesterfield Borough Council, said: "Chesterfield Football Club has been an integral part of life here in Chesterfield borough for over 150 years. "Football has the power to change people's lives for the better. At such a difficult time for all of us, we believe the club and trust have key roles to play in supporting Chesterfield's social and economic recovery. "We've been impressed by the trust's approach in looking at all aspects of the club's financial and business affairs, and we think it's the right thing for the council to do to back the trust at this time." And Councillor Barry Lewis, leader of Derbyshire County Council, said: "We're confident that the trust can breathe new life into the club."

Before their press conference, the trust had been encouraged not to make any big headline-grabbing statements that could come back to bite them; like saying they wanted to reach the Championship in five years. That advice would also be passed on to the Kirk brothers a few years later. Instead, the trust went for a more sensible and measured approach. Give us a chance, they said. We want to make the club sustainable, they explained. It's not going to be easy, they admitted. They played it just right. And when you look back at what they said at the time, they were true to their word.

"To have the club back in the hands of the supporters I think is a tremendous thing for Chesterfield and the surrounding area," Goodwin told the room. "It means the world to me because I have been a supporter for over 60 years. And to be able to influence it and to be able to help save the club, help make it sustainable for the future, is personally very satisfying. It is going to be difficult and I know people are going to be sceptical, particularly around finances because people want success on the field. But it's not all about success on the field. It's a large part and I accept that. People will judge us in future on what our league position is and I hope we can deliver on that. But it is important for me that this club is preserved for future generations. My grandchildren will come down, and this club will still be here for them. Sustainability is a key factor for me."

He continued: "One of the first things I want to do is talk to the supporters. I want to get them down here and I want them to ask open and transparent questions, and I want to be open and transparent with them. That is something that is not just important to me but to the whole of the board. Nobody wants to hide anything. There will be no surprises with us. What you see is what you get. We are all supporters of the club. We want it to feel like a family, community-owned club where everybody's happy to come down. We want to put some goodwill and some good feeling back into Chesterfield Football Club. It has broken my heart over the last five years to see us drop into non-league football. And if I can do anything to stop the rot and push back the other way then I will do that."

When the trust got the keys to the club, they found it pretty much mothballed. On the day of the press conference, the poor state of the pitch stood out like a sore thumb. The grass had not been cut and there were daisies poking through. When the trust rang the contractor, Premier Pitches, to find out what was happening, the response was that they were owed money. So the first thing the trust did was pay the bill. It wasn't the only pressing issue. The majority of the stadium's safety certificates had expired, there were weeds growing in parts of the stadium and £20,000 had to be spent on clearing up after the pigeons.

The trust had also been expecting to receive £150,000 from Leeds United following their promotion to the Premier League. When defender Liam Cooper moved to Elland Road in 2014, the Spireites negotiated a deal which meant they would get the six-figure sum if Leeds went up and Cooper made enough appearances. They did, and he did. The trust thought that they would get the money, only to find the club had already received it before they took over. Goodwin said at the time: "We are naturally very disappointed to have missed out on receiving a six-figure sum from the sell-on clause, but the matter was out of our hands.

"Having been assured that the payment was due to be received by the club this week, it was a great surprise when we took charge of the company bank account to learn that the money had already been transferred prior to the community trust taking ownership. It is disappointing, but we had factored in the possibility that this sum of money may not be available to us as it was all down to the timing of the payment and we had no way of influencing that."

In response, Allen said in a statement: "The long and protracted takeover has consistently been delayed by the community trust and the councils, not us. If they had got all their ducks in a row earlier then they would have obviously had the benefit of the money. If they had also conducted a final audit prior to purchasing the club they would have seen that the money had been already received before they went public in the press conference. You don't buy a house without taking a final meter reading. During the delays I had to inject a further £500,000 into the club, so I don't see a problem. They will of course benefit from any sell-on of Sam Morsy in the future, so I guess we are even."

When the trust took over, there were many sleepless nights about paying players' wages on time and the overall finances of the club. They saw themselves as custodians of the club and they didn't want to be remembered as the ones who took it under. When they first started putting their business plan together, they thought long and hard about whether they could do their calculations based on home crowds of 4,000. Attendances had been well below that — in fact, the last home game before the trust took over, against Harrogate Town, had a gate of 2,912. That number only further highlights the feeling at the time and the trust wanted to be cautious in their approach. Scarily, a home game against Yeovil Town in December 2019 saw only 1,700 come through the turnstiles.

Things were made even more difficult when coronavirus put the country into lockdown and ensured that the majority of the 2020/21 season, the trust's first in charge, was played behind closed doors without fans. The club would later secure a £1million loan from Sport England and there would be further funding from the National Lottery, although the National League was criticised for the way it distributed it. Rather than hand the money out based on lost gate receipts, a different formula was used, one which has never been revealed. What is known is that some clubs did a lot better out of it than others, despite boasting much smaller attendances. "That was shocking," Goodwin said.

Looking forward, the trust knew they wouldn't be able to run the club forever; the plan had always been to move it on to someone who could take it to the next level. Initially, they didn't know if they could get past two years. That is what their business plan told them. All they knew was that if they didn't take it on, then there might not have been a football club. They were told that the club was about a week away from its future being in serious doubt.

From the boardroom looking out over their beloved club, the trust had helped set the foundations for a successful future. What they probably didn't know, however, was that the good times would come sooner rather than later, albeit with a sprinkle of pain in between. "When we first took over four years ago, if you had said that we would be the driving force to get the club back in the EFL, we would have said you are crackers," Goodwin reflected. "We just wanted to make sure that there would be a football club for the future. The fact that we took it on was a huge personal risk to me and the rest of the trustees, because we could have been the board that took the club into oblivion. And that would have stuck with us forever."

On the pitch, the trust had been impressed with the job John Pemberton had done as caretaker manager and he was rewarded with a 12-month contract. But things didn't go to plan, and six defeats from the first eight league games left Chesterfield third from bottom when he left by mutual consent in November. Pemberton took a while to come out and speak to the press after a disappointing late 3-2 defeat at Altrincham and he was really down in his interview. So it didn't come as much of a surprise when his departure was announced the next morning. It also happened to be his birthday.

Goodwin had asked to meet him for a chat, with the intention of providing enough funds to bring in three loan players, but Pemberton had already made his mind up and he left. To his credit, rather than stick it out and pick up a wage when his heart maybe wasn't in it, he stepped away and was very reasonable when discussing terms. That night, Pemberton texted this author, thanking him for being fair with him, which meant a lot.

Rookie manager James Rowe, just 37 at the time, who had been top of the National League North with Gloucester City, was appointed in late November. He had blown the interview panel away with his enthusiasm and presentation, in which he showed clips of what his Gloucester side had been doing and compared it to what the Spireites had not been doing. Former Grimsby Town, Ipswich Town and Scunthorpe United manager Paul Hurst was also interviewed, but it was Rowe's energy that shone through.

Although he wasn't everyone's cup of tea, Rowe did have a knack of winning football matches and he ripped up the squad, making several new signings throughout the season and guiding Chesterfield from 21st to sixth. Eventually they lost 3-2 away to Notts County in the play-off elimination round, which was the first of three successive play-off heartaches for the club.

4

SAFE HANDS

It was Christmas 2021. The presents were under the tree, the crackers were ready to be pulled and *Home Alone* was on the TV. Ashley Kirk, having just sold his business, was looking towards the future. It just so happened that his brother, Phil, was also thinking about stepping away from his.

Over the years, whenever they had got together, the family had always teased the pair, in a light-hearted way, about them investing in the Spireites. It was a bit of a running joke but it had become a serious possibility. If anyone was going to get them involved it was Phil, Ashley laughed. "Because he's got the 'football money.'"

That Christmas, over a nice glass of red wine, Phil turned to Ashley and said: "Would you ever be interested in being a non-executive at Chesterfield Football Club? I am just thinking about investing." At the time, Chesterfield were top of the National League and Phil was planning on giving them some money to help get them promoted. "I was like: 'Wow, that would be really interesting … wouldn't that be nice?'" Ashley said.

As the festivities passed and 2022 arrived, along with the dark, cold January mornings, Ashley had not heard anything else about the idea. And then Phil rang. "I was skiing in Italy, up a mountain and I got a phone call from my brother saying: 'Right, that's it … I have made my mind up. We are going to do it.'"

The person linking all this together was the Spireites' chief financial officer Andy Fantom, who happened to live next door to Ashley and Phil's parents. Andy had been talking to Ashley and Phil's dad, over the garden fence, explaining that the community trust had saved the club, but now needed investors. "He was just talking to my dad about it, and then he was talking to us about it," Ashley said. "And then things aligned up for both my brother and I and things fell into place."

When Ashley came back from Italy, he and Phil went to meet Andy, chief executive John Croot and chairman Mike Goodwin to discuss how it might work and how they would want someone on the board if they were to give them some money. Everything was agreed, the legalities were completed and they decided to announce it at the next annual general meeting in March. In the past, when someone had expressed an interest in buying the club, it had not taken long to find out that they were a wrong 'un. But when fans researched the Kirk brothers, they heard nothing but good things. A quick Google search of Phil threw up positive articles in the *Financial Times.* Right from start, the signs were promising.

"We met them and straight away I could tell they were genuine," Croot said. "I have been in football a long time and I have spoken to a lot of people who said they had come to invest in this club. Generally within two to three minutes of meeting them I can tell they were not right."

Initially, they invested £1million into the club and Ashley joined the board. "Our only wish is to do good for the town and for the club," Phil said at the time. "There are no skeletons – look me up, it is all good." A year later, with the club's accounts showing a loss of £2.3million, they put in another £1million and took up a stake of 25 per cent. Reassuring supporters of their intentions, Phil told shareholders: "I am not going to change the team I support. I am here for the long haul."

A few months down the line, in October 2023, the club was still burning cash and another £1.4million was handed over, their stake increasing to 40 per cent. The further cash injection was for building a squad capable of achieving promotion, paying off some players who were not part of their plans, improving the training ground and repaying the loans to Chesterfield Borough Council, Derbyshire County Council and Sport England.

As time went on, the brothers realised that the club would need more and more financial support. It was running on fumes. So they had a decision to make whether they were going to go for it or not. Had the brothers not invested in the first place, the club would have had to cut its cloth and the budget would only have been enough for a mid-table finish in the National League.

"It became clear that the club was in some sort of peril and needed some more serious help," Ashley said. "As the seasons rolled on it became clear that having a charity, i.e. the trust, owning the club was not really feasible. We had a long, hard chat and came to the conclusion that someone had to do it so it might as well be us. The conversation was: 'Are we pushing ahead?' We decided that we were and here we are."

So, at the AGM in March 2024, proposals for them to invest another £2million and become the majority owners with a share of 80 per cent, with the community trust owning 15 per cent and the fans the remaining five, were approved. But as proceedings got underway, you could feel things becoming a bit skewed. People were missing the point. The latest accounts showed a loss of £2.1million. It was acknowledged as a significant loss but it was not a massive surprise. Whilst ever Chesterfield were in the National League they were always going to struggle to balance the books.

Based on what was said the year before, some people had expected a better set of results and there were one or two questions directed at the top table about that. But like all good leaders do, Phil steered the ship back in the right direction. He stood up, grabbed the microphone and said: "The club is now in a really good place. We are living the dream. I can't remember anything like this. It feels really special. I hope you are all cherishing this. It is funded. We are not going bust. We will have a hell of a time."

Those words settled everyone down and put people at ease. They weren't empty promises. You could tell by the tone that they came from the heart; anyone who has spent time with the Kirk brothers will know they are genuine people who are in it for the right reasons. The community trust had done its job by saving the club; now it was time to go to the next level. "Why would we do it? Because it's Chesterfield," Phil said. "There is no other club, obviously, that we would have done this for. I promised my dad to never do this because I know it can be a bit of a rabbit hole. But it is the right time, right place and right opportunity for the club, for me and for me and my brother to have a bit of fun and help the town. We are so incredibly proud to be from Chesterfield and what a special time. Hopefully, we can help the trust, who rescued the club, help it rise like a phoenix hopefully back to the Football League."

The likeable brothers are lifelong Spireites fans. Ashley has always lived in Chesterfield while Phil, who was part of the Chesterfield Football Supporters Society (CFSS), moved away during the mid-1980s and is based down south. A report in the *Financial Times,* who had earlier described Phil as "New King of the North Sea," described how he had turned Harbour Energy into the largest UK-listed independent oil and gas group, with a market capitalisation of £3.36bn. Ashley's recruitment firm CK Group, which he co-founded in 1991, was also very successful.

When Phil said his goodbyes, his offshore crews sent him a video of them all pictured in blue tops with "Spireites" emblazoned across the front of them. "They knew that once I walked away from that business that I loved, the first thing that I would be doing would be looking after my beloved Chesterfield," Phil said. "And here we are — living the dream."

The brothers are very close and they trust each other deeply. They agree on 95 per cent of things and have a good, honest, fair discussion about the rest. "We don't really have any ego between us … it works really well," Phil said. As well as financial backing, they set about changing the culture of the club, which was stuck in its ways. "The attitude was: 'We have always done it this way,'" Ashley said. "There was a hangover, some stuff from the Saltergate days. Everything was a bit of a mystery. Departments didn't talk to each other. People needed to start trusting each other again. It was a culture change that needed to happen."

The brothers look back now and laugh at Phil's promise to his brother that he would only have to attend one boardroom meeting a month. Instead, Ashley works most days at the club and gets calls from Paul Cook at half past six in the morning! They chuckle at the idea that they thought they would just come along to matches, have a few beers and have a bit of fun. They never intended to take it over. They liked the community trust part of it and still do. But the more they got involved, the more they got involved, if that makes sense. And they caught the bug. The club gripped them both. They got a taste for it. And they've never looked back. "Once you're in, it is a bit like a drug," Ashley added.

Phil said: "People talk about Ash and I as businessmen and we are businessmen, but we are not in this to make money. We are in this for the town and to have a club that we are proud of, that lasts the test of time. I still do think we are fan-owned, because I am a fan. I didn't have much money 30-40 years ago but through a bit of luck and some hard work I've got some money — and wow, I can help my football team. Me and

Ash talk about the 10 or 20-year view, where the club will be and what if something happens to me or Ash now. How we would manage those sorts of things happening. It is an evolution, not a revolution."

In the time they have been at the club, they have proven to be a great pair of safe hands. Honest, humble, genuine people with the club's best interests at heart. And they don't half know what they are doing. In the modern era of Saudi and Abu Dhabi backers, the Kirks' ownership is a throwback to good local people doing good things for their local area. Good on them. As for the trust, they did their job. They and the councils came to the rescue before last orders were called. There aren't any sleepless nights anymore.

Chairman Mike Goodwin said: "To get two people like Phil and Ashley to want to help with the club was amazing." Company secretary Peter Whiteley added: "It does feel like a dream. You probably couldn't have picked better owners. They are people who love being part of it and certainly have the resources to make it successful."

5

4-2-3-1

It was raining. Of course it was. It always rains in Manchester. Chesterfield chief executive John Croot and chairman Mike Goodwin were on their way to a Manchester Airport hotel to meet the man they hoped would be the Spireites' new manager.

Croot had always kept in touch with Paul Cook, just as he had other managers like John Duncan, exchanging texts and phone calls here and there about football, players and things generally. Cook had always been a person they could go to for sound advice and he was happy to help.

After James Rowe's departure from the club at the start of February 2022, Croot dropped Cook a message to see if he would be willing to meet up. Although he agreed, the prospect of being able to persuade Cook, their former manager whose stock was much higher than National League level, to come back and drop down into non-league was a long shot, and they knew it. They had other options, because they understood the chances of being able to tempt Cook, who had been sacked by League One Ipswich Town just two months before, were slim. But he was the one they wanted. They felt they needed to bring a big personality back to the club. And you would have your work cut out finding a more larger-than-life character than Cook.

"Basically, I rang him one day and asked: 'Can we have a chat?'" Croot said. "We had a few telephone conversations and we arranged to meet. I thought we'd got a chance because I don't think he would have taken us over to Manchester Airport if he wasn't seriously considering it. There were rumours at that time that this club and that club were after him, and they were all EFL clubs. So it was hope rather than expectation I would say."

Goodwin was similarly enthused. "At the time we thought it was fantastic that he had agreed to meet us," he explained. "Because we knew it was a stretch for him to come from League One down to the National League. The only thread that we had was that Paul had been here before and he has always said that we gave him his first chance. So that was the only thing we were clinging to."

On the way to Manchester, Croot and Goodwin were plotting their game plan, their strategy, to try and pull off a massive coup and get Cook to return. They would tell him about their future plans and how he would be in charge of the whole footballing department, an autonomy he had not been afforded at Portman Road. At the same time, they knew they didn't have to "sell" the club to him because obviously he knew it inside out from his last spell.

Cook's feelings towards Chesterfield were still so strong that, during their meet in Manchester, he offered to lend a hand in any way that he could. Even if they couldn't strike a deal for him to be manager, he was happy to help caretaker Danny Webb with whatever he needed. He just wanted what was best for the club and that was his message right from the beginning of the talks. It was a sign of his love for the Spireites. Chesterfield held Webb in high regard and so whoever was to come in, whether it be Cook or someone else, they would make it clear that Webb was staying. "Danny had stood in the breach for us when we needed it, really," Croot said. "It was never even on the agenda that Danny wouldn't be here, that was just a given. He had been a loyal employee for us."

The discussions took place for a couple of hours but within five minutes, Goodwin knew he was the right man. He and Cook hit it off straight away. Understandably, Cook was a bit wary at the beginning. It was a risk for him. If it didn't work out, then that would have potentially left his managerial career in a tricky spot. Chesterfield, now in their fourth year in the National League, were second in the table at the time. There was only one place higher they could go, but plenty of room for them to fall. It was an unusual situation; normally a manager is hired when a club is struggling and the only way is up. But the Spireites were flying — and anybody coming in would not want to be seen as the person who messed it up.

"He was concerned that he didn't have a great knowledge of the league at that time and that was bothering him a bit," Croot said. "But knowing Paul as I do, I knew it would not take him long to get a grasp of it. I think, in truth, he knows leagues anyway. I think his idea of not knowing the league and our idea of not knowing the league are different things. I think that was the thing that was playing on his mind a bit. There was a big element of risk in it for Paul, but we had full trust in him."

The initial chat had gone well and both Croot and Goodwin had an inkling that they might have half a chance of persuading him to come. And the odds started to turn more in their favour when Cook agreed to meet them again at the same hotel. This time he brought Spireites favourite Gary Roberts, who had been his first-team coach at Ipswich, with him. In the second meeting, Goodwin and Croot were joined by chief financial officer Andy Fantom. There were more talks about their vision for the club and Cook explained where he wanted to take it and how he would do it. He spoke passionately about getting the building blocks in place, such as the training ground and recruitment team. "He said: 'There are no secrets to it,'" Goodwin said. "He said: 'If you build from the bottom upwards, you will have success.' And he has proved to be absolutely spot on with what he has said."

On Tuesday, February 8, Chesterfield were at Stockport County in a top-of-the table clash. Rowe had got the Blues competing for promotion before he was suspended, eventually leaving by mutual consent. His assistant, Webb, had been put in caretaker charge, and they beat both Eastleigh and Dagenham and Redbridge before the trip to Edgeley Park to face the Hatters, who were top by one point. Chesterfield were fantastic in the opening stages, scoring two great goals in the first 21 minutes, and they were heading for the summit. Town fans had packed out the open away terrace behind the goal and there had been some wild celebrations when the ball hit the net. By coincidence, in the *Sky Sports* studio that night was Cook, who was being ribbed by some of the other guests on the show. The banter was along the lines of: "Cooky, your new team has just gone 2-0 up."

Before the game, Cook had texted Croot about the match itself, emphasising especially the importance of keeping 11 men on the field. Just four minutes into the second half, Jeff King was shown a straight red card. After that, the game swung and Stockport scored twice to draw level with 25 minutes to go. They piled on the pressure in the latter stages, creating chance and chance, and it just felt like a matter of time before they got a third. But Chesterfield somehow managed to hang on and escape with a point.

The next morning, Cook had just stepped off the train after returning from his media shift, and he rang Goodwin to tell him he would take the job. The chairman was delighted. "It was like winning the lottery," he said. Croot, meanwhile, was walking around his house grinning from ear-to-ear. "I couldn't quite believe it. Sometimes in this game you have to keep things to yourself. I remember my wife saying: 'What are you smiling at?' And I came up with some excuse. But I think she had worked it out!"

Cook initially joined on his own and was officially appointed on February 10, with Roberts linking up later in April. "The fact that we talked him round is testament to how much we wanted him to come," Goodwin said. "I knew after that it was only a matter of time before he delivered us success — I had that much confidence in him."

As a kid, Cook grew up in Kirkby in Liverpool and he was football-mad right from a young age, going to Reds matches with his dad, Chris, week-in, week-out. When he was nine, he cried when his dad couldn't take him to Rome for the European Cup final against Borussia Mönchengladbach in 1977, which Liverpool won 3-1. As he grew up, he would sit in the back of a van with all his mates going to away games and he loved the camaraderie that would bring. As he got older, going to the matches became more difficult because he was trying to become a footballer himself.

Over the years, he has travelled the world watching Liverpool, where he is still a season ticket holder to this day. Unsurprisingly, his standout moment is the stunning 2005 Champions League final comeback against AC Milan. Cook was there with all his family as the Reds came from 3-0 down at half-time to draw level, before winning on penalties. It is regarded as one of the greatest comebacks ever, and everyone remembers where they were when it happened. Cook was right there in Istanbul.

Liverpool winning the Premier League, their first top-flight title in 30 years, in 2020 was dampened because of the coronavirus and fans not being allowed inside Anfield to celebrate. But there was a big party outside the ground and Cook attended with a load of his pals.

As a central midfielder, Cook's playing career spanned 23 years and more than 600 appearances, most notably at Wolves, Coventry City and Burnley. He loved it. He felt it was an honour to play football. He counts himself as someone who is very lucky because, in his words, he hasn't had to "work" a traditional job. Although after two-and-a-bit years in the National League, his stress levels have probably gone up!

He played at Anfield against Liverpool for Coventry and Norwich, which he said was surreal. One of his favourite moments came when he was playing for Wolves against Blackburn Rovers, who were managed by Liverpool legend Kenny Dalglish at the time. During the game, Dalglish swore at him from the sidelines; Cook was about to turn around and give him some back, until he realised who it was! Years later, when Cook's dad was sadly ill, Dalglish came to visit him, which meant a lot.

Towards the end of his playing days at Accrington Stanley, he got his first experience of coaching thanks to John Coleman and Jimmy Bell, and Cook got an insight into what it was like to be a manager — from preparing for a game to negotiating contracts with players. It is something that he is very grateful for. Coleman and Bell love their football, so it was a perfect match. From that point on, Cook always knew he wanted to be a manager and he never looked back.

His three main principles are culture, habits and trust. Although they don't guarantee success, they give you a platform to be able to work from. The culture is one where everyone works hard to improve, the habits are how you apply yourself in training on a daily basis and then the trust — which is the big one — will follow. Trust is something Cook speaks about often. He wanted to be able to stand on the touchline and feel comfortable that his players would attempt to do the right things. They might not always work, but the correct decision-making, the thought process, was there. Players could have bad games, but if the trust was there, they would keep getting picked.

"I felt like I was always a player that needed trust," Liam Mandeville said. "He has played me three or four games in a row where I haven't played well but he has stuck with me. He kept starting me and then out of nowhere I would score and then my confidence would be back and I would be playing well again. He has been the perfect manager for me. He doesn't just judge you off one game. If he trusts you, he gives you a chance."

Cook's preferred formation has always been 4-2-3-1. He likes attacking full-backs, wingers who come in off the line and a lone striker who would bring his flair players into the game. He's always rated the importance of having three in midfield to dominate the ball. It doesn't guarantee that you win, but it definitely helps you control a match, is his view. Possession-based attacking football is probably how best to describe it. Play out from the back, but not for the sake of it. Get after the opposition. Press from the front. Win it back. Make them pay. Whatever you do, don't give the ball away cheaply, or plastic cups of tea will hit the ground. It is press, press, press; pass, pass, pass. Make the pitch big when you have the ball and make it small when you don't. Fitness is vital. All his players, current and past, tell stories of lung-busting runs and boxing sessions in the gym. None of this came from coaching courses. Cook's style is all his own ideas on how he wants the game to be played.

"I have learnt so much from him," Webb said. "He does all the shape the day before a game, that is when he comes into his own. He is so comfortable doing that. It is so mechanical and structured. He is very good at that. He likes to name the team two days before a game, normally, and he will do the 11-versus-11 work so the other team will get set-up like we think the opposition are going to set-up. Within the week, he and us as staff will go through clips of the opposition and individuals. He likes to do a lot of that with individual players to try to improve them. It all works well, he leads it. He will have the final say on everything, but he does offer us all an opinion and he does listen to it and takes it in. And it means a lot."

In his first managerial job at Southport in 2006, who were in the old Conference at the time, Cook had a weekly wage bill for the full squad of around £2,500, with most players on about £50 to £100 a week. It was a real eye-opener when it came to budgeting. It was a bit like passing your driving test. Then you get your first car, that is when you really learn how to drive. In his next appointment at Sligo Rovers, where he won three pieces of silverware in five years, his weekly budget was about £15,000, so he was able to offer players £500-£600 a week — which made him feel like Jose Mourinho under Roman Abramovich at Chelsea!

After returning home from Ireland and turning down the opportunity to manage St Johnstone in Scotland, he took over at Accrington Stanley in 2012. Ironically, it was a 4-3 defeat against Chesterfield that landed him the Spireites job the first time round. Accrington came to Derbyshire and were excellent on the day, leaving a big impression on everyone — including Blues owner Dave Allen, who made the move to bring Cook in just one month later in October that year. Allen said at the time: "I think Accrington are the best side we've seen here this season. That impressed me and we were asking ourselves: 'Why can't we play like that?' The wage budget at Accrington is about half that of Chesterfield."

In Cook's two-and-a-half years at Chesterfield, they won the League Two title, reached a Johnstone's Paint Trophy final and the League One play-offs and played some sublime football with a group of players who are still adored now, and will be for a long time. Unfortunately, it had a sad ending. No matter what the result was against Preston in the play-off semi-final, Cook knew he was leaving. Allen wanted to sell the best players, while Cook didn't want to have to build a new squad again. Cook, understandably, had his own ambitions. The club had taken him as far as it could and he wanted to leave as well. After the defeat to Preston, Cook took all the players out with him in Liverpool and when the night came to an end and he left the pub, he cried all the way home. He knew he was leaving some good people behind and he would miss them. His tears weren't the only ones, with the fans feeling exactly the same. For him, there was no one to blame. It had just reached its natural end. "Imagine how I felt, knowing that I had left the club that I love," he later told *1866 Sport*. "It is painful. It is not nice. It is not what you want. But sometimes things happen for a reason."

When Cook returned in February 2022, it was like flicking a switch from what the club had just had before. He gave everyone a lift on and off the field with his energy, positivity and how he had time for everyone. He makes players feel 10 feet tall and want to run through brick walls for him. He values the opinion of those around him, such as his coaching staff. Although he always makes the final decision, he encourages people to be honest and not just say what they think he wants them to say. His passion and knowledge of football is unrivalled. To say he loves football is an understatement. He is an absolute football nut. If you were on *Who Wants to Be a Millionaire?* and the final question was about football, he would be your phone a friend option. Having said that, he probably wouldn't answer because he'd be at a match.

He is honest enough to say that he doesn't really like people who don't like football. So take note, any player who might be signed by him in the future … whatever you do, don't just say it's a job! There's a meme on social media where a young lad starts a new job and a colleague asks him who he supports. He answers by saying he doesn't like football and the response is: "Well, we'll just sit here in silence for the next eight hours then. Nice one." That would be Cook. He loves his footy and he gravitates towards people who do as well.

In his last job, at Ipswich, he felt he should have been given more time, that his record of success at building clubs should have warranted him being given longer. He had been appointed in March 2021, but was let go after just 20 games of the new season after a rebuilding job in the summer. He didn't have the control that he had had at all his previous clubs, where he had won league titles at each one. While Cook was managing the Tractor Boys his dad Chris, who was his biggest footballing influence, sadly passed away. It had been an extremely upsetting and difficult time.

Cook has always spoken passionately about how managers should be given more time. He doesn't like the "hire and fire" culture. He is a builder of clubs. How can a manager implement a culture, habits and trust in a short period of time? He thinks managers deserve more respect and that people who shout abuse or write vitriol online need to remember that managers have families as well. In terms of the modern-day game, he doesn't like social media, how matches are dissected kick by kick and he believes the meaning of being a football supporter has been lost slightly. The key word being *supporter*, with some folk turning up and getting on the players' backs right from minute one.

After everything that had gone on, Cook just wanted to get back to enjoying being a manager again and Chesterfield had been the club that had given him his first real big job in football. He felt he had unfinished business. In the past, Cook had had offers from National League clubs but he wouldn't have dropped out of the Football League for anyone else but Chesterfield. They had given him his big opportunity when he was a young manager at Accrington and he had never forgotten that. After leaving in 2015, he had always kept an eye on results and had been as disappointed as anyone when they suffered defeat after defeat on their way to successive relegations. Cook had discussed coming back with his family and he weighed up the pluses and minuses before opting to take the plunge, with the aim being to take the club back where he left it — in League One.

"When the opportunity came around to come back here, I was sitting at home thinking: 'Why not? Why not go back and try and help them?'" Cook said in his first interview after rejoining. "My love for Chesterfield is purely based on what they gave me. I have got an opportunity to make those supporters happy again. They will know how committed I am coming back here." Asked what his message to the fans was on his return, he laughed and answered simply. "4-2-3-1!"

6

TROUBLE BY THE SEA

Paul Cook was slumped on a chair in the tunnel area with his head in his hands. It was May 7, 2022, and Chesterfield had just put in a lightweight performance against Torquay United. In sweltering conditions at Plainmoor, the Spireites had conceded twice in the last 20 minutes to lose 2-0. What made it worse was that almost 1,000 fans had made the 500-mile round trip for the lunchtime televised kick-off. Many had spent a lot of money on hotels and travel and they had been let down badly.

Had Chesterfield won, they would have secured a play-off place. Instead, they chucked in their worst display of the season, barely laying a glove on the Gulls. Luckily, Dagenham and Redbridge lost 3-1 at Solihull Moors, which meant the Spireites' play-off destiny was still in their own hands heading into the final game of the season.

Cook stood on the touchline that day at Torquay and he hated what he saw. He had never been more embarrassed watching a football game in his life, he later admitted. He didn't like how often his side gave the ball away, their lack of threat going forward and the soft goals they conceded. Since his return, he had not been enjoying watching his team play and had openly admitted as such numerous times. He had found it painful. "He's not coming out," was the feedback the press received after the full-time whistle in Devon. "He's not coming out and no-one will be speaking."

Since Cook's return, things had been very testing. The squad had been crippled by several long-term injuries, including top goalscorer Kabongo Tshimanga, who had suffered a fractured leg and dislocated ankle in Cook's first match, against Weymouth. It would keep him out for six months. Another problem was that Cook was a 4-2-3-1 man and he wanted his team to play expansive attacking football. But the players at the time had had 3-5-2 drilled into them under James Rowe. In Rowe's tenure, particularly that season, the game plan had been to remain solid, nullify the opposition and let Tshimanga do the business down the other end. It wasn't pretty, but it was effective. It had got them in contention for top spot.

There had been flashes of Cook's style rubbing off, most notably a 3-1 home win against Notts County, but overall performances had been clunky and victories had been hard to come by, as they dropped like a stone from second to seventh. "We all felt one of the lowest points was Torquay away," chief executive John Croot said. "I could tell by talking to Paul that he had got to grips with what he felt we needed, where we needed strengthening and what sort of players we wanted, because he started talking to me about it then."

Chesterfield stumbled into the play-offs on the final day despite only managing a 0-0 draw at home to Woking. Had they lost, they would have fallen out of the top seven and been replaced by the Daggers. In all honesty, there wasn't much hope going into the play-offs. They were bang out of form, performances had been a tough watch, the injury list was long. They had a manager saying he didn't trust his players or enjoy watching them. It was hardly a recipe for success.

But on a memorable night in Halifax in the elimination round, Chesterfield played ever so well and won 2-1 to book their place in the semi-finals. Out of nowhere, they had produced a really good performance against a side who had finished fourth and 10 points above them. They had had time on the training ground and it gave people a flavour of what Cook was trying to achieve long-term. It had been chalk and cheese from Torquay.

Five days later, they visited Solihull Moors, who had finished third, guaranteeing themselves a home tie in the semi-final. Having to beat two sides away from home to reach the final was a huge task, but that win at Halifax had given everyone a lift. And people started to believe Chesterfield could do it when Joe Quigley gave them an early lead, but the Moors had too much firepower and they turned it around to lead 2-1 at half-time before adding a third in the second half which gave the Blues too much to do. It was a second play-off defeat in two years, but a summer rebuild under Cook gave everyone optimism as they departed Damson Park.

As Croot touched upon, Cook's planning had already started. He wanted a squad smaller in numbers and players who were fit and always available for selection. He also wanted younger, faster, stronger, athletic and technically better players. Full-backs who could get up and down all day long. Midfielders who didn't give the ball away. Flair players who would get fans out of their seats. He wanted the club to have assets on the pitch. Lads who he could work with and improve. People who could take information on and buy into his culture.

When Cook first arrived and he examined how the club had been op-erating, he couldn't understand why they kept signing loads and loads of new players. Where was the continuity? Where was the willingness to improve players? He couldn't get his head around it. And yet, for all the new signings, there was no recruitment room, no designated place where the coaching staff could bounce ideas about players off each other. Where they could watch clips, analyse stats and view reports.

As well as taking charge of the first team, Cook had been given the freedom to shape the whole football department. A recruitment room was one of the first things he identified as being of great importance. The training ground had also seen better days, with consistent problems with waterlogged pitches. The training ground is where players pick up their habits, one of Cook's big three principles; if players put the work in during the week then come matchday, more often than not, he believes the efforts in the week will be rewarded.

So that was another area that needed improving, as well as beefing up the number of backroom staff to provide a stronger framework and more support for the players. For Cook, it was all about building the foundations first. Then success on the pitch would follow. Reflecting later in an interview with *1866 Sport*, Cook said: "I couldn't understand where we had got to as a club. I just felt our standards as a football club had dropped. For me, the quicker I could implement the changes that I believed were the right ones, the better. I have got to add that I have had the full support of the board above me."

That summer, he set about rebuilding the squad to suit his style and culture. Not all his signings would work out — that's just football — and sometimes it's out of your hands. But the majority of them would play a part in the success that was to come. In came attacking full-backs Ry-heem Sheckleford, Branden Horton and Bailey Clements, who were seen as good profile fits. They were in their early twenties, were full of energy and would provide overlapping runs and plenty of crosses. They could also get better. Cook had been aware of Sheckleford since his Fulham days and knew all about Clements from his time at Ipswich. The club announced Clements as a Chesterfield player in the big Tesco on Lockoford Lane, near the stadium; a nod to the running joke among the fans, that all new signings always get spotted there. The gag went viral and even made the national media.

By chance, Clements' girlfriend had family who lived in Chesterfield. "When the gaffer took the job and I was still at Ipswich, I was like: 'Oh, it would be funny if I ended up there,'" he said. "And a few months later that's what happened! It helped me having people there that I knew and who I knew would look after me to help me settle in."

Darren Oldaker was a central midfielder, again in his early twenties, who Cook had been tracking from when he was manager at Wigan Athletic. Oldaker had been at Gillingham at the time, before dropping down into part-time football with Dorking Wanderers. Cook's son Kieran, the chief scout for Chesterfield, and head of recruitment Neil Hornby had both been to watch him, and they liked what they saw. He was a lovely footballer, a good technician; very smooth in his approach and kept possession nicely.

Playing alongside Oldaker in midfield would be Ollie Banks, who would need no introduction to Spireites fans having spent three years at the club between 2013 and 2016 and winning the League Two title under Cook. Banks, then approaching 30, had been at Barrow but a move back closer to home and an opportunity to play for Cook again suited him perfectly. He was another excellent technician who could play cross-field passes with his eyes shut and score worldies with one arm tied behind his back.

At the opposite end of the age scale to Sheckleford, Horton and Oldaker was Mike Jones, a former winger turned midfield destroyer who had spent his career in the Football League with the likes of Bury, Carlisle United, Crawley Town, Oldham Athletic and even a short spell at Sheffield Wednesday. After two miserable years at Barrow which were ruined by injury, he was having to come to terms with the possibility of having to retire. He got in touch with Cook via text and it would end up being one of the most important messages he ever typed out. Cook gave him a chance and he initially came in on trial in pre-season and Jones impressed enough to earn himself a one-year deal. It's probably fair to say that his arrival didn't create much noise, but he would turn out to be one of the first names on the teamsheet and become a fan favourite. When he played, Chesterfield would win.

Jones, who was training with Farsley Celtic to keep himself fit, said: "It was tough. No one was interested, no one was picking up the phone. No one was getting back to me. Nothing was coming up. It was a case of: 'Bloody hell, this could be me done.' I am really grateful that he gave me that opportunity because no one else really was going to. Once I got that opportunity I knew I could still play and I was still fit. I just needed that one person to give me a chance and look at me. And Cooky was that one person."

The most exciting signing of the summer was Armando Dobra, who was just 21 and an attacking player who Cook had worked with at Ipswich Town. Dobra, who had been capped by Albania at youth level, had high potential and was clearly very talented. Cook had given Dobra his chance at the Tractor Boys so the pair had a good relationship and that helped in securing his services. Former England midfielder Kieron Dyer who had been working in the academy at Ipswich while Cook was manager, was also influential in persuading Dobra to join the Spireites.

When the local newspaper, the *Derbyshire Times*, heard about the interest in Dobra and published a story, this author got a call to say that such reporting might have put the deal in doubt. As you can imagine, when Dobra was officially announced as a Chesterfield player, there was one almighty sigh of relief! Further additions in Ash Palmer, who had won the National League title with Stockport County months before, and direct Altrincham winger Ryan Colclough, who Cook had worked with at Wigan, would be made as the season progressed. Brick by brick, the foundations were being put in place. A team which reflected Cook as a manager.

Chesterfield now had a side which was more youthful but still had a nice balance of experience. They had players they could improve and sell for profit if they had to. They had a clear style of play, an experienced and talented manager who knew how to build title-winning sides. Off the field things were stable, with the ownership between the community trust and the introduction of Phil and Ashley Kirk and the connection between the fans and club was on the up. The only roadblock back to the Football League was that Hollywood-backed Wrexham, and fellow promotion contender Notts County, were further along in their journey. And they would take some stopping.

7

NEVER GIVE UP ON YOUR CLUB

Wembley is not a place for losers, that is for sure. As Chesterfield's team coach weaved its way out of the home of football and onto the streets of the capital, the bus was not exactly a bundle of joy. Some had tears in their eyes. Others tried to get some rest. Some leant their head on the window and just stared into the distance. They were replaying the game back over and over in their heads. How well they had performed. Could they have done this? Should they have done that? They were drained. It was torture. A whole season, a year's work, had come down to one match. One penalty shootout. God, football can be cruel.

And then came the rubbing of salt in fresh wounds. The gloating. A bunch of Notts County fans, walking back to the pubs and hotels to celebrate, had spotted them. They banged on the side of the vehicle, they waved their flags, sang their songs and mocked them. It was hard to ignore. It was difficult to stomach. To make matters worse, there was bad traffic, so that prolonged the agony. "We were basically sitting ducks," assistant manager Danny Webb said. He told the players to remember the feeling and use it as fuel.

As the coach sped off, there was a bit of peace and plenty of thinking time. Calls to family. More mulling over what had just happened. That was until Webb suggested they stop off at a services on the M1 to let the players get some refreshments. Unfortunately, it happened to be a place brimming with more Notts County supporters. Most of them were fine, coming over and shaking the hands of some of the beaten players, but a small minority crossed the line and things got a bit heated. Home could not come quickly enough.

"They were singing things like: 'You'll always be National League,'" captain Jamie Grimes said. "And that kind of stuck with us. We had to go and do it after that." The day before, the squad had looked around Wembley to get a feel for it. They took pictures, videos and spoke to their friends and family via FaceTime.

They walked up the famous steps and imagined themselves lifting the trophy. They had the freedom of the world-famous arena. After growing up dreaming about playing at the 90,000-seater dome and playing "Wembley" on the fields and the parks as youngsters, there they were — running around the real thing, roaming wherever they wanted. From pitch side, to dressing rooms, to the chill-out lounge, ice baths and tunnel area. It was like having your own personal grand tour. It was like breaking into the stadium in the middle of the night and having it all to yourself. "Better than Wealdstone, this" and "not a patch on Maidenhead" were some of the light-hearted comments as the players wandered around.

The tickets for the players' families had arrived after they had already left for London, so Ashley Kirk got to drive his car right underneath Wembley and deliver them to the squad. It was a special moment for him. This author was lucky enough to be invited along and see all of this with his own eyes. Sitting under the arch, a few rows back on the north side in the "posh seats," it evoked a lot of memories. You think about the great goals that have been scored, the late winners, the mistakes, the penalties, the red cards, the managers, the celebrations, the heartache and all the history. All your childhood memories were instantly unlocked. You didn't want to leave. You could have stayed there all day. But in the back of your mind, you were wondering what was going to happen on that very stage in just over 24 hours.

That night, this author had a nightmare before he'd even gone to sleep. While sinking a few pints in the Green Man pub, Sheffield Wednesday, the team he'd supported all of his life, were trounced 4-0 at Peterborough United in the first leg of the League One play-off semi-final. After the hammering at London Road Wednesdayites had, unsurprisingly, written off their chances of overturning such a deficit. Many had said they couldn't be bothered to go to the return fixture at Hillsborough, even though they had tickets.

In the days leading up to the second leg, "Tom the Chesterfield fan" rang up *BBC Radio Sheffield's Football Heaven* show and gave a passionate rallying cry to Wednesday fans. "Never give in," he said. "Never give up, never give in on your club. Never turn your back. Never, ever say: 'No, I've had enough.' Because it's your club and you should be proud whatever the situation. It's not the players, it's not the manager, it's you and your badge. And never forget that, because I certainly won't."

His call went viral on social media, it was shared everywhere and it inspired a whole fanbase to believe again. It made the hairs stand up on the back of your neck. It gave you goosebumps. He had done Owls manager Darren Moore's team-talk for him. Unbelievably, in the second leg, Wednesday came roaring back. Everything that had to happen for them to win did. Everything fell into place. One-nil up after nine minutes. Two ahead before half-time. A third with 20 minutes to go. And then, with the last kick of the game, with some fans having trickled out of Hillsborough believing it to be over, they scored in the 98th minute to take it to extra-time and cause pandemonium in the stands. It was incredible.

It looked like being all for nothing when an unlucky own goal put Peterborough back in front for 5-4 on aggregate. Until another twist saw Wednesday make it 5-1 on the night and 5-5 overall. On what was an unforgettable night, one that many say is the best they have experienced, Moore's men ended up winning 5-3 on penalties. Spireite "Tom" could take credit for the greatest comeback in play-off history. In more dramatic circumstances, Wednesday then beat Barnsley in the play-off final at Wembley, with the winner scored on 120+3, to secure promotion back to the Championship.

Amusingly, "Tom" is actually called John Connaughton. When he first rang *BBC Radio Sheffield* many years ago, they misheard his name and logged it as "Tom" and he has gone along with it ever since. He told *The Star*: "I've spoken to people who said fans were talking about my call in the ground – it's mad! People have said they went to the ground because of what I'd said. It's crazy!"

***

Back to Wembley and spots of rain tapped against the hotel window on the morning of Chesterfield's big day. Downstairs, it may have been early, but a queue was forming at the bar. Both Spireites and Notts County fans were having liquid breakfasts to calm their nerves. Both teams had reached the final after epic semi-final victories. Chesterfield had beaten Bromley 3-2 after a gruelling 120+ minutes, which included the 10-man Ravens equalising in the 99th minute of normal time, before Liam Mandeville struck the winner in the first half of extra-time.

The other semi-final was remarkably similar. Notts County came from two goals down against Boreham Wood to draw level in the 97th minute of normal time, before incredibly scoring the winner in the 120th minute. County were the favourites for the final, there was no doubt about that. They and Wrexham had played out one of the most exciting and tightly-fought title races ever. County achieved 107 points, smashed in 117 goals, lost just three times, but still only finished second behind Wrexham. They got 111 points, a record for the National League. The Magpies also had the best striker in the division in sought-after Macaulay Langstaff, who had rocketed in 42 goals.

Chesterfield had topped the table after being unbeaten in the first 10 games but they couldn't keep pace with County and Wrexham, who were relentless and finished third on 84 points. It was their highest finish since dropping out of the Football League. They'd had a good season themselves.

To the final itself. Chesterfield's game-plan had been to get after the Magpies and it worked. They didn't give them any time on the ball, they got in their faces and played at a high tempo. The Spireites were the better team on the day and deserved to win. But they didn't. It was hard to begrudge County promotion, because they had been outstanding all season, but Town really should have won. Had it not been for an error from goalkeeper Ross Fitzsimons and another fluke goal, they would have been the ones celebrating. Chesterfield were well on top in the opening stages and missed chances in that period also cost them.

Having led 1-0 after just five minutes through an Andy Dallas penalty, they were three minutes of normal time away from sealing promotion until John Bostock, who was County's standout player on the day, caught Fitzsimons out with a wide free-kick at his near post. It was a cheeky attempt, but it should have been saved. The Magpies' goalkeeping coach Tom Weal had apparently noticed that Fitzsimons sometimes left big gaps and told his players to be aware of that. Bostock disguised it cleverly and it was brave to go for it rather than just put it in the box for one of his teammates to attack, but the risk paid off. As the ball crept under the diving Fitzsimons and over the line, Chesterfield's players put their hands on their head in disbelief. Fitzsimons sat on the floor, looking white as a sheet.

All their hard work had been undone in one moment of madness.

And so to extra-time. As they say, it's the hope that kills you. And that was certainly the case when a wonderful run and curling strike from Armando Dobra put the Blues back in the driving seat again in the first half. It made you believe that it was back on. Dobra ran over to Paul Cook on the sidelines and the pair embraced. Cook had given him his chance at Ipswich Town and now at Chesterfield, and Dobra was grateful. This was his way of thanking him, by scoring the winner at Wembley to earn promotion. So he thought. We all thought it. Up in the stands coach Kieron Dyer, who had worked with Dobra from when he was a teenager, was very emotional. From watching Dobra develop at Ipswich, from someone who couldn't kick a ball very far to curling one in the top corner at Wembley … it was a proud moment.

But you just knew it was not going to be Chesterfield's day when, early in the second half, Fitzsimons' punched clearance from Kyle Cameron's cross was mishit into the ground by Ruben Rodrigues. Having looked like it was going to land on the roof of the net, it looped over Fitzsimons' head and in. Again, it was another avoidable and soft goal. In what was a bold move County then substituted goalkeeper Sam Slocombe — who had started the game very nervy, giving away an indirect free-kick just yards from his goal in the opening minutes — for 6ft 4in penalty-saving expert Archie Mair in the last minute of extra-time. It would ultimately pay off.

Reflecting back on that change in goalkeeper, Banks felt it was a clever move — even if he can't remember the substitution being made. "Even if he wasn't any better at saving penalties, by doing it they automatically get a little bit of a psychological edge." Liam Mandeville recalls thinking Mair was "humongous. It was almost like a psychological thing. When you see they are bringing on a keeper for penalties, you think there is one thing he is going to be good at — and that is saving penalties. I think it was well played on their part. I think it was a good tactic." Jeff King wasn't fazed, though. "I was never changing what I was doing. I tried not to look at him too much."

Chesterfield had practiced penalties in training that week, including walking from the halfway line to try to recreate what it would be like and even having teammates heckling each other from behind the net. But in truth, nothing could probably prepare you for that wobbly legs moment.

When it came to spot-kicks, Grimes believed he was sixth or seventh on the list to take one. He had actually played the whole game with painkillers because of a freak accident, injuring his knee in the celebrations at the end of the semi-final win over Bromley. Fans ran on the pitch and someone accidentally slid into him and knocked him off his feet. When it first happened, he was concerned that it might be serious, but it settled down and he was never a doubt to miss the final. But because of his sore knee, he avoided practicing penalties; he was worried that if he put his foot through the ball that it might flare up. The day before the final, when the players were doing their tour of Wembley, he jumped in one of the ice baths for 10 minutes. When he got back on the bus, shivering cold, all his teammates were wondering what the hell he had been doing.

Standing arm in arm on the halfway line, Chesterfield's players huddled together. They had a front-row seat for what was about to happen. "You feel their emotions as they are stepping up," Grimes said. "You feel their nerves. You feel every step when they are on the run-up. I was kicking every ball for them when they were doing it."

Mandeville, who was playing in the No.10 position on what was his first time playing at Wembley, hobbled off with cramp just after Bostock's equaliser. His job was to deal with Bostock and Matty Palmer and he ended up running seven kilometres in the first half. With his average around 11-and-a-half in a full game, he had covered a lot more distance in the first 45 than he normally would and his legs caved in. "By the time it got to the 90th minute I was absolutely finished," he said. "I wish I was still on because being off the pitch was way worse than being on it. I was kicking every ball on the sidelines. Notts County are a passing side and they are unbelievable at it, to be fair to them. I think a mixture of that and the emotion of the game absolutely finished me off.

"Looking back, I shouldn't have been trying to press two players at once, I probably should have reserved my energy a little bit more than I did. I was a penalty taker when I was at Doncaster when I was 19 so I definitely would have wanted to take one of the first five. That is one of the disappointments on my part, because I felt like I let the team down in that regard. Especially when I am supposed to be one of the fittest players. To come off before extra-time was a disappointment for me, 100 per cent."

When Notts County won the toss and understandably chose to take the penalties in front of their own fans, it was another sign that it was going to be their day. Chesterfield went first and Banks put his foot through it to get them off to a good start. Despite the whistling and the off-putting tactics of the rival supporters, the midfielder was as cool as a cucumber. "I wasn't nervous," he explained. "It was weird because I have taken quite a few penalties in the last few years and it is a bit of a nervy thing to do. It is all on you basically. When we were talking about who wanted to take a penalty, I just said I wanted to go first and the gaffer was happy with that. I didn't feel nervous one little bit. It was strange. I just knew I was going to score."

The week before, Banks had been listening to a podcast featuring Southampton legend Matt Le Tissier, who scored 47 out of 48 penalties in his career and his advice helped. "He said that 90 per cent is your mental attitude towards taking it," Banks continued. "He said that if you get that in the right place then that is the main thing. And as I was walking up to take mine I was like: 'I am going to score.' I probably enjoyed it. I enjoyed the pressure. I have always been the same.

"I played golf at a decent standard when I was young. You would be stood with loads of people behind the tee and I loved that pressure. I always seemed to hit a good shot. I thrived off that pressure. When I was taking penalties for Barrow I would go off a system where if I went down the middle, then next one I would go left and then the one after I would go right. But obviously, when it is a one-off situation, I just went with the one that I felt most comfortable with."

After Banks had scored, so did Langstaff, before Darren Oldaker's effort was well saved. He had hit it with plenty of power and direction but Mair had guessed right and it was probably a nice height for him. Rodrigues then drilled home to give Notts County the advantage. Laurence Maguire, with his last meaningful kick in a Spireites shirt, slotted in before Jodi Jones went the same side, low to the keeper's left, to keep County in front. Then up stepped King. Like Banks, he struck it ever so well, but Mair somehow kept it out with a high dangled leg. No matter how many times you watch it, it is hard to believe he stopped it.

Reflecting back, King said: "Building up to the game, I usually think about moments that could happen and the thought of having to take a pen crossed my mind. But that thought in my head was worse than actually doing it. I remember thinking that it was going to be really difficult because of the pressure and everything. When it went to pens I was relieved because I thought we had run ourselves into the ground. So I didn't get to the point of feeling nervous, I just felt really free.

"I have never really been a penalty taker but I have always been a personality where if there are younger players in the squad, especially in games like that, I have got to put my hand up. Because I can't be letting these types of players take the pressure on their shoulders. As silly as that might sound, you do get people who shy away from them.

"In the build-up to the game my pens were really good. I didn't change anything in the final. Fair play to the lad, because he made a great save. It is only a good pen if it goes in, I suppose, but I speak to people and they go: 'That was a great pen, you couldn't have done much more.' It was not nice at the time and I was gutted but when I reflect I would not change anything, really.

"I just told myself to connect with the ball. I just thought: 'If I connect with it and it is travelling at that pace, then there is not a big chance that he is going to save it.' Especially if I went with height. To be fair, he dived at height. When I looked up I thought: 'B******, how has he saved that?' It was a great save, fair play to him. I spoke to him after the game and he had stats on most of our players. I think it was only myself and one other lad who he didn't really have stats on."

King's miss gave Bostock the chance to win it but his ballsy Panenka-style penalty was too high and it came back off the crossbar, giving Town a lifeline. 'What was he thinking?' was the shocked response from *TNT Sports* commentator Adam Summerton. Joe Quigley thumped his spot-kick down the middle with an air of confidence to pass the baton back over, but Cedwyn Scott did not repeat Bostock's mistake as he sent Fitzsimons the wrong way and Notts County won the shootout 4-3.

Weal was again the mastermind, presenting manager Luke Williams with incredible amounts of detail about penalty takers and which goalkeeper would give them the best chance of winning.

Referee Matthew Corlett blew the full-time whistle and while County's players all raced towards Mair, Chesterfield's sunk to their knees. "It was devastating," Mike Jones said. "It took me a long time to get over it. It was really hard to take, hard to accept. Although we probably deserved to win on the day, I kept telling myself, convinced myself, that Notts County probably deserved that bit of luck because they finished so many points above us. But you can't hide how close we were, how we played on the day and we should have got the job done. It hurt for a long time because it was there. It was so close … we should have got over the line."

Bailey Clements had similar views. "I think we definitely deserved to win," he said. "Coming so close at the end of normal time and then so close at the end of extra-time … it was just gutting. On the flip side, taking away not winning, getting the chance to play at Wembley isn't something that everyone gets to do. The atmosphere on the day, the actual moment of the day, was probably one of the highlights of my time at the club. I had my family there. When I came out of the tunnel, I looked up and saw them all there. I couldn't feel any prouder of myself of what I had achieved for them. It was just gutting that we couldn't get the win to make it an even more special day."

Mandeville added: "All the hard work you have put in was for nothing in the end really, as horrible as it sounds. You are still in the National League and you have got to do it all again next year. I remember thinking that I didn't want to do it that way again. I'd rather just get it done."

Many of the squad have never watched the match or penalties back. They couldn't face it. It was too painful. But Jones had no choice — his young son had it on loop on YouTube for days and weeks after. "He was doing my head in," Jones laughed. "Honestly, for months after I would come down in the morning and he would have it on. In the end, I had to say: 'Mate, that's it.' It was haunting me for so long and he wasn't helping!"

As Notts County's players headed for the steps, the applause from the 16,000 Spireites fans, who had sang their hearts out all afternoon, for their own team said it all. They had seen a group of players go to war for them. The squad got into a huddle on the halfway line and Cook told them how proud he was of them and that they had given a good account of themselves. He told them to remember the feeling and to use it as motivation for next season. That picture would appear on social media throughout the next 12 months.

The players then broke away and put their hands together for the supporters. As much as they appreciated the response the fans had given them, they couldn't wait to get off the pitch. There was no need to hang around and prolong the agony. Before heading down the tunnel, Jones remembered watching Notts County celebrate. Rather than ignore it, he wanted to have those images burnt into his mind.

"You don't want to see every bit of celebration but you want to look and see what it means and what could have been," he said. "You have just got to suck it up and be man enough to take it. At the end of the day, we would have been celebrating just like they were. It just spurred you on even more. Watching them celebrate, their fans knocking on the bus … I just wanted to look and remember how much it hurt. And make sure I took that the right way into the next season."

As he was walking off the pitch, Jones' teammate Banks saw his little boys. They were devastated, which understandably really upset him. "That was my worst moment in football," he said. "I have had bad times in football, like where you've not been playing or you've been treated poorly, but that is the single worst I have ever felt. It was more for my family than anyone else. When you get older and you become a dad, football changes for you. As you get older it means more. Your life tends to revolve around football more with your kids and your family coming to games. That moment really got to me."

Back inside the dressing room, the boots and the shin pads came off and everyone was down in the dumps, with different players remembering different things about what happened. Those who were not involved went around and consoled those who had played, offering some words of comfort and a little handshake. Many of those whose kits were muddied sat and just tried to take in what had just happened. Generally, it was very quiet. Cook spoke briefly and was very positive, whilst understanding nothing he could say would make anyone feel any better. Him and his staff then went into another room and had a debrief.

Grimes said: "It was very solemn. I remember a moment on the pitch when Danny Webb gave me a hug and I felt the tears going. I had a bit of a blubber. I managed to fight it back all the way round. In the dressing room, you didn't know what to say. Everyone had given everything. I can't really remember what the gaffer said. I just remember it being absolutely horrible."

Jones explained: "Personally, I was pretty angry. I was upset and disappointed that we as a team did not finish the job which I felt was a little bit of an Achilles' heel that whole season — that we could not see games out. We weren't mature enough and we didn't have that nous about us. We let it happen at the worst time, not once but twice we let it slip. That wasn't aimed personally just at Ross, but it was as a team and a collective group. It kind of summed it up that we weren't able to see a game out on the day and time and time again in the season."

Clements said: "It was silent. There were a lot of tears and heartbreak. It wasn't really a space to say anything to anyone at that time. I think everyone wanted their moment to take it in and try to deal with it however they best wanted to."

Banks recalled: "I think I just went in and said that we were unbelievable on the day. I wouldn't say there were arguments but it was like: 'How have we lost that game?' Because, let's be honest, we should never have lost that game. We had them right where we wanted them. Yes, they had more possession, but we never looked in any threat. But, you can look at it two ways, Notts County had an unbelievable season and if you are going to be completely honest, they did deserve to go up. But on the day they didn't at all. It wasn't our time, it wasn't meant to be. I always go back to the time I got promoted with Tranmere through the play-offs. Everything was just destined for us to get promoted that year. I am a believer in that. Notts County were meant to go up that season and they probably deserved it."

Up in the players' lounge, the County players were still in their kit, medals on, bottles of beer in hands, laughing, joking, high-fiving their families. Chesterfield's lot had their head in their hands and were absolutely distraught. Mandeville, who played in the same Sunday League team as Langstaff, shared a word with the striker. "You could see the joy on his face," Mandeville said. "It was tough. Part of me did think that they deserved to go up after the season they had. It just felt like they were meant to win it that day. Their second goal was the luckiest goal ever. It gave me motivation to do it next year — without Wembley, to be honest."

Cook was okay with the defeat. Disappointed, yes. But Chesterfield had turned up, given absolutely everything, but had just fallen a bit short. When it comes to a final, there is nothing more gutting than when a team does not turn up, when they don't show the best version of themselves. But that could not be an accusation thrown at the players on May 13, 2023. They left everything out there, but small details in big games matter.

The Spireites were a good side that season and had improved from the year before. But the loss of three games in a week in October, and a run of nine games without a win, including six defeats, during February, suggested their journey was still ongoing. Destination Football League was just out of their reach. One thing that Cook later reflected on was how Chesterfield needed more firepower. Wrexham had won the league scoring 116 goals, while the Spireites had notched 35 fewer with 81, and he would address that in the summer.

"I wasn't bad after Wembley," Cook later said. "We didn't let our supporters down. There was no problem losing on penalties for me because it wasn't our time. Now if we had lost to the ones who had finished below us it would have been a painful defeat because you'd have expected to go up." Chief executive John Croot had a similar opinion. He said: "I sort of felt it was perhaps a year early. We were still rebuilding. Of course, if the chance comes to get promoted then you have a really good go at it and that's what we did. Before the game at Wembley I thought if we don't do it, then we have got a hell of a chance next year. I always felt it was a window of opportunity for us."

In the mixed zone, the area where journalists wait to secure their post-match interviews, it was like being in two very different places at once. You were at the party of the year, but also a funeral. The emotions could not have been more contrasting. Fitzsimons walked by with a look of absolute devastation. There was no way he was stopping to have a chat. He wanted the ground to swallow him up. He wanted to sneak by in Harry Potter's invisibility cloak. You could not help but feel for him as he marched towards the team coaching waiting at the back entrance.

Dobra had a face like thunder. One of sadness, anger and frustration. When a reporter gently asked for an interview, he gave him the side-eye, slightly shook his head to indicate it was a no, before also climbing the steps onto the bus. It was a while before he spoke to anybody that sum-mer — he couldn't face anyone. Then Cook emerged and gave a short interview. He said his players had given everything and that they had no regrets, preferring to focus on congratulating Notts County than to go into any specifics about the match.

Grimes fronted up and when asked by this author to sum up his feel-ings, tears filled his eyes. He said that he couldn't. While all of this was going on, every now and again, a Notts County player would appear with a beer in their hand, a medal around their neck and a smile that would be there for weeks. Their players were lining up to speak to the media and who could blame them? It had been their day. While they were cracking the cans open, a trolley of undrunk lager emerged from the Chesterfield dressing room and was wheeled away. Wembley is not a place for losers.

Back on the coach, there was a lot of reflecting. There was a whole range of emotions, but no-one was playing the blame game. There was no criticism and, despite the gut-wrenching feeling in their bellies, the seeds were being sown for the following season. Banks, who shed a tear or two on the way home, remembered: "One of the lads said: 'Let's get some music on, we've not done it, but we've got nothing to be ashamed of, we've had a good season and we'll go and win it next year.' And we did that. I feel like we knew we were going to win it straight after that play-off final."

Sitting at the front of the coach, Webb was surprised, but proud, of how the lads had been able to show such courage. He explained: "Believe me when I say this, by the time we got back to the stadium, a lot of the lads were actually looking forward to next season. It is hard to believe that but that caught me out really. Even the lads who missed penalties, they obviously weren't laughing and joking, but they were positive about going to make amends next season."

By the time the coach arrived back in Derbyshire, the mindset had switched. The group headed into Chesterfield for a few more drinks and the welcome they received blew them away. Not one person went up to any of the boys and gave them any criticism. They were all very sup-portive and respectful. "They were buying us drinks and saying we had done them proud," King said. "It was nice that they appreciated what we had done all season. That is something I remember personally. Ross

Fitzsimons was out with us and he'd had a tough time with the mistake. He was a little deflated but people were saying what a great season he'd had. It was really nice that we weren't going back to somewhere with people on our backs, saying that we had let them down. Everything was really positive. I think people understood that we were dead on our feet in that final."

They were given a couple of days off to let the dust settle before they all met up at the stadium again. Cook spoke to them and understandably, there was still a lingering flatness. But Cook felt it was important that they didn't just go their separate ways after Wembley. It helped a bit with closure and to refocus minds for the next season. It was time to finish the job.

8

NOTHING WILL BE LEFT TO CHANCE

I t was absolutely baking. It was 35 degrees. It was beer garden weather. It was not the sort of climate you wanted to be doing timed runs in. It was not exactly ideal for running the full length of a football pitch, there and back 15 times, with the sun beating down when you are struggling to catch your breath. And it was definitely not the conditions you would want for a game of "murderball" — an intense training activity which former Leeds United manager Marcelo Bielsa is credited with creating.

The rules are simple. It's 11-versus-11 on a full-sized pitch but the ball is always in play. When it does go out of play, another ball is thrown back in instantly. Each player has a cone and when the ball goes out for a throw-in, for example, everyone has to run back to their specific cone. It's basically non-stop sprinting. Quite simply, it's hell. And Kieron Dyer loves it. Those taking part, however, do not.

"If you get on a team who are not keeping the ball, you are in for a tough, tough time," Mike Jones explained. The lads don't exactly like it but it is game-related. If you can do murderball in 30-odd degrees then when you come back to Chesterfield it is going to make it miles easier. It sets great foundations."

The following pre-season after Wembley, Chesterfield went to a four-star sports resort in Colina Verde, Portugal, about 30 minutes from Faro, for five days of warm-weather training. Leyton Orient had used the same facilities the year before and Aberdeen's under-21s were there too. It was well-known for sports teams to go there and get their fitness work underway but there were also locals staying there on their holidays. It was a nice relaxing place with a lovely big pool; you could take a walk along the harbour and there would be some live music on. The players could enjoy some downtime with some fun games and one volleyball match got a bit lively. But there were also double and sometimes triple training sessions. Make no mistake about it; the players were there to work.

Paul Cook puts great importance on such trips because of the camaraderie and togetherness they bring. They allow new players to gel and get to know everyone else in the squad. Despite the heat, you probably would prefer to start your hard graft with the sun on your back rather than running up hills in the Derbyshire countryside with the rain lashing in your face. It wouldn't exactly be a nice welcome back to work, especially after the heartache of the play-off final. A trip away was just what the doctor ordered. And, at the end of the week, when the first sessions are in the bag, there's time for a beer and a night out.

Ollie Banks said: "The gaffer is a big believer in getting everyone together and having a trip before we come back to do pre-season at home. There is a lot of hard work, it is not just a jolly-up, but it gets you together. You learn about your teammates, you basically live together for a week, they essentially become your second family."

Jamie Grimes explained: "As much as we worked really hard, it gelled us together really well. In pre-season, you kind of bond over how hard it is. Sometimes the harder it is, the more you bond." Liam Mandeville added: "It was hard work but we were given our time to do our own thing and have fun and we made some great memories while we were out there. And we spent most of it as a full team. I know they say you don't have to like each other but I do think it is a big thing to like each other. It makes such a difference.

"Another thing is, nowadays people think that people are too soft, that you can't have a go at people. But I feel like when you are so close together as a group, you are not having a go at people, you are advising them, I think you say it in a better way when it is someone you like. People don't take it to heart and they know you just want the best for them. And when you are down, when you are not playing so well, the lads are picking you up rather than letting you think about how you haven't been playing well."

Jeff King said: "There is always going to be a night out or a day out drinking and when people drink, they connect more. When it gets to pre-season I don't actually drink alcohol, because I like to get myself as fit as I can. So I was sober the whole time but I stayed out with all the lads and connected with everyone. Liam Mandeville was on the karaoke and Will Grigg, who had never met any of the lads, was making jokes around the table while we had a big meal. You could just see everyone coming out of their shell and it was really important. The work we got put through was a benchmark for how fit you needed to be because this was our year and we weren't going to miss out."

Mandeville, by the way, was said to be brilliant on karaoke. The rap song, which no one could remember, was not one that many would go near. But he nailed it. He knew it word for word without looking at the TV. He is, by all accounts, a great laugh on a night out and it's not hard to imagine why. A typical day out there would involve everyone having breakfast together, while the coaching staff would have a meeting about their plan for training. There would be a lot of running, ball work and then lunch. Some players would then have a little nap or go for a swim before the afternoon session would start and later on there would be some gym work. On their rest day, some of the lads played golf and others went on a boat trip.

Danny Webb explained: "It gets everyone together, there is a bit of social. It is not a stag do, but the boys can go out for food and a few drinks on the last night. It is not a holiday but it does keep everyone in good spirits. The training is hard. It is very, very tough. It is a good trip for a lot of reasons. It is a work trip. If the gaffer felt that it was slipping into a fun week away then it would be stamped out. Luckily, we did not have a group of players who tried to take the mick and turn it into a holiday. They start getting judged on that first day of pre-season. We are all seeing who is fitter than who and there is a pressure that comes with that. A lot of managers had watched us and realised how we kicked-in in the last 10 or 15 minutes of games with fitness and I think a lot of that was down to that Portugal trip."

In the days that followed the play-off final, some players posted on social media to express their disappointment. Grimes and King said they were "gutted." Darren Oldaker explained how it had been a "horrible" few days, how he was "devastated" and that he was "sorry." There were other messages, all equally as sad, but one that particularly stood out was from Jones. It ended: "Next season, nothing will be left to chance!" Those eight words gave the fans the lift they needed. That is what everyone needed to hear. And they ended up ringing so true.

When asked what he meant by that, he said: "That pain we all felt, we had to take it in a positive way. We were favourites from the off for the next season. From day one, the minute we came back, the gaffer's mentality was: 'We win this league and we win it as soon as we can.' That was my mentality, the lads' mentality. That was everyone's mentality. The only way to put the hurt right was to go and get the job done and win the league. That was the plan. It wasn't just to win it, it was to win it in style and win it as early as we can. The hurt and how close we came … nobody wanted to go through that again."

In the weeks after Wembley, when it came to adding to the squad, Cook's focus was on quality over quantity. Recruiting players in key areas who could really make a difference. In Tom Naylor, Grigg and Michael Jacobs, he captured three marquee signings. Between them, they had almost 1,500 appearances and nine promotions. They were far too good for the level. "From day one after Wembley we set-up for what we wanted to try to achieve," Phil Kirk said. "Paul and his staff, I think, got what they wanted. We talked about what money we had and where we were going to spend the money."

Naylor, who was the first of the trio to arrive, had just made 36 appearances in the Championship for Wigan Athletic, where he had won the League One title in 2022. Cook had worked with Grigg and Jacobs before at the Latics so he knew what he was getting. When it came to Naylor, he sought the advice of his trusted former assistant Leam Richardson, who was Naylor's manager at Wigan at the time and received a glowing reference.

A day later Grigg, a five-time promotion winner capped 13 times by Northern Ireland and the second highest all-time goalscorer in League One, was announced. In 2019, Grigg had joined Sunderland for £4m. He was a "big name" signing and needed no introduction. As well as his goals, he was well-known because of Gala's 1996 dance song *Freed from Desire*, which was adopted by Wigan and Northern Ireland fans. The well-known new lyrics went: "Will Grigg's on fire, your defence is terrified!"

"For me to drop down into the National League, it had to be something special," Grigg said. "Having worked with Paul Cook before and having had such a great time with him previously, it was a massive pull." Jacobs, who had won promotions with Wigan and Wolves, was the last of the trio to put pen to paper, signing on the eve of the new season.

Cook had also tried to secure his services at Ipswich Town. "Paul Cook always got the best football out of me in terms of the way I played," he said. "I have had my most successful seasons under him."

All of them had reservations about dropping down into the National League, but the lure of playing under Cook was appealing and they could see that the club was ambitious. They helped improve the standards on and off the pitch and they impressed everyone with their professionalism. The younger players were told that if they wanted a long and successful career, then they should watch how those three conduct themselves and they wouldn't go far wrong.

"The first thing I look at is a person's personality," said Webb. "And they walked into a dressing room with a lot of lads who have played lower league or National League football and they didn't look down on them or give it the big 'un. They really fitted in and I think they got a lot of respect from the other lads for that approach to their work. On the training ground, their effort and their quality shines through. You can see why they have had such good careers because of their attention to detail; whether it be a passing pattern or not cutting corners when they are running around pitches. That is why they have maintained a high level of performance for most of their careers."

King echoed those views, saying: "Once we assembled the squad, saw the personnel and played a few pre-season games, I thought: 'Yeah, we are good ... very good.' Throughout the season you never really saw the likes of Naylor, Grigg or Jacobs get too high or too low. They were always level-headed. Maybe inside they were, but they never really showed emotion. You see what they are doing and they are just getting on with the next one. And obviously the gaffer was experienced to know how you win leagues. So when we lost games ... don't get me wrong, he wasn't happy, but he would say how well we had been doing. After a few sessions Grigg said, and he meant no disrespect: 'Bloody hell, you lot are good aren't you? You are really at it.' That was so important to hear. That was the standard we had."

In terms of recruitment, the story behind the signings of Jacobs and James Berry, a young, direct winger from Macclesfield, is a funny one. At one point, it looked like both deals were slowly disappearing. But then the club got a call from Berry's agent saying that they had managed to strike a deal which meant that he could leave the Silkmen. And then

10 minutes later Jacobs rang Cook to tell him he would be coming too! "We had been talking to them both on and off and trying to get the deals done," Ashley Kirk said. "Both of them were difficult deals for different reasons. We could have said no but we wanted them both and it was a bit of a statement of intent."

Grigg went into his first few training sessions not really sure what to expect regarding the standard and quality that he was coming into. "In that first week I was pleasantly surprised," he said. "There were a lot of unknowns. The standard, quality and professionalism were all surprising but pleasantly surprising. I think I was really excited with that first week and I sensed there was such a good feeling about the place. I was a little bit anxious because the boys had lost a play-off final and you don't know how they are to react from that. But I think the new signings helped with that and definitely gave everyone a positive outlook going into the new season.

"I think I sensed quite early on that it could be a successful year if we got it right. If I had not known that they had lost a play-off final, I would not have been able to tell at all — that was one of the surprising things. I lost one myself and it is hard to bounce back from. The gaffer spoke about it the first day of pre-season and that was literally it. That was credit to the dressing room. One of the strengths the gaffer has is signing the right characters and the dressing room was full of people who weren't going to dwell on the past."

Chesterfield signed highly-rated goalkeeper Harry Tyrer from Everton, thanks to Cook having the respect of those in power at Goodison Park, on a season-long loan deal and with the goals of Grigg, the leadership of Naylor, the creativity of Jacobs and the potential of Berry, the Spireites looked stronger in all areas. They had also managed to do the majority of their transfer business early, which would prove to be vital. After a couple of days in Portugal, Chesterfield knew they had the right ingredients. They could tell they were onto something exciting. After a few sessions, Dyer turned to Cook and his fellow coaches and said that if they didn't go up this season, with the quality of players they had, then as staff they weren't doing their jobs properly. The talent and quality was that obvious.

"The gaffer recruited so well," Jones said. "To bring in Naylor and Grigg, who had been there, done it, got the T-shirt, to add to what we already had … it was a match made in heaven. They are such good lads. The gaffer only recruits good lads, first and foremost. They settled in and got on so well with everyone straight away. Everyone knew the calibre of players they were and what they had already achieved." Joe Quigley added: "From day one of pre-season you could see how well we had recruited and how good of a squad we had got in terms of personalities."

As the plane touched back down in the country, the building blocks for a title push had been put in place. In fact, those days away were the making of what was to come. Everyone came back with a spring in their step. They had washed the Wembley demons away and they were ready to finally get out of the National League. "It was just a really good trip," Jones said. "We had a couple of nice meals and little nights out. We didn't half work hard and then we socialised as well. It got everyone in good spirits again."

Highlighting the togetherness that was formed on that trip, Grimes explained: "When we got back, someone said: 'We've only been in pre-season seven days but it feels like six weeks.' It felt like we had a head-start because when you spend 24 hours a day with your teammates you get to know them a lot better. You bond with them. When we got back we felt close."

Webb said: "A lot of people doubted us after the Wembley defeat and sometimes there is a hangover. Even I was pleasantly surprised in the first week of pre-season to see the vibe and the enthusiasm of the players to say: 'Let's have another go at getting out of this league'."

In their first pre-season outing, Chesterfield hammered Matlock Town 9-0. The Gladiators play in the Northern Premier League, two divisions below the Spireites at the time, so they are no mugs. Previous friendly encounters had seen Chesterfield win narrowly by a couple of goals, so to nearly hit double-figures was a sign of their firepower. Four days later, Derby County, who would be promoted to the Championship, went to Matlock and only won 2-0.

Derbyshire neighbours Alfreton Town, of the National League North, had also proven to be tough opponents during friendlies over the years, but again they were brushed aside 5-1 while Chesterfield would also win 3-2 at League Two Accrington Stanley. They also ran Sheffield Wednesday, Sheffield United, Derby County and Bristol Rovers all close. Watching on from the press box, it was obvious that Chesterfield were in a really good place. They had a slick pre-season, looked incredibly fit, had not suffered any major injuries and looked like they had fire in their bellies. It just felt like all the pieces fitted into place.

Another person who could sense that success was just around the corner was club media assistant and fan, Bron Jenkinson, who had got a closer look at preparations for the new season than most other people. "They were on another level in terms of mentality, work ethic and determination," Jenkinson said. "I felt confident from the first day of pre-season that promotion was beckoning – the lads just wanted it – and you could just tell that there was nothing that was going to stop them getting that promotion after the heartbreak of Wembley."

9

'HOUSERY

I t was a grey, overcast day. The first game of the new season is usually met with glorious sunshine but Saturday, August 5, 2023, was a bit dull. It was drizzling. It didn't feel like the first day of the campaign. All of the talk from the outside was about whether there would be a hangover from the play-off final defeat. And the weather kind of reflected that. Just 85 days after those Wembley tears, it felt too soon to be starting again. The sun was not ready to come out yet. Some were still mourning. The heartache was still heavy. It still stung. Replays of Archie Mair's ridiculously outstretched limbs were still doing the rounds on social media. It was hard to escape it. The mute button came in handy. Fans were asked if they had got over it. Most hadn't. It was lingering.

Pre-season suggested there was no hangover, but you can never be sure. Sometimes you can win all your friendlies and get off to a stinker. Other times you can lose them all and start quickly out of the blocks. It's very strange. Chesterfield had been three minutes away, plus stoppage time, from celebrating promotion in the home of football. The party of all parties had been about to commence. But less than three months later they were about to host part-time Dorking Wanderers. They were going to have to slog it out for another 46 matches across nine months in the National League. Aargh!

With Wrexham and Notts County now out of the way, the path back to the Football League had been cleared. But with that came a lot of pressure. The Spireites were massive favourites to be crowned champions. There was an expectation from all corners that they had to win the league. And Chesterfield had been quite bullish themselves on the topic — they had made no secret that that was their aim. No play-offs this time; it was all about the title. But the history books showed that play-off final losers don't tend to do well the following year. They don't bounce straight back up off the canvas. It takes them a while to get themselves off the ropes and out of a daze.

As mentioned, those inside Chesterfield's camp reported a different story. They told one of positivity, vibrancy and excitement. There was no moping. There was no sulking. They were up for it. They could not wait to get going again. There wasn't a hangover. They weren't struggling to get out of bed. They weren't eating last night's manky kebab. They had clear heads. They were determined to replace the Mair memories with magical ones. They were ready to put on a show.

The smell of fried onions and burgers was in the air. Pints were being slurped. The smart new replica shirts, with the Crooked Spire proudly blazoned across the front, were being worn on a competitive matchday for the first time. It was down to business. Town were back. And they were going to have a right go. The turnstiles clicked. Old friends reunited. Bums on seats. "It's good to be back," and "The pitch looks well" the types of small interactions being shared as the gates opened.

Captain Jamie Grimes, with those Wembley tears now dry, led the Spireites out before turning to his left and putting his hands together in acknowledgement of the home faithful. Harry Tyrer practiced his quick footwork, while fellow new signing Tom Naylor did a little jump. Sports scientist Jordan Hardy applauded the players as they came out of the tunnel, while long-serving club photographer Tina Jenner side-stepped across the SMH lawn to capture the first images of the new season. *Snap, snap, snap.*

Across town the Dorking Wanderers manager, Marc White, was experiencing a very different type of matchday. Serving not only a touch-line ban, but a complete stadium suspension for his bad behaviour at the end of the last campaign, the Del Boy-type character had checked into the Holiday Inn. The entertaining personality, who is also the owner of the club, was wearing a black hoodie and cap with some bright white pumps. In his hotel room, the bed sheets were slightly ruffled and he was sitting at a light-coloured wooden desk, mobile phone in hand, waiting for the live stream to start on a giant TV. It was such a bizarre way to start the new season for him.

Earlier his coaching staff, along with Chesterfield's, had been briefed by the match officials about new rules which included only one person from each team being allowed in the technical area at one time. The idea behind that was to stop those in the dugouts putting too much pressure on the fourth official and the referee, and to maintain respect levels. However, that became problematic later in this game when assistant manager Danny Webb and first-team coach Gary Roberts were both trying to innocently issue instructions to the players, but were told one of them had to sit down! The other main regulation was a big clampdown on time-wasting. But, predictably, after the first month of the season, that was forgotten about.

In the build-up to the fixture, White, who had guided Dorking to 12 promotions in 23 seasons and from a club which hired a pitch for £50 when they first started out to one now mixing it with some historic ex-EFL sides, had claimed his team were "nowhere near ready" for the season to begin and that he was having "sleepless nights" about facing Chesterfield. It felt like an attempt at some early mind games and everyone saw through it.

Dorking were actually unbeaten in pre-season, but had only faced lesser opposition and had conceded a lot of goals. White, who does not have the required coaching badges to manage in the Football League and has flatly ruled out taking them should they ever achieve such a feat, should not be "underestimated," said Webb in the pre-match press conference. "Only Marc and his missus know if he has been having sleepless nights," he said with a cheeky smile.

"Come on you f****** Wanderers. Let's av ya. Don't write us off," White boomed as the live stream he was watching whirred into action and the two teams lined up, ready to go. The couple in the room next door must have been wondering what on earth was going on. The game got underway and Liam Mandeville blazed a good early chance over the bar. It was the type of opportunity you would expect him to score, or at least hit the target with. But his moment would come. A rough, late tackle in the first 20 minutes from Dorking's Josh Taylor on Armando Dobra, which went unpunished, got the juices flowing and tested the new rules. Webb, normally of a polite and gentle nature, chewing gum in mouth, was prowling the touchline with the body language of a nightclub bouncer. That tackle had angered him. His eyes had glazed over. Two seasons ago, Chesterfield's players had been on the end of a number of dreadful challenges that wouldn't have looked out of place in the MMA world, with no action taken by the officials. Webb hadn't forgotten that and from that moment he took it upon himself to protect the players like a father figure.

At the midway point of the first half, Chesterfield took the lead when Mandeville's corner fell to Ryan Colclough and he hammered home into the top corner. Colclough celebrated in front of the Kop, thumped his right hand against the club badge on his shirt and clenched his fists. Naylor pointed and blew a kiss to the East Stand. The Spireites were up and running and it had come from a set-piece — a method that would prove to be very fruitful throughout the campaign. The advantage lasted just four minutes, however, when Jason Prior volleyed in Taylor's cross from the right. In the Holiday Inn, White, now standing up, slapped his hands together in a slightly tame celebration for someone usually so loud.

Before the mid-interval, Dobra had a big chance to put Chesterfield back in front but his close-range shot was straight at goalkeeper Harrison Male. Meanwhile, referee Ruebyn Ricardo, who made history when he became the youngest referee from the black community to be in charge of a League Two game in April 2023, aged just 25, was noticeably stopping his watch quite regularly. "It's not f****** basketball," White sassed. More on basketball later.

On the stroke of half-time, former Spireite Joe Cook, who only made two appearances the previous season before being sold to Dorking, recklessly chopped down Dobra near the corner flag, which would come back to haunt him later on. The pair had to be kept apart by Tyrone Williams as they headed down the tunnel. It was a tackle which was labelled "stupid" by his own camp. Having watched some of the challenges on their own players back on a laptop, Chesterfield's coaching staff spoke to the referee at half-time to make him aware of their concerns. Ricardo had tried to let the game flow but, in doing so, had been inconsistent in some of his decision-making.

White, now with his cap off and his hands on his hips, was a happy man once again on 52 minutes when Williams was judged to have pulled the shirt of Prior from a corner and referee Ricardo pointed to the spot. "Come on Jase, come on Jase, son," White cheered as Prior converted down the middle to put Dorking in the lead for the first time. "Yes, f****** yes," White yelled. Thoughts of a Wembley hangover for Chesterfield started to creep in again. A defeat on the opening day would not be the be-all and end-all, but there would have been a lot of chuntering on the way home.

But 12 minutes later, it was 2-2. Colclough had managed to squeeze in a low cross from the left and Mandeville, Chesterfield's player of the year in the previous campaign, had snuck in at the back post to tap in. He ran over to Colclough to celebrate and the duo hugged. On the touchline, seemingly in response to some earlier dark arts from the Dorking bench, Paul Cook pointed and smiled in their direction, giving them a thumbs up before punching the air in delight. Dorking's assistant manager, Dean Milton, responded by calling Cook a 's***house.'

As the game reached the latter stages, Milton instructed Wanderers to slow the match down, but things had only just started. Dorking's Cook received his second yellow card and his marching orders after hauling down Colclough on the edge of the box. Cook left the field with his arms stretched out wide and with a confused look on his face, suggesting he was totally innocent, but replays showed he had let Colclough spin away from him before hauling him down. And it ended up being a double punishment for the visitors as Mandeville stepped up to superbly curl in the resulting free-kick to make it 3-2. Mandeville ran off in delight, his hand slipping on the greasy surface as he did his best to copy former Spurs striker Robbie Keane's iconic cartwheel and forward roll celebration, before being mobbed by his teammates. "F****** shambles," White groaned. "This is why we are part-time, mate."

As Dorking tried to change formation for a second time to get themselves level, 13 minutes were added which, along with first half stoppage time, meant that nearly 20 minutes of extra football was played. Fitness levels were being stretched on the very first day. In the second minute of the 13, Seb Bowerman pounced at the back post to make it 3-3 and give Town fans that sinking feeling again. There had been more ups and downs than a ride on Blackpool's Big Dipper and this was game week one of 46.

Normally, a 92nd-minute goal would be considered to be a late equaliser but, with 11 minutes still to play, there was still time for a winner. And Chesterfield got one. Although nobody knew it back then, it was a similar type of goal that they would score multiple times across the season. The move was patient, there was lots of probing, there were opportunities to shoot that were not taken as they waited for the exact moment to strike. Dobra to Ollie Banks, to Michael Jacobs, to Naylor, back to Banks, who then got the eyes from Joe Quigley. He clipped in a clever cross and the man the fans call the "White Pele" got in front of his marker to nod into the bottom corner in the 98th minute to spark wild scenes. The SMH erupted, while expletives were rife in White's hotel room. Roberts was smiling from ear-to-ear with both arms held up pointing at the sky, while Quigley ran over to the West Stand with his arms held out wide in Gladiator style, as if to say: "Are you not entertained?" That was his first goal in 26 appearances since his double against Scunthorpe United on Boxing Day 2022. It had been a long wait, but it wouldn't be his last.

It was too much excitement for one Town fan, who ran onto the pitch and had to be restrained. "He goes by the name of Joe Quigley" rang around the Sheffield Road arena. Chesterfield were up and running; 4-3 winners in front of a crowd of 7,657.

It was "nutty" and a "humdinger," Webb said post-match, explaining that this season was all about the "end result." They wanted to win "by hook or by crook," whilst adding that it was important that the new rules did not make the sport "regimented" and suck the fun out of it. Hitting the nail on the head for what was to come, Webb also said: "It takes a while sometimes to be the finished article within a season. Sometimes it is early to mid-September when you are ticking all the boxes."

In the end, the match was a microcosm of the season ahead. Finding a way to win. A last-gasp winner. Goals from set-pieces. Fitness levels shining through. Conceding soft goals. Mandeville scoring and assisting. Quigley netting off the bench. All with a bit of 'housery thrown in. Football was well and truly back.

10

LET'S GO WIN THE LEAGUE

Five words. Five words that would provide fantastic entertainment and social media content for Chesterfield fans in the months to come.

The Boundary Park pitch was in pristine condition, glistening in the Greater Manchester afternoon sun. It was like a new, yet-to-be used snooker table cloth at the Crucible. Standing on the touchline just in front of the leather-seated dugouts a bearded and moustached James Norwood, in a fresh white clean T-shirt, had just been handed a camera phone by Oldham Athletic's media team. "Can you just do a short video introducing yourself to the fans please, James?" they asked. "Sure, no problem, lads," came the reply.

Tilting the camera slightly down on himself, Norwood pressed record and the red light started to flash. With a little grin, he opened up with: "Hiya lads, it's James here," before panning to his left to show his location. He put the camera back on himself and continued: "I'm looking forward to the new season." Norwood then flicked his head sharply to the left before returning to face the lens. And then came those five words. "Let's go win the league." Five words that were clearly innocent and were meant in goodwill, but would haunt him for a long time. He wanted to create some excitement and show his intent from the beginning. Nothing wrong with that. But boy, did they not age well. It didn't matter how many times the video appeared on your timeline; you just had to watch it again. And again. And again.

Norwood had signed from Barnsley two days before the start of the season. The experienced forward had scored plenty of goals in the Football League, including 11 in League One in the season just gone, which ended with that last-gasp play-off final defeat to Sheffield Wednesday. Norwood came on as a sub in that game and had Barnsley won, Norwood could have been a Championship player. He had also banged in the goals to help fire Tranmere Rovers to promotion from the National League in 2018. He was a marquee signing for the Latics. It was a coup.

His arrival at Boundary Park brought a lot of noise, with many wondering how they had managed to persuade him to drop down two leagues and speculating whether he could be the difference between Oldham winning the title and not Chesterfield. The stocky striker had actually played under Paul Cook at Ipswich Town and he had been "gutted" when he was sacked. He said they had a "great relationship" and that Cook was a "top man." Norwood would get one over on Chesterfield in the first month of the season, but the Spireites would have the last laugh.

***

On the eve of the first away game, speed merchant Jesurun Uchegbulam was sold to fellow National League side Rochdale for a small fee, with a sell-on clause included. The Nigerian, once of AC Milan as a kid, had signed his first professional contract at the Spireites a year before, again for a nominal fee, after impressing in a pre-season friendly for Matlock Town. Cook knew he wanted to bring him in after five minutes of watching him and he set the ball rolling the very next day.

During his time at the club he had mainly been used as an impact player off the bench, with just four of his 38 appearances being starts. He managed just two goals, although one in a 5-1 win at Torquay United was a beauty. The reasoning behind letting him go was explained as the need to try to strike the right balance between having players for the future but also for the present. The Spireites of course wanted players who they could develop and had potential but there was also some consideration, with this being Chesterfield's sixth season in non-league, that the requirement for more proven pros was greater.

On the same day that Uchegbulam was sold, another winger, James Berry, was finally announced as a Chesterfield player. He arrived from Macclesfield for a fee on a three-year deal, having scored 25 goals in 36 appearances to help the Silkmen win the Northern Premier League West Division. He also collected five individual club awards. He had only trained on the Friday before the game and was included among the substitutes but he did not come on. Swapping one 22-year-old winger for another 22-year-old wide man and then putting forward the "here and now" argument might have raised some eyebrows. But it would soon become clear that Berry was a far more productive player in the final third than his predecessor.

Newly promoted AFC Fylde provided the first away test. The Coasters, then managed by former promotion winning Mansfield Town defender Adam Murray, had clinched the National League North title on the last day of the previous campaign, with ex-Spireite Joe Rowley, who had played on that dark day at Forest Green Rovers, scoring in a 2-0 win at Bradford Park Avenue. Sadly for Rowley, who had played a big part in their promotion success, he was denied the chance to play against his former side due to injury and would be restricted to just a handful of appearances on his return to the National League before being released the following summer.

Fylde were back at this level after three years away and were fancied to hold their own, but they ended up being in a relegation battle and Murray was sacked in October after just two wins from the first 15. Before the game there had been some questions asked by the local media about the three goals conceded against Dorking, but there was no need to overreact. It was just one match, after all, although further scrutiny would come.

Unlike on the opening day, the sun was beaming down on the 6,000-capacity Mill Farm stadium. It is fair to say the 1,163 in the away end, in a crowd of 2,395, had taken the opportunity to have some "refreshments" before taking up their position in the shaded standing terrace behind the goal which was draped in Spireites flags. It was a rare away day where shorts and T-shirts could be worn and the football on the pitch was pretty scorching, too.

Town got off to a flying start when from a second phase set-piece, Ollie Banks floated a cross in, Jamie Grimes headed back across goal and Tyrone Williams swept home to put the visitors in front after just six minutes. The Coasters played some neat football at times, with the talented Nick Haughton having a free-kick superbly tipped onto the crossbar by Harry Tyrer, who later said it was one of his favourite saves of the season. Amusingly, Everton manager Sean Dyche would find out how Tyrer was doing throughout the season by ringing a Chesterfield matchday security figure, known as "Tank," for updates on how he was progressing.

Chesterfield continued to have the better chances, with Will Grigg and Armando Dobra both going close. Another easy-on-the-eye move doubled their lead on 37 minutes when Banks, Branden Horton and Dobra linked-up smartly to tee up Liam Mandeville who slotted into the bottom corner. The former Doncaster Rovers man had clearly spent most of the summer practicing his celebrations as this time he opted for a bow and arrow type triumph to mark his third goal in two games. "Da, da, da, da, da da, Liam Mandeville," belted out the travelling Blues.

And Chesterfield were gifted a third goal during five minutes of added time when Grigg pounced on a loose back-pass from ex-Spireite Josh Kay before nipping around goalkeeper Theo Richardson to score his first goal for the club. That gave the packed away end a perfect opportunity to perform a rousing rendition of "Your defence is terrified ... Will Grigg's on fire," for the first time after one of his goals. It was a noise that would be heard on loop throughout the season.

The National League's streaming service, introduced during the Covid era, allowed clubs to broadcast matches and Fylde's own commentators responded to Grigg's goal in comical fashion. "Are you allowed to swear on these things?" one asked. "No, let's keep it broadcastable," came the reply.

Just four minutes into the second half, a mistake by Danny Whitehead allowed Mandeville to slip Ryan Colclough through on goal and he made no mistake, firing across Richardson into the far corner in front of the away faithful. Just like against Dorking, he slapped the badge before going over to hug a familiar face in the crowd. "Easy, easy, easy," bellowed out from behind the net. Colclough had been working hard on his finishing and he was being backed to go on and get double figures, as were many of Chesterfield's attacking talents.

That should have been that, but the latter part of the encounter was far from straightforward despite the comfortable looking scoreline. A rare misplaced pass by Tom Naylor was intercepted and speedy substitute Jonathan Ustabasi, a summer signing, raced clear down the left and pulled a goal back despite the best efforts from Ryheem Sheckleford who was hot on his heels.

The spirited hosts got some encouragement from that and they almost grabbed a second as Gold Omatayo slipped a shot wide, before Danny Philliskirk was denied by Tyrer and then Banks nodded Emeka Obi's header off the line. The midfielder was clearly chuffed, celebrating it almost like scoring a goal. But Fylde kept on going and they eventually did get a second when Harry Davis headed in a corner on 86 minutes. That made it 1-1 on set-pieces, but the Spireites had the advantage in the only stat that mattered — the scoreline.

From being in cruise control, there was some panic in the Chesterfield ranks and only a stunning block from Grimes stopped Omatayo notching a third for Fylde. Six minutes were added and during that time Davis was shown his second yellow card for tugging the shirt of Joe Quigley. "Cheerio, cheerio, cheerio," sang the Town fans, who could now breathe a huge sigh of relief as the whistle was sounded on a 4-2 success.

It was two from two for Chesterfield with eight goals scored and it was the first time ever that they had bagged at least four times in each of their first two fixtures. The record-breaking stats were emerging right from the beginning. But the five goals conceded was a worry and it was a talking point on the message boards. Is this a title-winning defence? Could they win the league conceding so many goals? Does the backline need strengthening?

These were the sort of questions that supporters were asking. But the answers the local press were getting from the coaching staff was that it wasn't solely down to the back four and that it was more to do with players giving the ball away further up the pitch when they had committed men forward to attack. There was lots of intrigue as to how it would pan out. The players were being asked to do things that they had never done before. They were out of their comfort zone. Stretched to their limit. But the demands were high. And if you couldn't do what was being asked, then your days were numbered.

There was disappointment in the dressing room because the game had been out of sight at 4-0. Everyone knew that improvements needed to be made, but were confident that they would be. And despite scoring eight goals in two matches, there was a feeling that they could have been even more clinical, which showed the high standards being set.

**

Plastic pitches. Urgh. Chesterfield had never done well on them. The Likes of Naylor and Darren Oldaker hated them. Dobra's body had never reacted positively to them. And now there was another one in the league in Oxford City, who would be playing at this level for the very first time. They had come up from the National League South through the play-offs after finishing third. This was the Spireites' first-ever visit to the RAW Charging Stadium, which has a capacity of 3,100. With the lowest budget in the division, the part-timers were tipped to go straight back down. But their astroturf surface was a weapon that they could use to their advantage.

Cook had never been one for changing a winning team. He is a big believer in repetition and consistency, but this fixture was the first sign that he was more open to rotation this season. Williams missed out with that hamstring injury he suffered against Fylde so Ash Palmer was handed his first start, as was Michael Jacobs, while fellow new boy Berry was given his debut. One of the aims identified in the off-season was a desire to get more than the 27 league appearances out of Dobra that he managed in the previous campaign and, with the 3G surface in mind, he was on the bench.

As well as a flexibility in team selection, there was a tweak in formation as Chesterfield changed from a 4-2-3-1 to a 4-3-3. The thinking was that they could hurt Oxford in the wide areas and that Colclough and Berry could do a lot of damage one-versus-one. On paper, it looked like a very attacking line-up and some might argue that there can be such a thing as having too many forward players on the pitch, because it knocks the balance off and it can actually have the opposite effect. And that is how it felt on a nice summer's evening down in Oxfordshire for the first midweeker.

Wearing their orange and black away strip for the first time, there was not much to shout out about in the first half for the 641 supporters who had followed them down. The lively Josh Parker tested Tyrer, while down the other end Mandeville struck over the bar from distance. The blue-hooped hosts had been well-organised and given Town little room to work in. That was until a bright bit of play from Berry drew a good low save down to his right from goalkeeper Chris Haigh, who turned the ball around the post for a corner. And for the third match running, the Spireites scored from a set-piece when Naylor glanced in Berry's delivery just before half-time. Naylor, a former centre-back, had a record which suggested he could be an underrated goals threat and that was to be the case as the season unravelled. It was a first assist for Berry, too.

At half-time Webb had a sneaky look at the other scores in the division and he made a point of saying that if they could hold out for the win, then they would be top of the league. It was a little early incentive for the players. His belief was that it was important not to wait until 20-odd games into the season to get into first position. Do it now and thrive off the pressure. It was that elite mentality, alongside Cook's experience of keeping everyone grounded, that would stand Chesterfield in good stead.

The scoreline was harsh on Oxford, but they got themselves level just after the hour mark when Palmer's heavy touch on the halfway was pounced upon by Parker, who led a counter-attack, before drifting in behind Naylor to volley in Lewis Coyle's deep cross at the far post. With full-backs Sheckleford and Horton high up the pitch and possession given away cheaply, it was the type of goal that Chesterfield had already conceded and that they were keen to stamp out.

There were some nervy moments as the half progressed, including Tyrer saving from Parker and the hosts appealing for a penalty. A draw would have been fair, but the Spireites, who later returned to their preferred 4-2-3-1, found a way to win. A nice interchange of passes ended with substitute Oldaker, making his first appearance of the campaign, finding Grigg in the box to notch his second goal in as many matches and win the game. Oxford almost bagged an instant equaliser, but Tyrer made an excellent save to stop Parker's low shot from going in and ruining Town's 100 per cent start.

The result meant that Chesterfield went top of the table for the first time, as the only side to take maximum points from their first three fixtures. But Webb admitted afterwards that there were "still a lot of boxes yet to be ticked." He said: "We have got a few too many gaps when we lose the ball, but they will get plugged. The way we want to play is really attractive, attacking football which gets everyone off their seat and is really good to watch. But with that, sometimes there is going to be an openness to your play and it is about players reacting a bit quicker to fill the gaps that have been left by others. Hopefully, those things will come in a few months when we are top of the league."

Indeed ...

***

It's not often that you see a pitch invasion in the middle of August for a

1-1 draw. And when we say often, we mean never. But that is what happened when expected title rivals Oldham, with Norwood in tow, came to town. Everyone was tipping Chesterfield and the Latics to be going head-to-head for the one and only automatic promotion spot, so this fixture gave both sides a chance to get an early look at each other.

Oldham, then managed by former Everton defender David Unsworth, had ended the previous season strongly after finding themselves near the bottom for part of the campaign, eventually finishing 12th. Like the Spireites, expectations were high and they appeared to have made some good additions, with Norwood the most notable. The Latics came to the SMH Group Stadium on the back of losing 4-0 to Southend United on the opening day, before being beaten 2-1 at home to Halifax. But sandwiched in between those two results was an emphatic 5-1 victory against Aldershot Town. They were a team who were clearly still trying to gel. They were a bit unpredictable.

The *TNT Sports* cameras were in town for the Saturday lunchtime kick-off and they captured the moment a Chesterfield fan called Jamie bravely got down on one knee at pitch side to propose to his partner, Bethany. Thankfully, she said yes! Although the game had an intriguing look about it, nothing would be won or lost given it was the middle of August, although later antics from some of the 1,388 visiting supporters would have you think otherwise.

Oldham had won 1-0 in the same fixture the previous season, scoring after six minutes before sitting back and frustrating Town. And they went with a similar type of approach again. Unsworth, who was already under some pressure because of the early results and his style of football, knew it was a match he could not afford to lose. In truth, it was not a classic. Chesterfield controlled it but Oldham played on the counter-attack and probably had the better chances, particularly in the first half. Left-back Mark Kitching, who had been a threat in the win in Derbyshire six months before, made a raid early on and crossed for Norwood, who got in front of Palmer at the near post but headed wide, sparking sarcastic cheers from the Kop.

Kitching's opposite number, Horton, entered the box after a cool nutmeg and he picked out Colclough who headed on target but the delivery was slightly behind him. Soon after, the roles reversed as this time Colclough crossed from the right but Horton struck over the bar. The biggest chance of the first 45 fell to Norwood but he lifted the ball over after running through one-on-one. He had got himself between Grimes and Palmer and had managed to stay onside, but was wasteful in front of goal. The heavily-built striker turned around to face his teammates and put the top of his bright orange shirt into mouth. It was an expression of a man who knew it was a huge opportunity. He grimaced slightly, pressed his teeth together, before he put his head down and trotted back into position.

It was goalless at half-time but Chesterfield had to make a change with Sheckleford being forced off with a hamstring problem. It was an injury that would keep him out for two months and he would not start another league game until November. It was a shame for him because his appearances in his first season had been limited and now he had got injured when given his chance.

Oldham owner Frank Rothwell — who took over the club in July 2022 and who would go on to raise hundreds of thousands of pounds for Alzheimer's Research UK by incredibly rowing 3,000 miles across the Atlantic in 64 days, at the age of 73 — was with the away fans in the North Stand and he watched on as Chesterfield won a corner on the hour mark. Williams chipped a ball down the right flank for Mandeville to run onto and Liam Hogan headed behind for a corner as he tumbled to the ground. The Oldham captain claimed that Mandeville had clipped his heels, forcing him to lose his balance and concede the corner. He was furious at not being given a free-kick and referee Matthew Russell booked him for his reaction.

"Absolute bulls****," Hogan ripped as he marched back into his own box ready to defend the set-piece. Replays were inconclusive and Hogan's day got worse as seconds later Palmer's bullet header from the corner put Chesterfield ahead. The centre-back ran over towards the East Stand, his attempted knee-slide interrupted by a bump in the turf and he ended with his face planted in the ground and a pile-on commenced. Naylor, Grigg, Horton, Colclough and Grimes all jumped on top of him. It was a terrific header from Palmer, who had bullied his marker with an aggressive, determined, mazy off-the ball run before meeting the ball with his forehead. He had craned his neck muscles into a small gap to make contact. He had got where water couldn't.

Remarkably, he had already became Chesterfield's seventh different goalscorer of the season. That was a sign of things to come, with the goals being shared out all over the park. Oldham had struggled to defend from set-plays at the start of the season and Town had capitalised with their fifth goal from that method already. In the dugout, set-piece man Webb sprinted off before throwing his arms up in the air, while Cook lifted his right arm up towards the sky.

Chesterfield now had the momentum and they carved open Oldham with some slick build-up involving Oldaker, Mandeville and Jeff King, but Grigg got the ball caught under his feet in the box. That would have made it 2-0 and you just knew that was a big moment. It was the type of chance you would have expected him to bury. That could have put them nine points clear of Oldham already. Although he didn't net on that occasion, Grigg wouldn't let anyone down in the coming months. "Will there be late drama?" asked *TNT Sports* commentator, Adam Summerton, seconds before former Town man Charlie Raglan headed over from a corner. Everyone thought that was it. Chesterfield were in the clear. But they weren't.

Five minutes into added time, Kieron Freeman pinged a ball into the box from the right. Tyrer came off his line and chose to punch it rather than catch, but still got a decent distance on it. As the ball was in the air from Freeman, another former Spireite, Mike Fondop, fell to the floor, claiming he had been blocked off by Palmer. Play went on and with Fondop on the floor in an offside position and in the eyeline of Tyrer, Dan Gardner, who also used to wear the blue of Chesterfield, took aim from distance. Tyrer spilled it and Norwood pounced to slide in the rebound.

There was a deadly silence. Then it was chaos. Norwood, who had taken some stick for his body shape, to put it kindly, ran over to celebrate in front of the Chesterfield fans on the West Stand. He put his finger to his mouth in a shushing gesture. And then a couple of hundred Latics fans decided to join him on the pitch. It was one of those moments where time seemed to stand still. Was this really happening? Everything was in slow motion. People were looking at each other in disbelief.

In the pandemonium, Tyrer was pushed to the floor by an Oldham supporter, who would later appear in court and be slapped with a three-year banning order. That led to Cook leaving the dugout and going onto the turf to ensure his player was unhurt. It was a great show of leadership from Cook — and quite brave. This author remembered looking up from his laptop to see Cook marching onto the pitch, with hundreds of Oldham fans still going nuts. He was joined by his staff in Webb, Roberts and goalkeeping coach Dave O'Hare. They were worried that Tyrer might take further blows while he was on the floor, but thankfully he was okay. It was a bit surreal.

One Latics supporter, in a short-sleeved black T-shirt, had his arm around Norwood and was slapping him on the chest. Another got a selfie with him. Footage from the incident showed one Chesterfield fan in a red T-shirt and dark shorts having his cap knocked off his head as he and an Oldham supporter swung for each other a couple of times — but missed. Both of them also received three-year banning orders. While that was going on, Tyrer had gone over to the linesman and called for the goal to be ruled out for offside. "I can't see the ball," he said, with his mouth wide open in disbelief. Jacobs was with him and made the same point.

Eventually, the Oldham army got back in the stand. There was some confusion about what was going to happen next. Were the officials going to consult with each other and chalk off the goal? Was the last minute of the game going to be played? Oldham were trying to make a sub. In the end, referee Russell blew up early and that was that. It was one of the most bizarre finishes to a game and the points were shared. It would be the last time Chesterfield did not win at home for a very long time.

Webb described the late leveller as a "kick in the gut," and said he was disappointed that the officials didn't even have a discussion about Oldham's equaliser, believing that had the Latics fans not entered the field of play, then it probably would have been ruled out. At the same time, given the shock at what had happened, they were kind of relieved that the full-time whistle was blown because they feared more ugly scenes if Oldham had done the unthinkable and somehow scored again.

During the match, Oldham supporters had sang that Unsworth's football was "s***," but he said his game-plan had worked "perfectly" and that had it been a European encounter then it would have been a "masterclass."

Perhaps he was trying to put pressure on the Spireites, but his post-match comments that Chesterfield were the "best team in the league" and that they would "probably win the league" got under the skin of the Latics fanbase. Was he conceding the title just four games in on August

19? A couple of days later he tried to clarify what he meant, saying that if Oldham finished above Chesterfield then they would be champions. It was a failed attempt at smoothing things over. He also falsely claimed that Town had "double the budget" of the Latics. He was clearly a man feeling the heat and he was sacked one month later, with the club third from bottom. "The start of the current campaign has unfortunately not met the expectations of the club," Oldham said in a statement.

For Chesterfield, they were unbeaten in four, including three wins. Leaving the stadium, despite the gut-wrenching equaliser, you knew which dressing room you would rather be in. And it wasn't the away one. Four months later, the Football Association finally fined Oldham £5,000 for the pitch invasion and warned them about their future conduct. Bizarrely, they denied the charges, which stated they had failed to ensure that their supporters behaved in an "orderly fashion." But surprise surprise, the case was proven.

One line stood out from Webb's chat with the local media pitch side after the game and that was: "A win is much better than a draw, but a draw is much better than a defeat and hopefully come the end of the season we will have had the last laugh. We have got to crack on, keep winning games and win this league."

They would, indeed, have the last laugh.

11

BASKETBALL

The atmosphere was uncomfortable. It was filled with anxiety and frustration. It made your teeth grind and your toes curl. It was teetering on the edge. Borderline anger. It made you want to cover your ears. Shut yourself away. It was like being in a pub when you can sense trouble brewing. Or being at a party gate-crashed by those not invited. Side-eyes were exchanged across the press box. This could get nasty.

Social media was even worse. It was toxic. Every update was met by responses from people getting angrier and angrier. They were going redder and redder in the face. They were about to combust. The keyboards and keypads on their laptops and phones were taking a hammering. They were about to set on fire. You could be forgiven for thinking that someone had just walked into their front living room and thrown their TV through the window.

But they would learn. They would soon realise that this team was not like those of the past. This lot wouldn't curl up into a ball and hide away. This group wouldn't throw the towel in. These lads would stick their chests out. They would come back fighting like Tyson Fury. Why? Because they were bloody good players. They were fit. They had a togetherness. They had suffered pain. They had one common goal. And they had a manager who made them feel as tall as the Shard. These boys responded to going two goals down with the words: "Challenge accepted."

And whenever it happened again, those in the crowd wouldn't get tetchy. They wouldn't get ratty. They wouldn't shout abuse. They wouldn't boo. They would wait for the magic to happen. And it did.

***

The August Bank Holiday weekend brought about a double-header against Altrincham and Hartlepool United. Although it was two games in three days, Chesterfield did not want to use that as an excuse because they knew they had a strong squad with two players for each position. This is where their summer recruitment would come into play. They could use their strength and depth to their advantage.

Another challenge of the busy fixture schedule was making sure that enough homework was done on both opponents so that no stone was left unturned. Each member of the coaching team took on some of the workload and they took it in turns to watch Altrincham and Hartlepool with a fresh pair of eyes.

On the same bank holiday in the previous season, Chesterfield and Barnet both agreed to move the game from Saturday to a Friday night, giving both sides an extra day to prepare for Monday's match. But that was not a conversation that was had this time and so it would be two fixtures in 72 hours of "fun," as assistant manager Danny Webb described it. Like Town, Altrincham had also started the season unbeaten, but they'd done it with one win and three draws. They had a boss in Phil Parkinson whose reputation was growing and who will probably be in the Football League sooner rather than later, as well as one of the best young attacking talents in the division in midfielder Chris Conn-Clarke, who had already scored twice in four matches and would go on to hit 22 goals. He would earn a move to League One Peterborough United, who have a long history of plucking players out of non-league, the following summer.

The Robins had proved to be a tricky customer in the past and had beaten the Blues a couple of times at Moss Lane, so they would not be underestimated. A "freak" mechanical fault on one of the True Blue Travel coaches on the way to the ground prevented some Chesterfield supporters from attending. An apology was issued and a full refund on both the cost of travel and match ticket was given. A voucher to use on the concourses at a home fixture was also issued. They did not know it at the time, but those affected probably ended up having a better day.

Game number five saw Chesterfield's sixth goal of the season from a set-piece as Jamie Grimes headed in Liam Mandeville's deep corner on 16 minutes to put the Spireites 1-0 up. The visitors had not really been in any danger for the rest of the afternoon, but they had also not created much of note to grab a second. The second half was a bit of a sleepy affair and it seemed to be petering out for an uneventful narrow away win until a mad 10 minutes turned the scoreline around.

It was 1-1 on 82 minutes when substitute Dior Angus, a former Wrexham striker, played a nippy one-two with Justin Amaluzor before firing across Harry Tyrer into the far corner. Altrincham smelt blood, they could sense the panic in the Chesterfield ranks and they pushed for a second goal as Tyrer saved with his legs from Regan Linney, who then had another chance but he hit the side-netting. But the Robins would get a winner in the 93rd minute when Angus swivelled and finished from close-range after a loose pass by Branden Horton.

On the touchline, Cook had been yelling at Ash Palmer and Grimes to squeeze up the pitch for some time, but they appeared reluctant to do so and Chesterfield fell to their first defeat of the season. It had been avoidable, but it perhaps served as an early wake-up call. Cook urging his centre-backs to get up towards the halfway line was a familiar sight throughout the season. He wanted them to play higher because that was the best way for them to put pressure on the ball further up the pitch. But naturally, as is seen time and time again in football, defences tend to drop deep when trying to maintain a lead. Space in behind makes them nervous. It was totally understandable, but by not squeezing up, combined with giving up possession, they conceded two goals anyway, so there was a lesson learnt there. Cook has no problems with players making mistakes when doing things that he is asking them to do. It's when people make errors doing things he doesn't want them to do which frustrates him.

Since his return to the club, Cook had only spoken to the media after a defeat and he did so at Moss Lane. He gave an honest assessment, as he always does, saying that Altrincham deserved to win the game, as well as outlining his frustrations at not being able to at least get a point. He also gave some detail on his team's weaknesses — "softness, decision-making and not retaining possession of the ball." He said: "We have a softness about us that has got to change if we are going to be successful this year. We have this Achilles' heel. I never feel comfortable. I watch us getting deeper, sloppier, refusing to do basic stuff like clear your lines."

He knew what the problems were and you backed him to sort them out.

***

Bouncebackability is a word coined by former Crystal Palace manager Iain Dowie. He used it when explaining how his side had gone from relegation candidates to promotion-winners, as they remarkably won 17 of their last 23 matches in 2003/04 to win promotion to the Premier League through the play-offs. For Chesterfield, the ability to bounce back from a setback was something they had struggled with in the 2022/23 campaign.

After going 10 unbeaten at the start of that season, they then lost three on the bounce in a week. They also went nine games without a win from the end of January to the start of March. If they were to win promotion a year later, then those sorts of runs could not happen. The top teams very rarely lost successive matches and Chesterfield knew they could not afford to get in a rut this time. If they lost a game, they had to respond next time out. There was no margin for error.

Just 48 hours after Altrincham, Chesterfield had a chance to get back on the horse when they hosted Hartlepool United, who had just dropped back into the National League after two seasons in the Football League, on Bank Holiday Monday. Despite losing to Barnet on the opening day, they had then won four consecutive matches to top the table so they had adapted quite well. Mike Jones was brought in for his first start of the season and, although he would go on to help provide some stability to the side in the weeks and months to come, his inclusion was not enough to solve Chesterfield's problems immediately.

In front of one the biggest crowds of the season of 8,451, the Spireites got off to the worst possible start, conceding twice in the first six minutes after goals from ex-Town striker Mani Dieseruvwe and impressive French midfielder Anthony Mancini. Dieseruvwe bullied Chesterfield in the first 20 minutes with his physicality and hold-up play, slotting into the bottom corner for the opener. It was yet another goal conceded from giving away cheap possession and then being countered on.

Mancini, a left-footed winger playing on the right, was powerful, quick and skilful and really caught the eye. He would be one of the better opposition players that the Blues would face in the season. He doubled the lead after being involved in some quick play down the right, before finding himself unmarked in the box and he was allowed to take a touch, turn and roll the ball low into the net.

The Pools had sliced open Chesterfield twice in the opening six minutes and, having scored three times in each of their last three fixtures, at that point you would not have backed against them to make it four in a row. They were cutting through the Spireites like a knife through butter and fans were wincing every time they came forward. In response, the fans started to sing the name of out-of-favour Laurence Maguire. The defender had played no part in the first few games despite being a regular in the side in the latter part of the previous season, helping Chesterfield to clinch third position. The supporters had not seen their team keep a clean sheet yet and they were now 2-0 down after six minutes. They wanted their feelings to be known.

As mentioned already, the atmosphere was tense and fraught. Two goals behind and with frustrations in the stands, Chesterfield could have crumbled. They could have hid. But Ryan Colclough halved the deficit on 14 minutes, heading in Mandeville's cross at the back post to continue his bright start to the new term. Six minutes later, Mancini was forced off with a hamstring injury that would keep him out for four months. That proved to be a turning point in the game; from then on it was all Chesterfield and it seemed only like a matter of time before they drew level.

As much as the Spireites were conceding similar types of goals, they were also scoring lots from set pieces and a corner from Mandeville, headed in by Grimes, his second in as many games, made it 2-2 just after half-time. It was like watching a different match from the first 20 minutes, with wave after wave of Chesterfield attacks. Although no one knew it at the time, the Spireites would be a second half team as the season progressed, wearing sides down with their fitness levels and relentless pressure.

Colclough was a man on a mission, going close several times, including having a goal ruled out for offside. James Berry also had a shot cleared off the line and Will Grigg missed a gilt-edged header. Everyone would have taken a point at 2-0 down, but in a strange way it would also have been disappointing to only get a draw because of the chances they had squandered. But they weren't to be denied.

In the 95th minute, Mandeville played a free-kick short to Berry, who crossed into the box. The ball ricocheted off Grigg and into the path of Tom Naylor, who fired in. It was a scrappy goal but no one cared. *Limbs.*

The scenes were joyous. Just like against Dorking, they had come from behind to find a late winner. "That day, before Colclough scored to make it 2-1, was a big speedbump because there was unrest," Webb explained. "But then you sensed that once it got to 2-2 there was only one team that was going to win it and that was when our supporters really came into their own. Because when we needed it, they certainly gave it to us."

Having had a mountain to climb and threatening to fall further behind and with the crowd getting anxious, Chesterfield had shown some real stones to ride it out and then go on to win it. It was just one match, but one that would be marked under "important" come the end of April. It had been a memorable five-goal thriller and it wasn't the only one of the season. Grimes said: "We always believed that if we got to 70-75 minutes, teams would fall apart and make mistakes because we would keep the ball and move them from side to side a lot. We knew that we would wear teams down and get chances late on."

"I never doubted us," Colclough added. "We always finish strong. We never doubted that we were going to score or create chances. There are not many games we don't dominate." By the end of August, Chesterfield had already won three games by scorelines of 4-3, 4-2 and 3-2. Could they keep this up? Could they get promoted this way? Did everyone need to bring a defibrillator to the SMH because of all the heart-stopping moments?

"You have to be careful it does not turn into basketball," Webb told the media after the breathless encounter. "We don't want to have to score three every game to win it. I would like to think today is a nice turning point because at 2-0 there was a real courage and a strength to go and win the game. Sooner rather than later we need to start getting some clean sheets."

Mike Jones later reflected: "Conceding goals was a bit of an obvious concern and maybe from the previous season as well. The gaffer knew that, he wasn't alien to it. That is the way he likes his team to play — on the front-foot, quite open, expansive, scoring goals. And sometimes when you play like that you are a little bit suspect at the back as well. You have got to take the hit with the good. We were exciting to watch and we showed character to win games from a very early stage. We always knew we could come back. The year before, it always felt like we were going to concede and that's what happened at Wembley. But this year, if we were getting beat we were still like: 'We will still win this, we have got loads of goals in us and loads of time.' That was the character in the squad and time and time again we did it. The main thing was winning, no matter how we did it."

Jeff King added: "Everyone who was involved in that Wembley final, you could see this year had extra bite. It was no coincidence that we were winning games in the 94th minute. That was down to the grit, determination of not wanting that feeling again of missing out. We said that we needed to stop conceding goals because our front four aren't just going to keep winning us games. We thought that there would be a time when they are not firing and we need to help them. We were fully aware of it and so was the gaffer."

***

Back on the training ground, a lot of work had been going into defending and attacking corners and free-kicks. Webb was the man who led on set pieces and he would start by watching some recent examples of how the next opposition would set-up, whether it be wide free-kicks, corners or long throws. He would make detailed notes on how teams would organise themselves and he would come up with ways on how to counter that. Within that, he would look at whether takers were inswingers or outswingers and he would work closely with analyst Jack Stephenson to find out which players go in the box the most and who tends to make the most first contacts.

Webb would then allocate them a marker; for example someone like Grimes or Palmer would be put up against the opposition's biggest physical threat or best header of the ball. When attacking, if the opposition are towering above them, then they would be told to play a few more short ones. Mandeville was on corners for the majority of the season and they would get a lot of joy from his deliveries. "I think early on I found a technique that I liked and I stuck with it," he explained. "I always do the same amount of steps. It is almost like a golf or tennis shot, always the same routine every time. I felt like that helped and a lot of the time it was a similar sort of deliveries that were required. We were a big side last year and I think that went under the radar."

On a Thursday before a Saturday game, Webb would take away the starting line-up and walk them through set plays so they had a picture of where they needed to be. Then later on they would get shown some video clips to make things even clearer. The phrase "second phase" is a modern term in football which refers to when a set piece has only been partially cleared, for example when a header is only nodded to the edge of the box and a team keeps the attack alive. Later in the season, Darren Oldaker would win a penalty for Chesterfield after picking up a second ball inside Bromley's box. That had been plotted by Webb, who was diligent in his homework.

Chesterfield would go on to score the most goals from set pieces in the division and concede the second fewest, with Southend United pipping them on the final day. "There is a lot that goes into it," Webb said. "I can set them up and do the work but they have to take responsibility. I showed the lads a table from the previous season and we finished second in both categories. So I said if we can finish top of one of those tables I think we will be up there. Luckily for us it was a major factor of why we went up along with all the other boxes we ticked. Whether it was the gaffer's shape, or the coaches' training ground work, or my set pieces … they all married up to make a good set of players win games."

Grimes said: "Throughout the season, Danny Webb would put leaderboards up for goals for and against, for set pieces and he would tell us that if we wanted to go up then we needed to be top of both tables. He would do a presentation on what each teams' threats were and then on the training ground he would work us through it. There was a lot of detail."

***

There was another game of "basketball" five days later at Aldershot Town for the first fixture of September. It was one of seven that month, which would mean almost 30 per cent of the season would be completed already. The Shots were having a lot of successful shots. They were the top home scorers in the division, scoring nine in their first three outings at The EBB Stadium. Many tipped them to struggle, but they were a surprise package, challenging for the play-offs and reaching the FA Cup third round.

And you could see why, with lively attackers Josh Stokes, Lorent Tolaj and Jack Barham. Teenage striker Stokes earned himself a move to Bristol City in January but was loaned back for the rest of the season. Swiss forward Tolaj also attracted attention with his 20-plus goals. Webb had earmarked him as one of the better strikers in the league.

During midweek, young defender Miguel Freckleton, 20 at the time, signed on a season-long loan from Sheffield United. The left-sided centre-back, who could also play left-back, had been on the radar for a while. He caught Chesterfield's eye when he played for the Blades against the Spireites in pre-season and they had monitored him ever since. They liked his calmness on the ball, his speed and the fact he had already been on loan in the National League with Wealdstone. Unlike other top-flight youngsters, he arrived with no ego and adapted instantly to training. He was focused from the beginning and wanted to show what he could do.

Cook had been flabbergasted at the number of players Chesterfield had signed in the past when he delved into the numbers on his return. But that wouldn't happen under his watch. Freckleton, on August 30, would be their last signing of the season which, when you think about the scramble for players over recent years, was quite an incredible stat. It showed that they had got their recruitment bang-on.

With Freckleton and Tyrer through the door, it said a lot about Chesterfield as a club, their style of play and Cook, that two Premier League sides were willing to loan them their young stars. Interestingly, Webb indicated that Freckleton coming in could allow them to go to a three-man defence to see games out and that happened down in Hampshire. Having always been a back-four man, it came as a bit of a surprise, but it was another sign of Cook's willingness to be flexible tactically.

The message to the players before kick-off was to play in their style, their identity, get an early goal and then at a minimum come away with a 1-0 win. It was a nice thought, but it ended up being another mad game. Colclough tested goalkeeper Jack Bycroft twice early on, but a scruffy goal down the other end for Stokes following a counter-attack down the right put the hosts in the lead on 25 minutes. The wait for a clean sheet would go on.

But just eight minutes later, Colclough scored an even uglier goal, his fourth in eight appearances, to make it 1-1. And it came from a Mandeville corner. The meticulous planning from set-pieces continued to pay off. Two goals in eight minutes after half-time from Grigg and Naylor, the latter a header from a corner to continue Town's threat from set plays, gave Chesterfield a commanding 3-1 lead towards the hour mark. But two minutes later the game was in the balance again as Tolaj teed up Barham for a simple tap-in. And there was a narrow escape soon after when Barham's header hit the crossbar and bounced back down and onto the woodwork again before going out of play.

Aldershot's second goal was the signal for Chesterfield to deploy what would be described as a "lopsided back three" in a bid to tighten things up, with Freckleton coming on for his debut to make a three-man defence and Mandeville floating between right-back and right-wingback depending on whether Town had possession or not. However, on 83 minutes it was 3-3 when Barham glanced in a terrific header. All three of Aldershot's goals had come from crosses. At that point, with the momentum with the home side, most people would have taken a draw. Including Cook, who told his opposite number Tommy Widdington — whose son Theo was sent off late on for throwing Armando Dobra off the pitch — exactly that after the full-time whistle.

But the basketball bonanza swung back in Chesterfield's favour when Joe Quigley came off the bench to score his second winner of the season as a substitute, lashing home from close-range in the 87th minute. Not content with five-goal epics, the Spireites had somehow secured themselves a seven-goal three-pointer. It was fantasy football. That victory took them up to second in the table, behind leaders Barnet only on goal difference.

The post-match interviews followed a familiar theme as previous weeks, with Webb saying that just because they had won, "things were not being swept under the carpet," adding: "There is an openness to us. Players have got to make better decisions of when to press and when to stay. We don't want to turn each game into basketball. As a team and I must stress it is as a team, we want to be conceding a lot less goals than we are at the moment. The idea is that we look back on these days at the end of the season and go: 'Those three points got us over the line to the promised land', but that is a long way off."

Michael Jacobs, who was just getting used to the National League, said: "When I came in I was expecting a little 2-0 or 3-0 here and there but there was none of that! Even from the opening day of the season against Dorking it was frantic from the off until the end." Reflecting back, Mandeville said: "A lot of the goals we conceded were from being sloppy on the ball and then teams breaking and scoring. It is going to happen at our level. At the end of the day, we are not Man City, we are not going to be able to keep the ball 99 per cent of the time. But with the way we played, it did wear teams down and then with our fitness and quality, it was always going to be hard to keep us out for 90 minutes."

***

The win against Hartlepool had not been a turning point in terms of goals conceded and the fragility and softness shown against Aldershot was alarming, so Cook set about making his Chesterfield side more solid. He knew that something had to be done despite the positive results. He saw the bigger picture. On average, they were scoring three a game, but conceding two.

For the next match, a 3-1 home win against Dagenham and Redbridge, Mandeville, a player Cook trusted deeply and who had been influential higher up the pitch, was again selected at right-back. It was felt that Mandeville was someone who could do a job in most positions, was tactically very astute and would be able to start attacks from deep. From Mandeville's point of view, it was a position that allowed him to get into dangerous areas and there weren't many opposition wingers who had the same engine to track him all the way up and down the pitch.

"I think it was Kieron Dyer who suggested it," Mandeville said. "I think he felt I had good attributes for it. I feel like I am a steady right-back, rather than an attacking right-back, which is surprising given I am an attacking player. I was actually comfortable defending one-v-one. I was probably more comfortable defending than I was attacking in a strange way. I think I have got quite a good football IQ so I am quite good at understanding what a position needs and having played for the gaffer for a few years, I know where he wants players on the pitch.

"But I certainly found a new appreciation for the right-back role. Don't get me wrong, there are some games where it is actually the easiest posi-

A devastated Drew Talbot's body language says it all as Chesterfield are officially relegated from the Football League in 2018, away at Forest Green Rovers. Below: The Spireites fans in the away end for their side's first game back in non-league, a 1-0 victory away at Ebbsfleet United *(Tina Jenner)*

Nervous Chesterfield players watch the shoot-out drama as the Spireites lose the 2023 play-off final at Wembley, with Notts County prevailing on penalties. Below: Despair for one fan and for Mike Jones, the veteran who had signed earlier that summer after impressing on trial   (*Tina Jenner*)

Joe Quigley celebrates his dramatic last-minute winner against Dorking Wanderers on an exciting opening day which rather set the tone for what was to come during the 2023/24 season *(Tina Jenner)*

Left: The good form of the Spireites even saw fans travel over from Spain to witness Paul Cook's men storm their way to promotion and then the league title

(Richard Simpson)

The Spireites were backed in numbers throughout their time in the National League, with their fans enjoying the ride while their team put on a show
(James Briggs)

Right: Chesterfield had to work hard to bring Will Grigg to the club, but it proved to be well worth it
(Paul Brassington)

Below left: Club mascot Chester the field mouse gets in on the celebrations on a foggy winter's day
(Michael Parkinson)

Below right: The moment that Spireites fans thought they had won their cup tie at Watford, but Ryan Colclough's header went over the bar
(Paul Brassington)

An atmospheric sky over Hartlepool United's Victoria Park stadium after Armando Dobra's early goal gave Chesterfield a 1-0 victory, their fifth win on the spin after a rare defeat (*David Coupland*)

Below: A familiar sight for Spireites fans as striker Grigg wheels away after scoring to cap victory away at Kidderminster Harriers, one of 25 goals for the Northern Ireland international (*Tina Jenner*)

Joyous scenes at the SMH as Chesterfield's fans and players celebrate together after victory over Boreham Wood secured the National League title, with skipper Jamie Grimes fittingly scoring the Spireites' 100th league goal of the season. Below: The drinks flow in the dressing room (*Tina Jenner*)

Another view of the pitch invasion to mark Chesterfield's Football League return *(Will Shearstone)*
Below: Goalkeeper Harry Tyrer and assistant boss Danny Webb with their medals *(Liam Norcliffe)*

Paul Cook's Spireites return was vindicated when he led his side to another promotion *(Tina Jenner)*
Below: The flag says it all as supporters gather at the town hall for more celebrations *(Liam Norcliffe)*

tion on the pitch. I remember one game against Eastleigh and I literally had the full length of the pitch that I could run into and no one was closing me down. But there were other games when it was a full press and there were not actually that many options in front of me."

With Mandeville getting up and down the right, Freckleton came in at left-back for his first start but was often tasked with tucking in and providing a back three, which was another attempt at making things more secure. "Because we were conceding a lot of goals from counter-attacks and not being as solid as what we would have liked, we started rolling into a three," Grimes explained.

"Instead of going two centre-halves on the halfway line with two midfielders in front, we would roll into a three. It started to work and gave us the confidence to be more solid. The gaffer was always doing things like that if he felt we needed to be more solid in a game. Sometimes he would do the opposite if he felt we needed to be more expansive — full-backs pushed up, centre-halves defending one-v-one on the halfway line. That is the belief he would give you to go on and win games and score lots of goals."

In baking conditions, Ryan Hill went close twice for the visitors before Josh Rees, who had scored a winner against Chesterfield in the previous season for Boreham Wood, volleyed in from the second-phase of a free-kick. The match hinged on the 70th minute sending-off of Daggers defender Harry Phipps, who was given his marching orders after dragging back Grigg on the edge of the area. Just like against Dorking, it ended up being a double punishment, because Colclough curled in the resulting free-kick to make it 1-1 and notch his fifth goal in eight outings.

Berry had only made one start since signing but he had been making a big impression off the bench and he won a penalty in the 90th minute after a driving run into the area saw him clipped in the box. Grigg did the honours from the spot and then Ollie Banks, who was another who had struggled for game-time, added a third from distance when his powerful drive creeped under goalkeeper Elliott Justham. Those two goals meant Chesterfield had scored seven times after the 90th minute in eight games. They had already secured 12 points from losing positions. A clean sheet still eluded them, but not for long.

"I remember that we weren't playing particularly well in the games but we were winning," Grimes said. "When I look back at it now, we just kept winning and winning and winning. But a lot of the time it didn't feel like we were winning because we had conceded goals or not played well. We would win a game and there would be no music on in the dressing room or anything.

"It was like: 'Right, we have got to be better next week,' and that was the mentality we had in the dressing room. The gaffer set that mentality. It is not about the result, it is about the performance. You know the way he wants you to play, but if you don't do it you come off the pitch feeling a bit "urgh" because we didn't perform how we were supposed to but we won the game. That performance mentality, rather than results, was really healthy for us."

12

FULL CIRCLE

James Berry had fallen out of love with football a little bit. After leaving Wigan Athletic, the former Liverpool academy prospect had spent two years at Hull City, making his debut for the Tigers in the Championship in 2020. But it didn't really work out after that. The coronavirus struck and Berry was living up in East Yorkshire and he couldn't see anyone. Football wasn't going great for him and things started to happen which he didn't agree with. "I'd just had enough," he explained. "Decisions were happening which were unfair and I was like: 'What's going on here?' I was living there and I was miserable. I wasn't depressed or anything like that but I just wasn't happy with football, I wasn't enjoying it."

Berry left the Tigers by mutual consent in July 2021 and he was ready to call it quits. He was 20 at the time and had become disillusioned with the sport he loved and had played for most of his life. He said: "I remember coming home and saying to my mum and dad: 'That's it for me now.' I had worked so hard and for me to be let down that easy, I just thought: 'I can't be doing with it anymore.'"

Berry was out of the game for four months and during that time he went to work with his dad doing plastering. It was early mornings and late finishes. Long days. Hard graft. But he enjoyed it and they had a laugh together. And it would make him appreciate even more how lucky he is to play football for a living. Whilst thinking about what to do next, he also thought about going to America and doing some coaching.

After swapping football for plastering, he was ready to put his boots back on again and he spoke to Altrincham manager Phil Parkinson. Berry was reluctant to sign straight away and instead he said he would come and train for free. In a behind-closed-doors friendly against Stoke City, he remembered being really unfit. He didn't look out of shape, but his aerobic ability had decreased in his time off. He only played 45 minutes, but he was shattered. In the end, he did sign for the Robins but was immediately loaned out to Macclesfield until January 2022. Berry spoke to Macclesfield's director of football and ex-Premier League midfielder Robbie Savage, who told him all about the club being reborn from the ashes and having to start all over again in the North West Counties Premier Division — the ninth tier of English football.

Berry liked the idea of being able to play football with a bit more freedom and enjoyment like he did when he was a kid. His love for football soon returned and he was adamant that he wanted to sign for Macclesfield permanently, his wish eventually coming true. He would go on to win two successive promotions with the Silkmen, banging in dozens of goals and assists and claiming a number of individual awards.

Berry was first made aware of Chesterfield's interest three hours before a pre-season friendly against Buxton. Savage called him and told him that the Spireites had put a bid in. In the past, other National League clubs had tried to sign him while he was at the Silkmen but he turned them down instantly. He didn't give them much thought. But this opportunity was much more appealing. It was a big club with ambitions to get back in the Football League. "I put the phone down and my dad was there," Berry said. "I told him that Chesterfield had put a bid in and me and my dad looked at each other as if to say: 'That's a good club.' With all the other clubs, I said no straight away. But that one really did turn my head."

The negotiations started and took place over 10 days. In that time, Berry was desperate to sign. He had loved his time at Macclesfield, but Paul Cook had sold him the club and he wanted to move. It was an easy decision to make. As a Wigan Athletic fan, the lure of playing under Cook, someone who had had success at the Latics, was very enticing. Cook explained how he would make him a better player and Berry liked what he heard. Berry was at Wigan when he was 16 and he would go watch matches when Cook was manager.

Although their paths did not really cross in Lancashire, Berry was fully aware of what Cook was about. Not only that, but Will Grigg, Michael Jacobs and Ryan Colclough were in the Wigan first team at the time and sometimes some of the youngsters would go and train with the seniors.

Years later, Berry was teammates with them at Chesterfield. "It is a mad, full-circle thing," he said.

When Berry arrived at the Spireites, he was made to feel welcome by all his teammates but Tom Naylor, in particular, made sure he was settling in okay. It was another full circle moment for Berry; Naylor was another ex-Wigan player who he had watched play for the club he supports and now they were sharing a dressing room together. Grigg and Jacobs would also take him under their wing and wouldn't hesitate to help him when he came to them for advice, while Tyrone Williams was the first person to take him out for something to eat. "It is little things like that that I don't forget," Berry said. "They made me feel really welcome as soon as I walked through the door."

On helping the younger players like Berry, Grigg said: "If they are not willing to learn and listen and buy into what anyone has got to offer, whether it be the gaffer or the senior players in the dressing room, it is a waste of time. I can only offer so much but it is the boys who are willing to listen and learn. Growing up, I had some good characters who definitely helped me, so as you get older your view on certain things and your perspective definitely changes a little bit. It is not just on the pitch, I think I can help off the pitch as well. It is definitely something I have tried to add to my game and my personality, but it is credit to the boys in the dressing room for doing everything that they do, day in, day out. Everyone works so hard and that is down to the players putting everything into it."

The first three weeks of training at Chesterfield were really hard for the winger. It was more intense and sharper than it had been at Macclesfield. The biggest challenge was the physical aspect. He would wake up in the mornings and he would be sore from the previous day's workout. Not long ago he had been playing part-time football in the ninth-tier of English football but here the physical demands were much higher. Berry is close with his mum and dad but it would be his dad and grandad who he would always talk to about football. After every training session, every match, he would chat to his dad about how it went. One day after a gruelling session, they spoke over the phone about how it was going.

"I remember saying to him that it was going to take me time to adapt," Berry said. "It was not that I was struggling but it was difficult.

It was like: 'Wow, this is tough.'" His dad offered him some simple advice, explaining that it would take time for his body to adapt and he was right. But he would soon get up to speed and from then on he looked forward to the training.

There was another Wigan connection, in Chesterfield's first-team coach Gary Roberts. As an attacking player himself, Roberts is someone who Berry would watch closely. Now Roberts was staying behind with him after every session to do some extra work on his finishing. Left foot. Right foot. Volleys. Headers. Bottom corners. Top bins. Inside the box. Outside the area. Those days plastering with his dad had certainly put things into perspective when it came putting the extra work in.

Now at Chesterfield, in his eyes, he was living the dream. He was training every day as a professional footballer. He counted himself as being very lucky and he was loving every second. Others may have shied away from the challenge that lay ahead. Their head might have dropped. Their heart might have not been in it. But not Berry. He'd come too far to quit now. "When I do that extra training, I think: 'What's there to go home for? What do I need to rush home for?' I live on my own in my apartment. I like to perfect my shooting because finishing is one of my best attributes. I am obsessed with getting it nailed down.

"I do really appreciate it because there are not many people that get to this stage — it is really hard. Three years ago I didn't want to do it. I know how lucky I am but, at the same time, if it weren't for me having a bit of b****** about it and going down to that level and not worrying what people think and stuff, then I wouldn't be here. I always thought that if I did really well then I would be back to where I should be, because I know I can play football with the best of them.

"It is surreal, I know how lucky I am, but I also know how ballsy I have been. It is all through my own type of doing why I am here. People can open doors for you but, at the end of the day, you have got to walk through them. I always live by the saying 'live in the moment' because you never know when your life can be turned upside down. Every day I say to people: 'Enjoy it, because it's precious.'"

Berry would have to be patient for his chance when he first joined, starting just once in the first 10 games, but he would make a positive impact off the bench. "I knew coming from Macclesfield and part-time and coming into a great team like Chesterfield, that I would not obviously play as much as I did at Macclesfield," he explained. "I was realistic about what was going to happen. But I also knew I would get my chance."

And he would take it in the coming weeks and months.

***

The ninth fixture of the season finally brought a first clean sheet. It came away at newly-promoted Ebbsfleet United, whose previous eight matches had looked like this: WLWLWLWL. The Fleet, then managed by German Denis Kutrieb, had won the National League South title with ease, achieving 103 points, 20 clear of their nearest rival and scoring 110 goals. And they had used that momentum to get themselves in the play-off positions early on, although they would eventually end up fighting relegation, with Kutrieb sacked in January, before edging clear under Danny Searle.

Questions from the local media before the game centred on the use of the back three and whether selecting Liam Mandeville at right-back was a long-term plan. It was clear from the answers given that Chesterfield were going to be more flexible in their approach this season and that selections and tactical decisions would be decided on a match-by-match basis. They would stick to their core principles of how they wanted to play and wouldn't stray too far away from that but, at the same time, they would tweak things if they thought it would help them get a positive result.

Mandeville did indeed carry on at right-back at Stonebridge Road Stadium, while Miguel Freckleton started at left-back, as he would for the rest of September. He was seen as a "stay at home" full-back, someone who would help tighten up the left side, rather than bomb forward like Branden Horton would. In possession, he would tuck inside to give Chesterfield a three-man defence, allowing Mandeville to get on his bike. They wanted to be more rigid away from home, while still playing attractive football.

The game down in Kent was one of the most one-sided 1-0 wins you are likely to see. The Spireites totally dominated from start to finish, but they were denied by a string of superb saves by goalkeeper Mark Cousins. Fleet's dangerman was former Leeds United striker Dominic Poleon, who had hammered in 35 goals in their promotion campaign and had already notched seven goals in six appearances before the Blues visited. But he was kept quiet for the majority of the 90 minutes.

As Cousins kept Chesterfield at bay, on the touchline Paul Cook was bellowing "patience, patience" as his team kept on getting into dangerous areas. He would roar that from the sidelines throughout the season, so much so that it made you wonder whether he was shouting it in his sleep! The second half continued in the same manner, with Cousins' inspired goalkeeping performance showing no signs of letting up. He was having one of those matches that all 'keepers dream of. The former Colchester United man would just not be beaten. Until he was.

It was eight minutes from time when Berry's hard graft on the training ground paid off. The substitute had got in down the left before picking out Dobra, who stabbed home from close-range. It was a scruffy finish, but well-deserved. That was Dobra's first goal of the season, his first since Wembley and the "Albanian Arrow" was off the mark. Replays showed that Dobra may have been lucky not to have given away a foul for a push on Joe Martin in the build-up, which meant he was unmarked in the box. Martin ran over to referee Paul Johnson and flung his arms in the air, but his appeals were ignored. In fairness, it would have been a hard one for Johnson to spot in real time.

Jacobs, who had earlier hit the post, was shown a second yellow card for apparent time-wasting with a throw-in, but it didn't matter. Chesterfield had recorded their first shutout of the season — much to the delight of Tyrer, who could rest easy knowing his next appraisal from 'Tank' to Sean Dyche would be positive — and their fourth successive win since the defeat to Altrincham. It sent them back to the top of the table with 22 points from nine games. They would remain there for the rest of the season. From September 16, they would be unmovable.

Perhaps it was easy to say in hindsight, but it was the type of game that the Spireites would not have won 12 months previous. They might have even ended up losing it at the death. But those in the press box that day remember thinking that they would find the breakthrough, and they did. There wasn't a resignation that they would have to settle for a point. And it was an attitude that would blossom as the season progressed.

As for Berry, the next phone call to his dad was a lot happier. "When I was watching the game, I could see that there was so much space behind them and I knew the runs in behind would kill them," he said. "Me and Gary Roberts had been working on it all week with Ryan Colclough. I was itching to get on and I thought it could open up for me, and thankfully it did. Going down to Ebbsfleet and winning 1-0, those are the results that win you leagues."

***

It was one o'clock in the morning, at the Ringwood Hotel in Chesterfield, when Kieron Dyer woke up feeling extremely unwell. He was yellow. He was experiencing intense pain in his chest. The former England midfielder, who had been capped 33 times and selected for the 2002 World Cup and Euro 2004, had previously been diagnosed with primary sclerosing cholangitis, a chronic liver condition that has no cure. Ever since that day, he knew he would need a liver transplant. Now was that time.

He got a taxi from Chesterfield all the way down to Addenbrooke's Hospital in Cambridge. He left Paul Cook a message to tell him what was happening. "Gaffer, I won't be coming into training for a while," he said. Dyer was lying in his hospital bed and he felt lower than a snake's belly. He knew he needed a transplant, but he didn't know whether he would get one. His family were seriously worried. He was, he would later recall, more yellow than Bart Simpson.

Thankfully, on September 18, he did get a donor. But sadly, that meant someone had died. It was a big weight to carry. Dyer underwent a nine-hour operation and three weeks later, he was discharged. He had been in hospital for three months from July to October and, in that time, he had been visited by the likes of Cook and Ipswich Town manager Kieran McKenna. He'd even been given a hamper from Norwich City, the biggest rivals of his boyhood club Ipswich.

When Cook got the job at Portman Road, Dyer was working in the academy and the pair got on like a house on fire. They had the same ideas about how the game should be played and they bounced off each other. Dyer thinks so highly of Cook that he even said he puts him in the same category as Sir Bobby Robson, which is quite the compliment, when it comes to his man management. Although Dyer does recall that Cook was about to sack him before they had their first chat at Ipswich!

Such was Dyer's dedication, he had watched every Chesterfield game from his hospital bed and had kept in touch with Cook to pass on his analysis. He returned home with an optimistic outlook on life that he feared would never return. Dyer knows who his donor is, and his donor's family knows who Dyer is. They have written to each other. "The gratitude I feel for the position I find myself in has no bounds and I feel blessed," he said. "I'm not just living life for myself now. I am living life for my donor as well. Everything I do in life now, it's not just for me. It's for him."

In Dyer's absence, Chesterfield brought in UEFA A licenced coach Paddy Byrne. The Northern Irishman had been working in Everton's academy for eight years and had also been the first team coach at Macclesfield. He had also had roles at Wigan Athletic and Rangers listed on a very impressive CV. Belfast-born Byrne said: "I met Gary Roberts a couple of years ago on a course and we have remained in constant contact ever since. We share similar ideas on football in terms of how we think the game should be played. When Kieron was unwell I had a coffee with the gaffer and Robbo and it progressed from there."

***

In the middle of September, Chesterfield secured back-to-back 3-2 home victories against Halifax and Wealdstone. Despite the same scoreline, they were two very different games. The Shaymen encounter really was a humdinger, while the visit of the Stones was a little more straightforward than the scoreline suggested. The season ticket holders were certainly getting value for money, anyway, having seen Town win 4-3, 3-2, 3-1, 3-2 and 3-2 already.

Night games under the lights at the SMH had produced some fond memories since Cook's return. A 3-1 win against Notts County and a 3-2 (again!) cracker against Southend United topped the list, but the Halifax clash wasn't far behind. The Shaymen arrived in Derbyshire with the tightest defence in the league, having only conceded seven times in the first nine games, but they fell behind inside two minutes when Grigg slotted in from a couple of yards out. Mandeville provided the assist — more evidence that he could make an impact from a deeper position.

That was Grigg's fifth goal in his first nine appearances but he still felt he could have been doing better. Looking back in the summer, he said:

"Five in nine is probably not the best stat in the world. If you look at how I ended the season compared to how I started, it probably wasn't as positive. It probably took me a little bit of time to adjust."

Midway through the first half, it was 2-0. It was that man Mandeville again, who was leading the way in the assist charts, who swung in a corner and Williams leapt like a salmon to double the lead. It was looking like a routine win at that point, but it was anything but. Just three minutes later, Halifax halved the deficit when Mili Ali, who would go on to secure a move to Exeter City in January, calmly finished past Tyrer after Jamie Grimes' clearance had been intercepted.

Cook's message at half-time had been to be more ruthless and less wasteful in the final third. He wanted his side to put the game to bed early and show no mercy rather than to go through the motions and make it a nervy ending. But it didn't quite pan out like that as Halifax drew level when Tom Naylor was judged to have brought down Tylor Golden in the box and Luke Summerfield stepped up to make it 2-2 with 20 minutes remaining. As chants of "you're not fit to referee" were aimed at the man in the middle, Aaron Jackson, from the home stands, Cook was shown two quick-fire yellow cards for dissent and applauding sarcastically. Colclough was also booked for showing his frustration.

The anger towards referee Jackson then went up another notch when Naylor was shown a second yellow card and was sent off for his reaction at not being awarded a free-kick. Chesterfield had been 2-0 up, been pegged back to 2-2, and were now a man down and without their manager on the sidelines. Halifax were in the ascendency and at this point there only looked like being one winner. But they couldn't make the extra man count and then they were reduced to 10-men themselves when Adam Senior was shown a straight red card for a late tackle on Berry.

The pendulum had swung back towards Chesterfield and a huge roar went up. As seven minutes were added, Freckleton sent "super sub" Joe Quigley in on goal and he beat Sam Johnson at his near post to bag a third winner off the bench. That goal was Chesterfield's ninth of the season scored after the 80th minute. And it was still only September. The main reason behind that? The players' fitness and determination not to have to go through the play-offs again.

"The gaffer is not actually that bothered where you come in the runs, but it is in-built in yourself that you don't want to be miles behind everyone else," Mandeville explained. "So people are coming back fitter than they have ever come back before and that means the starting point is already higher than what it usually would be. I do feel we were the fittest team in the league which is why we scored so many late goals."

Reflecting back, Jeff King said: "We were really fit. Fair play to the coaches, every single one of them was really good at getting us to peak performance and peak levels. Even when you weren't in the team we had Saturday morning sessions sometimes, and on a Monday for the lads who didn't play the sessions were really, really good. There were always extra bits of running which, at the time and if you are not playing, it is a bit of a nightmare.

"But you appreciate it when you do get put back in the team because you are ready. You probably noticed that when we did make changes, no one really needed two or three games to get up to speed, because everyone was ready because of what we were doing through the week. I have spoken to friends who we played against and they said they were dead by 60 minutes because they hadn't touched the ball. We were that relentless. We had a lot of compliments from people we played against, which showed we were doing the right things."

Chesterfield could have collapsed, they could have felt sorry for themselves, and two or three years ago they probably would have been the ones on the end of a late gut-punch. But not this group. They were a winning machine. After 10 games, which has always been viewed as the first marker of the season, the Spireites were top by three points and had taken 25 points from a possible 30. Solihull Moors and Barnet were behind in second and third, respectively.

Four days after the Halifax thriller, Chesterfield were back on home soil against part-timers Wealdstone, managed by Stuart Maynard, who would get the Notts County job in January after Luke Williams left to join Swansea City. The Stones had a reputation for an easy-on-the-eye style under Maynard and they showcased that at the SMH. They were mid-table at the time, four points off the play-offs. The mood, understandably, was buzzing after five straight wins and Chesterfield were expected to make it six — despite facing a handy Wealdstone outfit who were underdogs but, on their day, could cause an upset.

The Spireites kicked towards the Kop in the first half, something that opposition sides chose to do more regularly if they could win the toss. King, Grigg and Jacobs all had sights of goal but those opportunities came back to bite them as a well-worked passing move between the thirds ended with Kyle Smith applying the finish to Jaydn Mundle-Smith's low cross. It was one of the better goals scored against Chesterfield in the season and it was the type that would have made Notts County sit up and notice of Maynard even more.

After the edginess from the crowd when 2-0 down against Hartlepool, whenever Chesterfield went behind, there was never any panic. Sometimes it felt like they actually waited to concede a goal or two, before deciding they had better score a few now! And three goals in 16 minutes, including two in two, had them back in command before the 70th minute. In-form Berry, making just his second start, took advantage of some indecision to sweep home his first goal for the club to make it 1-1, becoming the 12th different scorer for Chesterfield in the season already. He then created the second, Mandeville sliding in his cross. "I knew I would play really well because I knew how fit I was getting," Berry said.

Joining him in notching his first goal was Jacobs. Grigg won the ball back with a high press and then his former Wigan Athletic teammate took over, faking to shoot and sending Wealdstone man Charlie Barker for a hot dog, before composing himself and finding the bottom corner with the outside of his right foot. It was a classy goal and one that Cook was raving about on the training ground some days later, saying it deserved more credit than it got at the time. Sean Adarkwa grabbed a second goal for Wealdstone in the 96th minute with the last kick of the game, but thankfully there wasn't even time for the action to restart. *Phew.*

It was a bit of a strange clash, a little flat at times, and nothing like the 3-2 rollercoaster just days before. Such were the high standards and demands, the players came off the field feeling a bit disappointed that they had let in that late goal, knowing that things could have got nervy had there been a couple of minutes left. But it was another three points and it sent them five clear at the top after Solihull drew 1-1 against Bromley. It was the first time in 13 years that Chesterfield had won six on the bounce. It took their total points gained from losing positions to 15 after just 11 fixtures and it was the fourth successive home match that they had scored three goals. "You can enjoy the records broken when you have achieved your main objective and we all know what that is," Danny Webb said pitch side, when everyone had gone home. "We are certainly showing an ability to bounce back."

Reflecting back on the start to the season, when Chesterfield were winning games but conceding goals, Mandeville said: "I think it was actually more of a positive thing because that is what Wrexham did the year before. The amount of times they were behind in games and they would come back and win was unbelievable. Even though teams probably thought they could score against us, they probably didn't think they could win against us. Even when teams were leading against us, I think they were worried about what was coming back. I think it was a psychological thing more than anything.

"When you do it so early in the season, I feel like you end up carrying it all the way through. It is not something that you lose. You know at some point you are going to get a chance, you are going to score. And then with the players we have got at the back it was only a matter of time before we started keeping clean sheets. The goals were never going to stop, it was just about keeping clean sheets and that was always something we were going to be able to change. A lot of the games we didn't play that great but we had the quality going forward to make a difference."

***

On a bright Monday morning the local media and sponsors were invited to the club's revamped training ground to view the updated facilities and to watch Chesterfield's players being put through their paces. A new training ground had been one of the main aims when the community trust took over the club, but finding a suitable location — and of course, financing it — was always going to be a sticking point, especially while they were in the National League. The base at Hasland had a problem with drainage; but because the club did not own the facility, there had been a reluctance to invest much money into it.

Particularly in the winter months it would become difficult to train on because of the rain. It was so troublesome that players would not be able to stand up at times, because it was that sludgy and they would get back in their cars absolutely caked in mud. It was not enjoyable and was more like something you would see in Sunday League rather than at a professional football club. But after securing a long-term lease, around £300,000 was ploughed into it by the Kirk brothers to improve the drainage.

It was renamed the Erwin Training Ground in memory of the late Erwin Miller. Erwin's son, Karl, is the managing director of Motan Colortonic, who sponsor the South Stand at the SMH Group Stadium. Karl said his dad had helped many people and was a "great believer" in developing. It was fitting. The pitches looked great and, along with some little touches like club signage and some smart white fencing, it made it a much more appealing place which will no doubt help to attract new players in the future and develop the current crop.

They will not have to hide the training ground from prospective new signings anymore. Instead, they can show it off. It is a facility that the club will reap the benefits from, on and off the pitch. There are two full-sized pitches, which are the same dimensions as the one at the SMH and a designated goalkeeping area.

While the new facility was being developed over the summer, the squad had trained at St George's Park National Football Centre at Burton, at Matlock Town and at Staveley Miners Welfare. While they are all great in their own right, the players appreciated having their own top-class base to do their work. Throughout the season they would express their gratitude at just how much it had made a difference. It would also mean that they would have less travelling to do and they could train at the times they wanted, rather than waiting for a particular facility to become available. The aim in the future is to also add some buildings for changing rooms, a gym and a kitchen.

On this particular day, the Monday before Rochdale, the players who had played against Wealdstone were doing some light recovery work, while those who did not feature did some more intensive drills. As they arrived they all gave the media and sponsors a warm welcome, as did the coaching staff. They did that throughout the season. They were a very close-knit set of players and, unlike in previous years at the club, they were all good mates and were genuinely happy for each other when someone in their position played well.

"I put massive importance on what we have got as a group," Ollie Banks said. "The relationship that we have all got, staff included, is a proper special dressing room to be in. If there was a bad egg, or anyone who wasn't on-board, or fitted into what we want, then they wouldn't last two minutes."

Cook, with a cup of tea in his hand, obviously, held court and was more than generous with his time. He had been keen on a new or improved training ground from the moment he came back to the club. In the years that he had been away, it was still the same. Nothing had changed. It had not moved on. With a crowd gathered around him, he answered questions, had a laugh and a joke and gave his opinion on various different topics. With interviews not being his favourite activity, this was a rare chance to hear his thoughts. His leadership and passion for football shone through. You might think that you like football more than anyone else but once you hear Cook talk about the game, you soon realise you probably don't love it as much as him.

Every now and again he would break away to shout some instructions across, to let his players know that he was still watching their every move. The boss has eyes in the back of his head. There was no expectation for this to happen, but he also came over to chat with the local media. He spoke about how Jacobs had had his best week of training leading up to the Wealdstone match and how his goal had been a result of that. He explained how he wanted certain players to mark the likes of Jacobs and Grigg in training because it would be an education for them. If they could get to grips with their quick-thinking and movements, then they would have no trouble come game day.

He also gave some detail on how he wanted his players to be comfortable in possession when they were camped in an opponent's final third. He wanted them to go into deep water and not panic. It was a fascinating morning and much appreciated by everyone present. You could not help but be excited and impressed. As the season went on, the goals that were scored, the saves that were made, the patterns of play that were put together, it was clear that the training ground had already paid for itself.

Ashley Kirk said: "He [Cook] said that he has been in so many clubs and every club is the same. They all want to sell players but nobody wants to invest in making those players better. And the way you make players better is on the grass, with good coaches, working them hard. And surrounding them with experienced players who will make them better. He said that you can't expect us to be a good football team if we are training on pitches that were either rock hard or like a quagmire, depending on what time of year it was. It is no good expecting to produce footballers without having decent pitches to train on. And that was a point hammered home relentlessly by the manager and all of his staff."

Grimes could not agree more. "It was a game-changer," he said. "The standard of training just went through the roof. Passing drills were sharper and there weren't any mistakes because of bobbles or people slipping over. It made such a difference. The previous training ground was so boggy and heavy on the legs that you had to reduce your training time — or even when you did train, there was no quality behind it. I put a lot of injuries that we had the season before down to the training pitch. When the pitch got heavy, people started getting little calf injuries, hamstring injuries, because you are dragging your legs out of mud every day when you are used to hard ground."

***

Given what we saw that morning at Hasland, it was not a surprise that Chesterfield won 2-1 at Rochdale the next day. The Dale had been relegated to the National League after 102 years in the Football League and they found themselves in seventh ahead of kick-off, having only lost one of their last eight, but they were 10 points behind the Blues. To be fair, a play-off spot for a newly-relegated outfit showed they had adapted to the fifth tier steadily. As the Spireites had discovered, this was not an easy league to bounce straight back from.

Eight-hundred Town fans made the journey for the televised clash and they watched a really professional away performance. Chesterfield had opened up the hosts several times in the first half before showing a different side to their game after the break to see it out. Only six minutes had been played when Dobra headed in Jacobs' terrific whipped cross, but the goal had already been coming. After not scoring in eight games, he had now got two in four. "I was never afraid that I wasn't going to score, it was going to come eventually because of the quality of players we have," he said.

Not for the first time, former Spireite Kairo Mitchell scored against his old club to make it 1-1 after a superb defence-splitting pass from teenage centre-back George Nevett, who was another would be snapped up by Peterborough United the next summer. The Welsh youngster, just 17 at the time, played some excellent passes out from the back all night and reports later in the campaign linked him with a move to Crystal Palace. Mitchell, who had been booed by those in the away end, patted the Rochdale badge on his shirt while shouting "come on" in the direction of those who had been giving him some stick. It's fair to say that it didn't go down too well.

But it was only a brief setback as Mandeville and Dobra played a short corner and Naylor headed in the former's inviting cross on 25 minutes for his fourth of the season. Incredibly, that was Chesterfield's 30th goal of the campaign already and 10 of them had come from corners. Another ex-Town man, Jesurun Uchegbulam, was kept quiet and the Spireites secured their seventh successive win for the first time since 1967. It was hardly backs-to-the-wall stuff in the second half, it was quite comfortable actually, but without really threatening down the other end. Along with the clean sheet at Ebbsfleet, it was a sign that the little tweaks they were making defensively as a team were working.

It was a mature away display. It was one of those on-the-road wins on a Tuesday night where people would say: "That's what champions do." Those inside the camp were pleased that they were able to show a more uglier side to their game, because they knew that would be needed further down the line. According to Grimes, this was the last time they had music on in the dressing room afterwards. Such was their elite mentality, they immediately switched to thinking about the next match and how they could improve.

On the team coach back to Chesterfield, the six on the trot stat was mentioned by the coaching staff but they only had eyes for the big prize. Rochdale didn't take the points, but their press food did make a big impression on the local media. A giant meat and potato pie with chips and gravy went down a treat. It would be talked about for a long time. It's the little things in life, isn't it?

***

As September drew to a close, if Chesterfield could make it eight league victories on the spin, that would be the first time they had done so since

1933. But the next game was away to Maidenhead United — a ground they had never won at — so obviously their record was halted! At the training ground meet earlier in the week, Cook had hinted that Mike Jones "might" collect his fifth yellow card of the season in the latter stages against Rochdale if they were in a winning position and, would you believe it? That's what happened! So the midfielder, who had started all six wins on the bounce, would be suspended against the Magpies and be allowed to put his feet up.

Chesterfield had not won at York Road in their five previous visits, but they weren't the only ones who had struggled down there. The Magpies had a reputation for turning over some of the bigger clubs like Wrexham and Notts County as well. They were a difficult side to play against, very well organised and tough to break down. They also knew how to play their sloped, slanted pitch better than anyone else. They knew which areas to target, how the ball would bounce and run and they used it to their advantage. It was a weapon for them.

They liked to attack down the hill in the first half, get in front and then defend their lead after the break. It was a situation that left many opposition managers debating which way they would prefer to kick in each half. It was one of the many little nuggets in non-league that made you smile and roll your eyes at the same time. As well as a sloped pitch, there are also slanted press desks which leave you with neck ache and fearing that your laptop could crash onto the floor any second.

But they also deserved a lot of credit because they were part-time, had one of the lower budgets in the division and survived by developing players and selling them on. With West Ham favourite Alan Devonshire in charge, an FA Cup winner in 1980, they were a tough nut to crack, but it was felt that this was a different Chesterfield side to previous years; one that could play attractive football and also go toe-to-toe physically. With seven successive victories, surely they could finally put an end to the York Road hoodoo?

The match played out exactly how most would have expected with Town, kicking up the slope in the first 45, dominating possession, but clear-cut chances were not free-flowing. Banks, who was starting his first game since the second week of the season, dictated play with some wonderful diagonal passes, stretching the Maidenhead low block. Grigg had a chance blocked, while Colclough fired over.

The away side got let off the hook when Grimes threw his body in the way of a threatening strike from Reece Smith after intercepting a loose pass from Mandeville. However, on 30 minutes, they fell behind when Tobi Sho-Silva bundled in from close-range. It was a scrappy goal and one that was picked apart by Cook in his post-match inquest. He was frustrated at how three players had got involved in trying to win the ball back near the corner flag rather than just letting one person deal with it. In one sense, the willingness to win the ball back was admirable, but in doing so was to the detriment of the team. By the way, that was Maidenhead's first goal in more than seven hours of football. Of course it was.

The Blues continued to play their passing game and they drew level just before the hour mark when Mandeville teed up Jacobs, who was starting to make contributions, to curl a beauty into the corner from 20 yards. Incredibly, that was Mandeville's 13th goal contribution in as many matches. He had made it his aim to try to score or assist in each game and he was on track so far. He would later joke that Cook killed any hope of that when he started playing him at right-back!

Just two minutes later, Grigg had a great chance to put Chesterfield in the lead when he went through one-on-one, but his attempted lob was easily claimed by goalkeeper Craig Ross. It was the type of opportunity you would have backed him to score 10 times out of 10. But this was Maidenhead away, remember. And that probably explains why the Spireites were not awarded a penalty with 17 minutes remaining when Grigg was blatantly tugged back by Sam Beckwith. Grigg was about to pull the trigger from seven yards out — it would have been a clear shot on goal and there was no reason for him to go down in that position. It was clear as day. But referee Jason Richardson was having none of it. It left Cook and Webb with their arms out wide on the touchline in disbelief. Beckwith knew he had got away with one and said so behind the scenes at full-time.

It was horrible, it was a battle, it was everything you would expect from Maidenhead away. The winning run was over, but a point against a bogey side wasn't the end of the world. Interestingly, Cook came out and spoke to the press afterwards. Because he only tended to front up after a loss, it was a bit of a surprise. But looking back now, it was a clever move. He had not been happy with the performance and felt his side had gone back to the days of giving up possession cheaply and allowing teams to counter.

Perhaps sensing that some of those frailties were creeping back in, it was his way of making sure that standards did not slip. It was true leadership and an action that saw Chesterfield put their foot to the floor in October and November. Before the fun began, there was one outgoing as Bailey Hobson left to join Kidderminster Harriers on loan for an initial month which would end up being extended.

The summer signing from Alfreton Town had yet to make his debut so it was felt it was a good opportunity for him. They had received some enquiries for him from National League North clubs but Chesterfield wanted to send him out to the National League so he could test himself rather than drop back down to where he had come from. The former bricklayer, who was playing Sunday League with his mates only a few years before, would end up being one of Kidderminster's best players.

13

FREED FROM DESIRE

It was always football for Will Grigg. That's all he ever wanted to do. His best friend's dad ran a Sunday League team and he has fond memories of playing for them on weekends, in summer tournaments and the day he was scouted. He joined his boyhood club Birmingham City when he was seven and he went right through the academy system. From the ages of seven to 13 he was one of the better players and there were high hopes for him. He would always be the top scorer and would train with players older than him. But he broke his leg at 15 and that was a massive setback.

From that point onwards, his future in the academy was more in the balance. When it came to the final decision, two people said "yes," two others said "no" and he was released when he was 16. It was a choice between him and another striker, Jamie Sheldon, who was playing for England at youth level, but ended up falling out of the game and down the leagues. Giving his honest opinion, Grigg admits that at that time Sheldon probably was the better choice. But it still hurt.

"It was almost the worst thing but the best thing that ever happened," Grigg said. "I was sitting in the car on the way home with my mum and it was almost like the world had completely ended. That gave me a realisation that that was what I wanted to do."

But nothing was ever going to stop him from making it. He played non-league football for two months for Stratford Town and then he was signed by Walsall, which is where he made a name for himself. From being let go by the Blues, 18 months later he was in and around the first-team at the Sadlers at just 17. Anything can happen in football.

He was always going to be a striker. You hear stories of right-backs turning into forwards or wingers ending up in the net but there was none of that for the Solihull-born man. It wasn't even a conversation.

It was goals, goals, goals. His son is seven-years-old and he is trying to turn him into a striker but he is more interested in being a tricky wide man at the moment. "I was always at the top end of the pitch," he explained. "It was all about goals and I think that carried on from a really young age."

Growing up, Grigg idolised 'R9' Ronaldo and Alessandro Del Piero. He had a goldfish called Del Piero. Yes, you read that correctly. He only had one pet and he named it after the legendary Italy and Juventus striker because he liked what he saw when he watched Serie A highlights show *Gazzetta Football Italia* on *Channel 4* on Saturday mornings.

When it comes to football, all of Grigg's family are actually Aston Villa fans. He was bought Villa kits up until the age of six but when he joined the Birmingham academy he would get free tickets to games. He did the unthinkable and changed his team to the blue half of the second city. "I shouldn't be telling you that," he laughed. When it comes to family dynamics on derby day, Grigg chuckled that they don't play each other that often anymore and that they are probably more "smug" than him given the difference in success levels. He always checks for their result but, in his own words, he isn't a "diehard" Blues fan. The affection for them is from his time at the club in his younger days.

So how did he sign for Chesterfield? It was a chance encounter with Paul Cook at the wedding of former Wigan Athletic chairman David Sharpe, which was held abroad in the summer. They were sat on the same table and Cook asked what he was doing next season and if there was any possibility that he'd be up for coming to the Spireites. It was very informal, very relaxed, nothing too serious. Cook was just testing the water.

Being the friendly guy that he is, Grigg gave Cook the impression that he might be open to it but deep down he didn't think it would be for him. When they got back to England, they had another chat and arranged to meet. Again, Grigg wasn't really thinking that this was a move for him. In fact, on his drive up to Chesterfield, he rated the likelihood of him actually signing at "lower than five per cent."

"I didn't want to drop down to the National League," Grigg said. "I hadn't played in League Two let alone the National League." However, after having more talks with Cook and his staff and a look around the stadium, he drove back down south with a completely different feeling. "My opinion quickly changed," he said. "After that, it didn't take long to get sorted. I genuinely really enjoyed what I heard, the short-term and long-term goals for the club were really ambitious and it was genuinely something that I wanted to be a part of. It was something that really got me excited."

Cook and Grigg had enjoyed success together at Wigan, winning the League One title in 2018 in a season in which the striker bagged 26 goals in all competitions. There is a reason that many of Cook's former players signed for him again. "He is incredible," Grigg explained. "His management, the way he looks after his players. He is probably the best manager I have worked under. I have got so much respect for him. He understands me off the pitch and he understands me on the pitch as well.

"He knows how to get the best out of me. He understands that I am not going to get the ball deep, turn, take on two players and stick one in the top corner. He doesn't work the team around me but he makes sure the three behind me are effective and can feed me the ball and get the best out of me. I am a goalscorer, I spend a lot of my time in the box and he gets that. And he knows that if he provides the chances for me then I will deliver for him, like I have in the past."

Before Grigg signed, all Chesterfield fans would have described him as a goalscorer, a fox-in-the-box type. But as they watched him more and more they would have a new appreciation for his work rate, his clever movement and hold-up play. "I am not the biggest, strongest or quickest but I like to think I have got a bit of everything," he said. "I will always work hard for the team. It is my job at times to get hold of the ball at times and give everyone a target to work off. My strengths are scoring goals but I genuinely enjoy linking the play, having battles with centre-halves and just helping the team whenever I can."

On his ability to sniff out a goal, he added: "There is probably a lot of stuff that you don't realise like my reaction time and my anticipation. If we do a long run in pre-season I definitely won't be at the front but if we run to a pole and back and it is 10-15 yards, I will probably be one of the first ones. Which you wouldn't necessarily expect because I am not the quickest. But my agility in tight areas is impressive, so that definitely gives me a head start.

"I think it is a little bit natural but I have worked hard over the years to try to understand when the ball is going to come, the timing of the moment, the sharpness of the movement, learning what centre-halves want and want centre-halves do. I would like to think I have tried to get the best out of my career. I always say that footballers should be a student of the game and you should learn anything you can about the game. I am still learning every day."

***

Despite the eight-match unbeaten run, including seven wins, there were still some unanswered questions from September. Was the clean sheet against Ebbsfleet a one-off? Why were some games still like basketball? Does Cook know what his best team is? But October would provide the emphatic answers and leave everyone with crystal-clear clarity as to what this team could achieve. The message from the camp had been that once one or two concerns were ironed out, Chesterfield would start to go up the gears right about now and they were right. They went into full flow mode. Cook-ball was about to trample on everything in sight.

The month started with a home game against old enemy Bromley who, despite being unbeaten in 11, were fourth and seven points behind, which showed what a good start the Spireites had made. If they could open up a 10-point gap over the Ravens at this early stage, then that could prove to be a very useful barrier later in the season. "It could be a big three points and dictate where the season goes," Danny Webb said.

Andy Woodman's men had always been a tough opponent. Their style of football is not the prettiest, but it is effective. They ask questions of you, defend properly, play for set-pieces and long throws and are not afraid to throw in some dark arts. They've always been able to flick a switch and go into "operation chaos" late on in matches.

Going back to when James Rowe was Chesterfield manager, there had always been a bit of needle when the two sides met. They were always lively. And with Michael Cheek, the National League's all-time record goalscorer, in their ranks, they always had a chance. Chesterfield had found all of that out in their epic 3-2 play-off semi-final win against them just five months previous.

This was the third Saturday/Tuesday week in a row so the thinking behind the team selection was to bring the energy and see if Bromley's tired legs could cope. It was Cook showing his experience of knowing when to give players a rest. And those changes had a massive impact on the result. Chesterfield's first goal was a prime example of being patient and waiting for the right opening. "Patience with a purpose," was how Webb described it afterwards.

It started on the edge of their own box with Tom Naylor winning possession back. Mike Jones drove forward and found Ollie Banks, who switched play to the opposite flank to Jeff King. His cross was a good one but only partially cleared to the edge of the area. Jones was there to collect the second ball, heading into the path of James Berry, who found Branden Horton. He could have crossed but opted not to. As the ball came back to Jones, who had not scored in more than a year since signing, there were some optimistic cries of: "Shoooooot."

Instead, he played the simple pass to Horton, whose refusal again to cross was met with some frustration from the home faithful. Michael Jacobs and Banks then linked-up and this time Horton, who had not started any of the last six since the 4-3 thriller against Aldershot, whipped in a lovely-shaped cross which Joe Quigley met with a bullet header to make it 1-0 on 55 minutes.

During their reflections of the season, a lot of the players would comment on how they could sense and hear the frustrations of the fans as they went side to side and waited for their moment to go for the throat. But that was the way they were being instructed to play and it was working. Berry, Quigley and Naylor all went close to grabbing a second, before the latter headed in a corner from King to double the lead 20 minutes later.

Despite the Spireites having lots of success from corners, the manner of the goal took everyone by surprise — including former Town goalkeeper Grant Smith, who didn't react to Naylor's seemingly-savable header into the ground as Ryan Colclough, who was not offside, moved out of the way at the last second to bamboozle the away stopper. It was Naylor's fifth goal in 14 appearances. The summer signing was certainly making a big impression.

Banks almost slid in a third before the full-time whistle was sounded on a very good win against a likely promotion rival. A second clean sheet was in the bag and just like buses, they would all come at once this month. On the same night, Barnet scored a 97th minute winner to beat AFC Fylde 2-1 and so remained just three points behind. Webb said: "It would be great, wouldn't it, if we were top all season and only had one team chasing us? We would love that. We can't have it all our own way."

If only he knew…

***

Whereas the previous season saw the Spireites keen to get promoted by any means, this time it was all about winning the league. And with just one defeat in 14, they had given themselves every chance of doing so ahead of an away day at another old National League enemy in Boreham Wood — at a ground, in Meadow Park, where they had never won. Cook had been waiting to find out the outcome of his sending off against Halifax and he was slapped with a four-match ban which started here. The longer the wait went on, Cook had feared that referee Aaron Jackson was trying to get him "properly done" — and he was right.

When the team news landed, it made everyone sit up. Another five changes after just beating one of the strongest sides in the division convincingly. Cook had never been one to change a winning team, especially in those sorts of numbers, but from here on in several swaps on the team sheet would become the norm and would confirm a different approach from this season. It was one described as trying to catch teams "off-guard." It was a reporter's nightmare, scrambling around to work out who was in and out in short notice before a 2pm announcement, but Chesterfield had a squad capable of coping and it would ultimately be a big factor in their future success.

With Boreham having had one less day to recover, having played on Wednesday night, again the energy levels came into Cook's thinking. There was an understanding of the system and the roles within the team so it was like a jigsaw," Webb said. "As long as the piece fitted, you could keep swapping them over. With that year of working for him, a lot of players from the season before and the ones who had played for him previously, knew what was expected of them when they went back in the team. He didn't do it just to keep lads from moaning, but there is an element of squad happiness. When you have got such a good set of lads you want to keep them all firing, keep them all fresh and we did that."

Giving his opinion, Grimes said: "There was no issue with it at all. The way we were set-up, everyone knew what their role was in the team. There might be little tweaks but generally everyone knew their role. We had 22 players who should have been starting, basically. The gaffer would change it for different teams. If we were playing a more attacking team, he would put Mike Jones in there who would be a bit more solid and read the game. But in other games he would put DJ Oldaker in, who was unbelievable on the ball and who could pick a pass. It was never rotating for the sake of it. The gaffer put in people's best attributes for the game. It was always thought out."

Boreham — who, like Town, had suffered play-off heartache just months before, conceding in minutes 97 and 120 against Notts County in the semi-final — had made a slow start to the new campaign, finding themselves 17th and 20 points worse off than the Blues. Surprisingly, they never got out of trouble and ended up being relegated, with long-serving manager Luke Garrard departing at the end of the season. It just showed how difficult it could be, to bounce back from a massive play-off disappointment.

Like Maidenhead, this had not been a happy hunting ground, but Chesterfield breezed to a comfortable 2-0 victory with the goals coming from Liam Mandeville and Quigley, his second in as many matches. Unfortunately, he limped off late on with an ankle injury, which would require him to wear a big medical boot and he would miss the next three matches. Chesterfield managed to take the points despite Grigg skying a penalty over the bar before half-time and even Wood keeper Nathan Ashmore, who always seemed to have the game of his life against the Blues, couldn't keep them at bay.

It was a welcome routine win, at a place they had not won at in their five previous visits. When you win at a location you have always struggled at and put two past a goalkeeper who had been unbeatable in recent meetings, it made you wonder whether this was finally the year. He wouldn't be the last opposition manager to say something along these lines, but Garrard had no problem in telling the media that Chesterfield would probably win the league. It was only October 7, but with the Spireites being 10 unbeaten, including nine wins, you could see where he was coming from. It was nice to hear, but the last thing anyone in blue wanted was for someone to jinx it.

***

The league action took a backseat for a week as Chesterfield were pitted against seventh-tier Kettering Town, who were struggling near the bottom of the Southern League Premier Division Central, in the FA Cup fourth qualifying round. The Spireites had reached the third round proper of the competition for the last two seasons and they were aiming to make it three in a row for the first time in their history. Strangely, they had actually done better in the FA Cup in non-league than when they were in the Football League. They were also hoping that this would be the last time that they would have to qualify for a competition that they famously reached the semi-finals of in 1997.

Cook had always been a big fan of the FA Cup. He masterminded a shock 1-0 win against Pep Guardiola's Manchester City in the fifth round in 2018 when he was in charge of League One Wigan Athletic. City went on to win the Premier League and the League Cup that year, but missed out on the treble because of pesky Mr Cook. Who scored the winner that day? A certain Mr Grigg, who, believe it or not, outpaced Kyle Walker before finishing low into the far corner. The highlights are something Grigg points to regularly when people question his speed!

The FA Cup was second on Chesterfield's priority list, behind promotion, and although they knew they weren't going to be climbing the Wembley steps to lift the trophy, they fancied themselves to reach the third round again. They didn't want it to be at the detriment of winning the league title, but they were confident they could cause a few upsets along the way. Cook, not fancying being on the end of a result that would leave him red-faced, made eight changes, but it was still a very strong line-up, including Naylor, Jacobs and Grigg. Ryan Boot was also handed his first start since signing the summer.

In the opposition corner was former Spireites striker Leon Clarke, who was in his late 30s. He showed glimpses of why he had managed to play at a high level in his career, but he didn't have enough quality around him to make much difference and Chesterfield eased to an easy 5-0 victory. Grigg got on the scoresheet, but this one didn't mean quite as much to him as the one against Pep's men.

Darren Oldaker scored the goal of the game, curling home from the edge of the box via the post. It was a goal we had seen before; not in a match, but the club had posted a clip of him on social media doing exactly the same in training. Practice makes perfect, as they say. The new training ground was continuing to help work some magic.

Naylor's strike wasn't far behind as he crashed in a fifth to seal Chesterfield's passage through to the first round proper and bank themselves £9,375 in prize money in the process. Jacobs, also known as "Crackers,", continued his fine form with three assists. And they wouldn't be his last. The margin of victory also meant that Cook had been in charge for three out of four of Chesterfield's biggest FA Cup wins in the last 100 years.

With more than 5,000 in attendance for such a low-key fixture, it highlighted how much Town fans were enjoying watching their team and the momentum being built. Webb said he wanted a big club like Portsmouth in the next round and, funnily enough, that is who they got. That would throw up a number of intriguing storylines, but for the time being they had to park that and focus on getting back to league action.

***

A week later Chesterfield should have been taking on Gateshead at the SMH Group Stadium but the town was flooded by Storm Babet, causing devastating damage to homes and businesses. A major incident was declared with hundreds of homes evacuated. Footage showed cars completely submerged underwater and people being rescued from their properties by emergency teams. Sadly, one 83-year-old woman died.

The visit of Gateshead, who were sixth at the time and playing some attractive football, was one that had created a lot of excitement. And even though the stadium itself was fine, the surrounding areas would have made it extremely difficult for people to attend. On this occasion, there were more important things than football and the right decision was made to call it off.

The postponement meant that Chesterfield's next game after Kettering was 10 days later at home to York City, who had appointed former Notts County and Solihull Moors boss Neal Ardley as manager after sacking Michael Morton after six winless matches. It was no surprise that Cook reversed a lot of the changes that he had made in the FA Cup. Probably the biggest surprise was Boot keeping his place in net. Not because he had done anything wrong, but because most people naturally assumed that Harry Tyrer would come back in for the league outing. But the post-match discussion revealed that Tyrer had suffered a back spasm so he was not risked. Mandeville was selected at right-back again for the first time in four matches.

Not much happened in the first half apart from Armando Dobra and Jacobs having efforts on target. But the second 45 was very different. Grigg smacked a header against the crossbar from Banks' excellent cross, before the latter opened the scoring with an accurate, low, arrowed shot into the bottom corner on 49 minutes. It was an underrated finish, because the angle was tight. The ponytailed midfielder, who had been likened to a "s*** Andy Carroll" by the Minstermen fans, made sure they knew who the goalscorer was as he ran over to them with his finger to his lips to shut them up.

On the hour mark, it was 2-0. Naylor's volley from 20 yards zipped into the bottom corner. Just like his goal against Bromley at the start of the month, it took people by surprise because it initially looked like he had not connected with it that sweetly and it seemed to travel a long way before crossing the line. After the game, Ardley suggested his goalkeeper, Rory Watson, should have saved it, but replays showed it came through a crowd of bodies. Grigg put the game out of sight with a trademark tap-in, but again it was the slick build-up that made it. His one-two with Naylor in the middle of the park. Colclough's run to the byline and pick out of Banks. His touch, turn and shot. And there was the poacher to grab a third.

But his second goal and Chesterfield's fourth of the night, was very much unlike Grigg because it came outside of the box! He pounced on a heavy touch by Watson, swivelled and somehow, without even looking, rolled the ball in with his left foot from a ridiculously tight angle near the byline. Everybody was expecting Watson to block it or for it to hit the side-netting. It was a great goal. Normally, when an attack builds momentum, people rise to their feet in anticipation. But there was none of that. It came completely out of the blue.

No other striker in the league could have executed it like Grigg did. The noise inside the stadium was one of disbelief. "How did he get it in from there?" was the gasp around the ground. It was just his fifth career goal from more than 18 yards out. Talk about being a fox-in-the-box. It was a fitting way to mark Chesterfield's 40th league goal of the season by October 24. Bonkers.

And it was from this point onwards that Grigg really started to hit his stride, scoring at least once in every game that he started except four. "For whatever reason from Christmas onwards is when I tend to kick-on and score most of my goals," he said. "It just seems to be a little trend in my career — I am not really sure why."

After lots of questions at the start of the season about the leaky defence, Chesterfield had now notched four clean sheets on the trot. "As the season went on, we started to evolve," Webb said. "In the early days, it was just about getting ahead of steam, just winning games. I think at the beginning some of the criticism of the back lads was harsh on them because they weren't doing much wrong but we were giving the ball away quite easily and it made the back lads look a bit all over the place."

The evening was made better because Barnet and Solihull played out a 1-1 draw, the Bees equalising in the 97th minute. They slipped two points behind Town, who also had a game in hand. Solihull, who had looked like being real contenders for the first part of the campaign, were now 10 points adrift.

***

October finished with a first trip to Kidderminster Harriers in 23 years. The Harriers had won promotion from the National League North through the play-offs. It wasn't really expected and they were finding it tough to cope with the demands of a higher division. But so were the other three promoted sides in Oxford City, AFC Fylde and Ebbsfleet United. In fact, for large periods, all four were in the relegation zone.

At the time of the fixture, Kiddy were third from bottom, one point from safety. They were the lowest scorers in the league and had the worst home record. But they were good defensively. They had only shipped in six goals in eight games on home soil. Despite being at the opposite end of the table, they actually had conceded a very similar amount of goals to Chesterfield. Boot continued in goal for a third consecutive game, while Miguel Freckleton was preferred over Horton at left-back, despite the latter's impressive showings. As was the case earlier in the season, the thinking behind that was because with Mandeville bombing on from right-back, they felt they would need Frecklington to tuck in alongside Tyrone Williams and Grimes to make a back three.

In another little tweak, Banks was tucked inside off the right flank to create space for Mandeville to run into. So there was a lopsided three-man defence at times and a lopsided three-pronged attack behind Grigg. It was another example of their tactical flexibility. On paper, it looked like an away banker. But it was actually a very uncomfortable first 45 minutes. The Harriers were very physical, they put the ball in the box often and asked questions from long throws and set-pieces. They had five players over 6ft 2in.

In a 3-1 win, Chesterfield scored two fantastic goals on the counter-attack. The first through Banks, who again showed his laser-like precision to arrow one into the bottom corner to make it 1-0. And an added-time header from Grigg made it 3-1. They were both assisted by Naylor, who was showing week after week why he was probably the best player in the league.

In between, Zak Brown headed in a set-piece to make it 1-1 at half-time, the first Chesterfield concession in four matches, before Banks grabbed his second of the game and fourth in three appearances with a scrappier finish. He celebrated with a Robbie Keane-like forward roll, something his young son had asked him to do if he scored. He had forgotten to do it for his first goal, but luckily he bagged again to give him the chance to make up for it!

Since the Bromley game at the start of the month, the midfielder had been playing in a more advanced role as a No.10 and he was thriving in it. Giving a very honest assessment — perhaps too honest, he laughed — he admitted that he perhaps could not do what Cook wanted from his two holding midfielders. He was enjoying being more free and it had given him a new lease of life. Cook knew that Banks was a great striker of the ball, that he could cause some damage further up the pitch and he had been thinking about playing him there for a while.

He waited for the right moment and, once again, he showed his experience of knowing when to make the call. To cap off a brilliant month for him personally, Banks was rewarded with his performances by winning the National League player of the month for October.

"It is a hard one with me and the gaffer because we have a lot of discussions about stuff and we don't always agree with each other," Banks said. "He describes me as a bit of a maverick and I can definitely see where he is coming from. In that two in midfield, Tom Naylor came into hold in the middle of the pitch but obviously he had a fantastic goalscoring season, so the other one needed to be more disciplined.

"Whereas in the past I would have been the one who was less disciplined of the two in midfield. So it didn't work right for what the gaffer wants and that is fine. He likes the side of me when I play further up with the bits of creativity and goals but then he doesn't feel like I am disciplined enough at times. I love playing football and I love playing for Chesterfield, so I am happy to be of any help that I can."

Kidderminster finished the game with 10-men, Ross McNally receiving his second yellow card and his marching orders at 2-1 with seven minutes left, but the Blues had been more comfortable after the break and probably would have seen it out anyway. Make no mistake about it, this had been a tricky test, but they had come through it. They had proved they could have a scrap and that they could play football. Not that the latter had ever been in question.

Thankfully, Naylor, Williams and Dobra, who would have been suspended for the upcoming top-of-the-table clash against Barnet had they got booked, all avoided yellows. But there was a bit of an injury blow with Williams, who was a man-of-the-match contender at Aggborough, suffering a thigh problem which would rule him out for two-and-a-half months. All in all, the Spireites had enjoyed an extremely productive October. Five straight wins in all competitions. Just one defeat in 17 in the league. But they hadn't been able to shake Barnet off; the Bees had had kept pace and were just two points behind.

But it wouldn't be long before Chesterfield started to open up a gap.

Striker Danny Rowe also moved on, by mutual consent. He had been at the club for two-and-a-half years but sadly, due to a health condition, he had only made 26 appearances, scoring 10 times. The former Bradford City man had been loaned out to his old club AFC Fylde — where he is a legend for his goalscoring exploits, including netting the winner in the 2019 FA Trophy final with a brilliant free-kick — in a bid to return to full fitness, but it never happened for him.

A few days later Rowe, who has one of the hardest shots in football, signed for Robbie Savage's Macclesfield in the Northern Premier League, but less than a month later he left because of the same health concerns. It was a huge shame for Rowe, who, despite not playing much for Chesterfield, did create some fond memories, including a hat-trick against Southend United and a header in a play-off win against Halifax.

14

HE'S BETTER THAN ZIDANE

We've got Naylor ... Super Tom Naylor ...
I just don't think you understand ...
He's Paul Cook's man, he's better than Zidane ...
We've got Super Tom Naylor.

Tom Naylor was sat at home and his phone started to ring. It was an unknown number. Normally, you and I would ignore it. We get enough cold calls; we don't need another one from someone pretending to be from Three or *Sky TV*. But footballers can't do that in the off-season. Especially those who are free agents. They need work. So Naylor answered. And he would be glad he did. It was Paul Cook, and he wanted to bring him to Chesterfield. The pair had almost worked together before, but their paths had narrowly avoided each other at Wigan Athletic and Portsmouth. But now the timing was right. And he would go on to be one of the best free signings Chesterfield have ever made.

Cook had contacted his old pal Leam Richardson, who had worked with Naylor at Wigan and he had spoken glowingly about him as a player and a person. It was Cook's lucky day. Naylor wanted to get a move back closer to his family. After travelling around the country for most of his career, he wanted to settle down. Rather than hitting the motorway at the crack of dawn and arriving back when it was dark, he wanted to be able to take his kids to nursery in the morning and put them to bed at night.

"Being back at home with my family and being with my kids, day-in and day-out, is what I wanted to do," Naylor said. "I had offers elsewhere in the Football League but it wasn't for me. I have been at Portsmouth and Wigan and I have got two kids now. When Chesterfield came calling it was perfect."

Naylor had actually come through the ranks at rivals Mansfield Town and they also wanted his signature, but Chesterfield offered more favourable terms and Cook got his man. By November, it is fair to say that he was already a fans' favourite. In what had become a tradition, Naylor would give the Kop three fist bumps at the end of a game and they would respond in turn with a treble of cheers. It came out of nowhere, it was off the cuff, but it ended up being almost like a trademark celebration. Alan Shearer's right arm in the air. Peter Crouch's robot. Naylor's three fist bumps. People felt they couldn't go home until he had done it and they had joined in.

He arrived as a holding midfielder and Cook had always used two deep-lying midfielders in his teams, but Naylor would become a goal-scoring machine. Including against some old friends of his ...

***

The FA Cup has a history of pitting the haves versus the have-nots. The millionaires against the part-timers. David versus Goliath. It also has a habit of arranging a good old reunion. And at lunchtime on Sunday, November 5, that was exactly the case as Cook faced his old club Portsmouth in the first round of the famous competition. Ball numbers 57 and 36 had been drawn out of the hat three weeks before and now it was showtime. Everyone in the town had been excited about the game ever since and finally the day had arrived.

When Cook left Chesterfield for Portsmouth in May 2015 they were in League Two, but they had been in the Premier League as recently as 2010. They had won the FA Cup in 2008 which secured them European football the following season. Their UEFA Cup journey saw them lead 2-0 against seven–times Champions League winners AC Milan before 2005 Ballon d'Or winner, Ronaldinho, curled in a long-range free-kick and a late equaliser from Filippo Inzaghi broke their hearts.

Although it meant dropping down a division, the prospect of bringing the good times back to the south coast was too big a job for Cook to turn down. But it paid off because he led them to the League Two title in 2017 in dramatic circumstances. They were top of the table for less than half an hour, but results on the final day meant they were crowned champions. Just weeks later, Cook departed for Wigan Athletic. Contract talks at Pompey had not worked out and with the club on the cusp of a takeover, he made his decision to leave for the Latics for "footballing reasons" after being impressed with what they had to say after they made an approach for him.

Fast-forward to November 2023 and Portsmouth were still where Cook had left them — in League One — and any ill-feeling from some Pompey fans towards Cook had softened. He had always spoken positively about the Fratton Park fanbase since his departure and they recognised what a solid job he had done. On the day of the reunion in Derbyshire, there were no noticeable chants directed towards him from the away end. Everyone had moved on and both teams were absolutely flying at the top of their respective divisions.

Portsmouth, led by up and coming coach John Mousinho, a former Oxford United player in his first season in charge, were six points clear in League One after 15 games. They were unbeaten in 26 matches in the league going back to March in the previous campaign and they had also only conceded 10 goals. As well as Cook Gary Roberts, Michael Jacobs and Naylor were also former Pompey men. Roberts had been a player when they won the League Two title under Cook. Jacobs had only left a few months ago before signing for Chesterfield. Naylor had made more than 100 appearances for Pompey across three years from 2018 to 2021, winning the EFL Trophy in 2019. So there were lots of narratives at play.

Despite the size of the task facing them, behind the scenes the Spireites were quietly confident that they could cause an upset. There wasn't a silly giddiness. They were very calm and collected. The likes of Jacobs, Naylor and Will Grigg had played against this calibre of opposition and size of club all their careers. It was nothing new to them. And being in the trenches alongside that trio made everyone else feel at ease.

The phrase "free hit" had been bandied about in the days leading up to the game but Chesterfield did not see it that way. They did not want to give the impression that it was a day out and that it did not matter. They felt it was a reality that they could dump Pompey out of the cup. As many as 48 places separated the two sides in the football pyramid, but that didn't faze them.

"The gaffer just filled us with so much belief," Jamie Grimes explained. "He told us that if we did what we could do and if we did the things that we had worked on, week in, week out then we had a chance. Being an underdog was a nice change for us because in the league every game we were expected to win. The team talk before was like: 'We want to go up a league, let's see how good we are … let's test ourselves.'"

As you can imagine, a lot of the national media requested to speak to Cook in the build-up to the game and many asked about when he would be doing his pre-match press conference — only to find out that it would, of course, be Danny Webb who would be on media duties. He had a chuckle about it with the local press.

In front of a crowd of 8,377, including 1,566 from Portsmouth, Grigg set the tone straight away from the kick-off, chasing down goalkeeper Will Norris and blocking his attempted punt forward, forcing him to scramble the ball out for a throw-in within the first 10 seconds. On Bonfire Night, Chesterfield had lit an early firework. It was only a small moment in the game, but it was influential in getting the home faithful believing. It also made Pompey realise, if they didn't already, that they were in for a tough afternoon.

Mousinho certainly knew that would be the case because he named the same starting line-up from their win against Reading in the league the week before. He understood that Chesterfield were not your ordinary non-league team. Another incident which made people think it might be Chesterfield's day was when Grigg outmuscled defender Regan Poole off the ball in the Pompey man's own box. It was the sort of coming-together you see on a football pitch regularly but Poole landed awkwardly and had to be taken off. Scan results later revealed that he had suffered an anterior cruciate ligament tear in his knee and would miss the remainder of the season. The visitors were dealt another blow just before half-time when on-loan Chelsea midfielder Tino Anjorin had to be substituted with what turned out to be a serious hamstring injury which would sideline him for months. It was a costly afternoon.

Just after half an hour, Chesterfield took the lead. Liam Mandeville, fresh from signing a new contract until summer 2026 just the day before, delivered a superb inswinging free-kick from the left flank. It landed just on the edge of the six-yard box and it left Norris with a split-second decision whether to stay on his line or come and punch it clear. He went for the latter, but he was too late. Naylor got to the ball before him and glanced a header into the net. The midfielder had scored right in front of the Portsmouth fans, the same supporters who used to cheer him on. But he showed his class by refusing to celebrate. He jogged off, sticking out his right hand in the direction of the Pompey supporters as if to apologise. Grigg got him in a headlock. Mandeville and Ash Palmer mobbed him. But Naylor was unmoved. It wasn't a fake, empty gesture. He was showing genuine respect.

"When Mandeville puts in deliveries like that, it would be rude not to get on the end of them," Naylor said. "I knew I only had to glance it in because of the pace of the ball. I got between the two centre-halves, I timed my run well and got the goal." As for the ball from Mandeville, some of the best defenders at the top level would have struggled to cope with it. It was right in the middle of no man's land and it was the perfect way to celebrate his 10th assist of the season.

Surprisingly, there was not much of a reaction from Pompey in the second half. They didn't lay a glove on the Blues. They didn't throw the kitchen sink. There was just a nothingness about the League One leaders. They had run out of ideas. When they sent Norris up for a late corner, they didn't even put the ball in the box! There was the odd glimpse from their top scorer Colby Bishop, who was kept quiet all afternoon and from tricky Northern Ireland winger Paddy Lane. But other than that Chesterfield kept them at arm's length and collected a deserved and memorable 1-0 win to book their place in round two. If anything, they could have won by more.

A rousing rendition at full-time of *We are Sailing* was one of the best ever heard. Goosebumps galore. The result got everyone wondering whether this team could compete in League One on a weekly basis and the general consensus was that they could. It was just the second time in the club's history that they had beaten a team two divisions higher in the FA Cup. And the 48 places between them was the biggest gap they had ever overcome in the competition.

After full-time, Mousinho was very complimentary towards Chesterfield and he left a lasting impression on the Spireites' coaching staff. He spoke with real class and dignity. He admitted that Town had been the better side and deserved to win. He even went as far as saying that it looked like his team had 10-men because the Blues had run all over them. The result would look even more impressive come the end of the season when Portsmouth were promoted to the Championship as League One champions.

The draw for the second round was made immediately after the match and brought another home tie, against another League One outfit in Leyton Orient. Webb, who had worked under the late Justin Edinburgh at Brisbane Road, was taken aback when he was informed mid-interview. Normally, he was someone of chatty nature and in-depth answers. But he was visibly moved. A lot of raw emotion came to the surface. He mustered up a few words, but that was it.

The 2008 FA Cup winners had just been sent packing but there were no big celebrations in the dressing room. There was a much more important fixture coming up in just six days' time. Second placed Barnet, just two points behind, were next up at the SMH. Grigg recalled: "I think TV wanted to put a camera in the dressing room to film the celebrations and the boys were just sitting down — there was almost an expectation that we were going to win it so there was no celebration. It sounds slightly boring but that was just the mentality that we had and that was definitely a strength of ours throughout the season. That came from the gaffer and staff keeping everyone grounded and making sure we were focused."

Mike Jones said: "I think that came from the expectations we set ourselves at the start of the season. We expected to win the league, we wanted to win the league, we were adamant we were going to win the league. In the cup competitions, playing the likes of Portsmouth, we didn't fear them. The expectation in the camp was that we could beat them. We had lads who could play at a much higher level so when we were playing League One and League Two clubs, we were thinking we were going to win. So when we did, it wasn't like: 'Oh God, how have we won that?' We knew we could go toe-to-toe with anyone in the lower leagues, so it wasn't a shock to us at all."

Grimes added: "When we won, it wasn't a massive surprise. It wasn't like we had scored a lucky goal and held on for 90 minutes. In my opinion, you wouldn't have said they were miles ahead of us in any way. It was just a good game of football."

Expressing a similar view to his teammates, Mandeville added: "I think had the TV put the cameras in the dressing room, they would have been quite disappointed with what they saw after. It was probably the least celebrated game of the season. I think because we have got a winning culture at the club now, it was not a surprise to anyone that we had beaten them. I think that shows how far we have come because I remember in the early years we were celebrating draws which is just absolutely madness to look back on now."

And Jeff King said: "Inside the changing room was a real calmness. Most other clubs would have been having a party after the game but it was like: 'That's another one ticked off … now let's go'. We never went into games panicking, we were calm all of the time."

***

If Spireites fans had to pick one game to win out of Portsmouth and Barnet, the majority would have said the latter. The league was Chesterfield's bread and butter. Their eyes were firmly set on winning the league. They were never going to lift the FA Cup.

Cook had always been wary of the next match after such a headline-grabbing victory. Some players might take their foot off the gas. Others might think they have cracked it. Some might become complacent. So he made sure that no one was showing signs of having lost their focus in training that week. Even before Pompey rolled into town, the squad were made fully aware that the Barnet clash was more important. But, equally, there were no big speeches or extra meetings compared to any other match. Ideally, they wanted to win playing the style of football that they had in the first three months of the season but, if it was a scrappy affair which they came out on the right side of, then so be it.

To be fair, Barnet, who arrived 12 games unbeaten in all competitions, were one of the best teams to come to the SMH in the first half and they could have been out of sight at half-time. They had quietened a crowd of 9,677, which was the biggest of the season up to that point. Branden Horton blocked a close-range header from Dom Revan near the goal-line and Callum Stead had a similar attempt scrambled away. He then later hit the crossbar, with the rebound cleared off the line by Ash Palmer. The Blues, who had mainly been restricted to long-range shots, had been living dangerously. Dean Brennan's men had definitely caused them more problems than Pompey did.

But the second 45 was a completely different story as Chesterfield scored twice in 10 minutes through Armando Dobra and Grigg, although the latter would later have that goal taken off him and it was awarded to the former. Jacobs made it 3-0 after some fantastic build-up play and Joe

Quigley, who was back from injury, continued his knack of scoring off the bench by making it 4-0 on 86 minutes for his sixth of the season, five of which had come after the 80th minute. That was also Chesterfield's 12th goal which had been scored after that time. They could have been 3-0 down at half-time; instead, they were 4-0 up.

The Bees gave the Spireites a little scare, scoring twice in added time. Nicke Kabamba, who had scored a hat-trick against Chesterfield in the previous campaign, bagged his 12th of the season and former Sheffield Wednesday and Celtic striker Gary Hooper made it 4-2 before the visitors ran out of time. When reflecting on the season, the two matches against Barnet would be ones which would stick in the mind. This one certainly started to make people believe even more. "It was a game we had to win, no matter how it came," Webb said.

Interestingly, he felt that having another huge fixture after the Portsmouth one actually helped. Had they been at home to a so-called lesser team or a side fighting relegation, he felt, then it could have been flat and a bit of a slog. Instead, it was something for everyone to get their teeth into.

"The Barnet at home game was massive." Jones said. "They gave us a good scare in the first half but again we showed great character in the second half and we steamrolled them." That win took Chesterfield five points clear at the top and they had a game in hand. Webb wondered whether psychologically that defeat might knock Barnet off track and, surprisingly, it did. They crumbled in the weeks after, losing another three on the bounce. Had they won they would have gone top, but by the end of the month they found themselves 11 points adrift. They wouldn't get near Chesterfield again for the rest of the term. Again, there were no crazy celebrations in the dressing room. Just the usual pats on the back and "well done." There was a job to do, and they were determined to do it.

For the Blues, it was officially their best ever start to a season after 18 league matches. They were 15 unbeaten and had lost just once in 20 in all competitions. They had won 12 out of 13 in the league. They had also won seven on the spin for the second time already. It was only the middle of November. Make no mistake about it, this was a special group. They had a closeness and togetherness that those who know them said they had never seen in football before. They wanted to learn and get better, too.

***

"You couldn't write it." Four words that are used, mainly in a sporting context, for something that happens that is shocking and surprising. But, as football fans, we have trained ourselves to expect the unexpected. "I can't believe it, but I also fully can." "I'm shocked, but I'm also not." A trip to Roots Hall, to face financially-struggling and threadbare Southend United, was one of those moments.

Like Chesterfield the Shrimpers, who had been in the Championship in 2007, had also suffered successive relegations out of Football League. Their owner, Ron Martin, wanted out, their stadium was crumbling, they had been under a transfer embargo for more than a year. They had faced a winding up petition in the High Court over an unpaid £275,000 tax bill to HMRC and, as a result of that debt, had been deducted 10 points at the start of the season.

They were 16th in the table but they would have been in the play-off positions had it not been for the deduction. Manager Kevin Maher had been doing a grand job, as had his players, whose wages had not always been paid on time. Off the field, a takeover by Aussie Justin Rees and his consortium which had been announced, but not officially confirmed, had caught the imagination of the Southend supporters, who turned out in big numbers of 8,275 for the visit of Chesterfield.

But just days before, the game had been in doubt. Southend already had a small number of players and then it emerged that three of them — Daniel Kanu, Maro Vilhete and Noor Husin — had received international call-ups. Normally, especially in the Football League, that would have meant a match would have been automatically postponed. But no such rule could be found in the National League small print. Obviously. So the league ruled it should go ahead. As it happened, Husin didn't join up with the Afghanistan squad because of a dispute and he started against the Spireites. Southend had still, understandably, wanted the game postponed and because of their issues could only name two substitutes. But it turned out to be their day.

Grigg had actually swept in a cross from Jacobs to put Town in front just before the half-hour mark. At that point, most would have been confident that Chesterfield would tire the Shrimpers out and be able to use their subs to their advantage to extend their lead. But in the second half, a mad three minutes saw Branden Horton concede a penalty after a rash challenge on Harry Taylor and Jack Bridge tucked it away to make it 1-1. The second goal was very messy. Palmer passed the ball straight to Wesley Fonguck and he raced towards goal. Darren Oldaker tried to get back and, in doing so, accidentally deflected Fonguck's effort past Harry Tyrer. Tyrer should have still kept it out but it slipped through his fingers, hit the post and went in.

It shouldn't be forgotten that Southend had only lost one of their last eight, had won seven out of nine at Roots Hall and had the best defensive home record in the division. Their starting line-up was also very strong. Right-back Gus Scott-Morriss was always up and down the flank, Bridge was a tricky winger and Harry Cardwell was a good target man who scored goals. So this wasn't an embarrassing defeat, as such, but certainly unexpected, given Chesterfield's form and Southend's troubles.

The atmosphere on the Town team coach afterwards was flat and, such was their high standards, one or two players were sulking after their performance. But Cook told them that they had earned the right to have an off-day and he was right. This was their first defeat in the league since August. After losing at Altrincham, they had won seven on the bounce. After drawing against Maidenhead United, they won another seven on the spin. This was a group who could react to disappointment. And they would do so again.

It hadn't gone unnoticed by those in the Chesterfield camp that when they had lost this season, the opposition side had celebrated crazily. Southend, it was said, had celebrated like they had won the World Cup. You could forgive them, to an extent, after everything they had been through. The Spireites, meanwhile, had carried themselves professionally so far, ticking off one game at a time. A round of applause here. A word of praise there. But Cook was very much against his side banging on tables and doors. He would show respect to the opposition no matter what the score. It was all about recovering and focusing on the next match. Some of the over-top-celebrations from the opposition would not be forgotten.

"We felt like every time we played against a team we were getting the best of them," Grimes explained. "We would watch clips on the way they play and then when they played against us, they would run twice as hard and they would be in a more compact shape. They knew they had to, especially when they came to our ground, it just makes everyone raise their game. So when we did lose a game, it was like they had won a cup final. They would be celebrating like mad. Whereas if we drew a game, it felt like the end of the world. Those were the standards we set. So when we lost it was a really dejected mood. But with the gaffer and the way the lads were, we soon bounced back."

Thankfully, Barnet lost 2-0 at home to Gateshead so Town's lead remained at five points with a game in hand. They might not have extended their advantage, but it had not been cut either.

***

The fourth official put his board up and it was met by sarcastic cheers. Joe Quigley's number had gone up and he'd been dragged off. It had been a difficult afternoon. The pitch wasn't the best. The opposition had been climbing all over him. He'd had his shirt ripped to shreds. And the service into him had been lacking. It was another game without a goal. Some people just weren't having him. They'd written him off already.

Quigley signed for Chesterfield in January 2022 for a fee from Yeovil Town, but just three days later the manager who brought him in, James Rowe, was suspended by the club and later left. Quigley didn't score his first goal until his 14th appearance. But his new boss, Cook, knew he could work with him and improve him.

As time went on, Quigley became more appreciated. He still had his doubters and he was always an easy scapegoat after a defeat. But for those who watched him carefully, they understood his role was much more than just about scoring goals. He contributed a lot by dragging opposition players out of position and creating space for others. In November, he was rewarded with a new extended contract until the summer of 2025 after scoring seven goals in 16 appearances. Only four of those were starts. He had gone from being sarcastically cheered off the pitch to being affectionately referred to as the "White Pele."

"It was tough. I did not hit the ground running," Quigley admitted. "It can take time when you go to a new club and you are trying to settle in. It is about not giving up and the main thing is to keep working hard. If you work hard in the week, behind the scenes and on the training ground, it will pay off."

Cook responded to Chesterfield's second league defeat of the season by making six changes for another away day at Woking. It was a long trek in midweek but the squad had stayed down south after Southend, a plan they repeated later in the season to cut down on travel. Woking, who had finished fourth in the previous campaign before losing to Bromley in the play-off elimination round, were struggling this time around and had sacked manager Darren Sarrl, who had become a victim of his own success. Now with caretaker Ian Dyer in charge, Woking were 17th and just three points above the drop zone. They had won just one out of seven league fixtures.

It turned out to be a very productive night for the Spireites down in Surrey, winning 2-0 thanks to a goal in each half from Quigley and Dobra. It was a hardworking and ugly, but it deserved three points. On paper, it had looked a tricky fixture, especially after the Southend loss. But Chesterfield bounced back once again; partly down to having more quality but also the closeness of the players, who were all like best mates.

"Everything just went up a notch, including resilience," Webb said. "What happened this year is that we did bounce back very quickly. And that was helped not only by the players who we brought in, but the players who had already been here upping their game a tiny bit. And it made all the difference. This group was very committed to the cause. It was unique."

The next evening, Barnet were hammered 4-1 at home to Oldham Athletic, which meant that Chesterfield were eight points clear at the top and having played one game fewer. They had racked up 50 points and 50 goals from 20 outings. The previous season's champions, Wrexham, had been on 46 points at the same stage. Two points per game had always been seen as the required rate to win promotion. The Blues were blowing that out of the water.

***

November had started with a reunion for Cook and Co. against Portsmouth and it ended with another one with former Spireite Paul McCallum. He had been an unused substitute at Wembley and came to the SMH with Eastleigh as the league's top goalscorer with 15. During his short time at Chesterfield, at the end of the previous season, he managed just four goals in 19 appearances. He didn't set the world alight, but he was a popular figure and he contributed more than just goals on the pitch.

He was used as a lone striker and was a decent target man, strong in both boxes. But when it came to the summer, Cook only had eyes for Grigg. When it emerged that it would be possible to bring Grigg to the club, it was a no-brainer. He was Cook's number one target and he got him. McCallum was not short of offers either. Unsurprisingly, they both netted as the two sides clashed at the end of the month. Oh, and it was another 3-2 in Chesterfield's favour. The fourth home win by that same scoreline. It was turning out to be some season.

The Spireites, who must have had some special oranges or super-charged tea at half-time, continued their knack of blowing teams away in the second half, scoring three times in 15 minutes through Grigg and a brace from Ollie Banks, who assisted the opener, putting them out of sight. Or so we thought. Just like against Barnet, Town fancied giving their own fans the jitters and to make things interesting by conceding two late goals in five minutes.

McCallum got the first and it made for a nervy ending. It had got to the point where some were joking that this group preferred to live on the edge. They enjoyed the anxiety. They loved seeing people squirm in their seats. It felt like they were doing it on purpose at times. "What did you do that for?" "Funny," to quote a well-known meme from *The Inbetweeners*. They didn't, of course. They just had a weakness of conceding soft goals every now and again.

Grigg's goal was typical Grigg. His 12 for the season were from a combined total of about seven yards! He was very much on fire. Banks made it 2-0 from a superb quick-fire counter from just eight touches of the ball. Naylor intercepted a cross on the edge of his own area and played a first time pass into Banks, who nudged it on with one touch to Dobra. He drove forward, took three more touches, before a lovely weighted pass with the outside of his right foot teed up Banks, who had ran all the way from deep inside his own half, to take a touch before then curling home into the far corner. It was a tremendous goal.

And the second was equally impressive. Horton, right by his own corner flag down the left, played a short pass inside to Darren Oldaker, who fizzed a ball into Grigg, who delicately turned it around the corner for Horton who had carried on his run. The left-back, one of the fastest across the grass, steamed into the Eastleigh half, laid it off to Dobra in a central area, who again assisted Banks to finish across Joe McDonnell. They were two of the finest counter-attacking goals you are likely to see. They would not have looked out of place in the Champions League. After a stop-start beginning to the campaign, Banks had now got six goals in six games.

McCallum headed one back on 75 minutes and then five minutes later his striker partner Scott Quigley stroked in a second from 18 yards. But Chesterfield managed the last 10 minutes and added-time professionally to make it two consecutive wins. Incredibly, this was their 10th successive victory at home in all competitions. And they didn't stop there. When the players and management team got back in the dressing room they all checked their phones and were buzzing to once again find that Barnet had lost. In the 98th minute. They had scored many last-gasp winners but this time they were on the end of a late sickener. Bromley had now leapfrogged them into second place. But Town were 11 points clear of both of them with a game in hand.

Chesterfield had topped the table for a large period during the 2021/22 season but they had never managed to open up a lead like this. They were in a very promising position heading into December. But with two cup ties coming up there wouldn't be another league match for three weeks. In the meantime, Akwasi Asante's departure by mutual consent after three years at the club had been confirmed. The announcement was not a surprise to anyone. The Dutch-born striker had not made a single appearance in the season and was not part of Cook's plans. He had been placed on the transfer list a year earlier but he was then taken off it after impressing.

When he first joined in November 2022 from Gloucester City, he scored 10 goals in 14 appearances but he was then ruled out for eight months with a devastating anterior cruciate ligament injury. He was never quite the same player after that, although he did have little scoring sprees here and there. When fans hear his name in years to come, they will think of his blistering early form, his serious injury and his goal against then-European champions Chelsea in the FA Cup third round in January 2022. It was a tap-in into an empty net, but it was celebrated by the 6,000 Spireites behind the goal as if it was a last-minute 30-yard thunderbolt winner — rather than a late consolation after conceding five times in the previous 80 minutes.

Beaming from ear-to-ear pitch side at Stamford Bridge, Asante laughed with the local media that after scoring at the home of the Champions League holders, he "should be playing in the Premier League!" Just a week after leaving Chesterfield, he signed for Darlington — then struggling in the National League North.

15

CULTURE CHANGE

When people opened door number three on their advent calendar, they also swung open their curtains to find the ground covered in snow which had fallen overnight. But nothing was going to get in the way of Spireites fans watching their beloved team try to cause another upset in the FA Cup. Shovels at the ready, an army of volunteers — including some from Leyton Orient who had stayed in Chesterfield the night before the Sunday afternoon kick-off — marched down to the SMH to clear the pitch and ensure the footy was on. Town fans were rewarded with their efforts by what they saw from the next 90 minutes, whereas Orient's supporters probably wished they hadn't bothered!

In the frozen stadium car park, a snow plough could be seen shifting huge blocks of it so that the surrounding areas were safe. Inside the ground, volunteers had a bit of fun by building a snowman and kitting him out in a Spireites hat and scarf. His twig mouth was smiling and arms were celebrating, so he must have known what was to come. Even Paul Cook, a man not afraid to wear shorts and a short-sleeved T-shirt on the coldest of days, visited the club shop to get himself a bobble hat. Liam Mandeville was, of course, wearing gloves.

Orient, managed by former Blackpool and Doncaster Rovers midfielder Richie Wellens, were 16th in League One, 33 places above the Blues in the football pyramid. They won the National League title under the late Justin Edinburgh, with Danny Webb on the coaching staff, in 2019, so they were an example of a club who had been in non-league and then moved up the leagues. They were a decent template for Chesterfield to follow. But like in the Portsmouth game, Town fancied their chances. They had already beaten the League One leaders, so why couldn't they overcome a side in the bottom half of the same division?

The National League had grown incredibly strong in the last few years and the view from a lot of people was that there wasn't actually much difference between the top half of the fifth-tier and the bottom half of League One. And on a misty day in north Derbyshire, Chesterfield made it look like that was a fair argument. It wasn't a particularly great game, but the Spireites were the better side for large periods and goalkeeper Ryan Boot, making his first appearance in a month, was hardly stretched at all. Wellens' men had got into some dangerous areas early on but their final ball was lacking.

The match was settled five minutes before half-time through an own goal from Orient captain Idris El Mizouni, whose attempted headed clearance from Ollie Banks' cross looped in. It was another cup shock. Or was it? A lot of people had tipped Chesterfield to win. They had seen what they had done to Pompey and thought they could repeat the trick. This side were not a bunch of old-fashioned non-league sloggers. They were very good footballers who were very well managed and coached. There was no champagne spraying. No videos inside the dressing room of the players singing Adele. Pats on the back. Rounds of applause. On you go.

They had secured their place in the FA Cup third round for a third successive year, the first time they had achieved that in their history and earned a trip to Championship side Watford in January. Their run had banked them £117,00 in prize money and there would be another £105,000 up for grabs in the next round. And after the early season struggles with keeping the ball out of the net, they had now stopped the opposition scoring in seven of the last 11. There was a striking image of Webb celebrating on the pitch after the game. His frozen face was a mix of emotions. Joy at winning. Grief for his old pal Edinburgh. Anger at the changes he said took place at Orient when Edinburgh passed away. It was a time in his life of which he had fond memories, and others he wished he could forget.

There was another cup game six days later, this time in the FA Trophy third round against mid-table National League North Southport. Chesterfield had made no secret of the fact that this competition was not a priority. They had played a load of youngsters against Coalville Town the year before, losing 3-1 and were expected to take a similar approach when it came to the line-up this time. But they actually went really strong, with senior players Jeff King, Ryheem Sheckleford, Michael Jacobs and Joe Quigley all starting alongside young lads Ryley D'Sena, Sam Hooper and Jay Abudu.

Former Stockport County striker Richie Bennett gave Southport the lead but goals from Jacobs, Harley Curtis, his first for the club since signing in the summer after impressing on trial and James Berry made it 3-1 before the hour. Three more youths — Liam Jessop, Ali-Aftab Mohiuddin and Thomas Marshall — came on in the second half, taking the average age to 22 before Jessop grabbed himself a brace and Mohiuddin got in on the act from distance.

Progressing to the next round would have no impact on the league, either, because the promotion rivals Bromley and Barnet went through, so no ground lost there. The Southport game was a fixture which still attracted a crowd of more than 2,000 and, having arrived with low excitement levels, they left absolutely thrilled. Deep down most Town fans would not have minded losing. But their side ended up scoring six with five academy boys making their debuts and taking the mick. You had to laugh.

***

It was Monday morning and Jamie Grimes was down at Loughborough University, trying to make himself faster. Playing a high defensive line, as Chesterfield do under Cook, the skipper found himself sprinting back towards his own goal more than at any other time in his career. That was the risk-reward football that they were playing. He needed to be able get back into position quickly and to be able to defend one-versus-one regularly.

When he was at Hereford, they reached the FA Trophy final in 2021 and he received a bonus. And he was using that money to try to make himself a better player. Others might have used it to book a fancy holiday, put it towards a new car or a flash watch. But not Grimes. He was working with Speedworks — a team of experts who specialise in speed for athletes such as footballers, rugby players and sprinters. Through video analysis, they cast their eye over an individual's running style and give them key points on where they might be able to improve.

After undergoing some tests, it turned out that Grimes had one stride longer than the other so they helped to correct it. The result? He recorded his quickest-ever times. Honest as the day is long, Grimes admitted he could still get faster and that he wasn't the sharpest off the mark. He is a big unit, so it takes him a few seconds to get the tank moving. As well as being quicker across the grass, he felt he could jump higher and just move better all-round generally. It proved to be money well spent. He came on leaps and bounds, under Cook's guidance and through his own determination.

"I just do everything that I can to be the best I can be," he said. "I feel fit and strong and long may that continue. I still feel 25. I don't feel aches and pains, I don't feel tired. I am just going to keep squeezing every little bit out of myself as much as I can." The skipper's willingness to put his own money into something that would only improve his game by the finest of margins, the smallest of percentages, was an example of the culture change at the club. Gone were the days of players being overweight and arguing with fans on social media. Gone were the days of players seeing Chesterfield as one last big payday before heading for the retirement home. Gone were the days of managers swanning off early in the afternoon. There was now an elite mentality.

Some people only do the work when they are being watched. But not this bunch. Behind the scenes, this group were carrying themselves like the Special Forces. They had a military-like focus on winning promotion. There were no bad eggs. There wasn't a single personality that would upset the dressing room. They all had each other's backs. Although they all wanted to play, they were all genuinely happy when someone in their position had a good game. No one got too high after a win or too low after a defeat. Let the opposition blast out the music, sing and dance and bounce around if they beat us. Let them have their day; we'll win the war.

Grimes is a great role model, on and off the pitch. He always keeps himself in excellent shape and gets involved in the community side of the club as well. It may also be hard to believe, given his towering, physical presence, but he's actually someone who has struggled with confidence. Earlier in the season Cook tried to pump more belief into his captain, asking: "Jamie, why do you think you have started so many games under me?"

Grimes replied: "I dunno ... because I'm an alright player." Cook responded, with another example of his excellent man-management skills: "No! It's because you're a bloody good player!" You could only imagine what it would be like to play for someone like that. The story also opened your mind to what different players might be going through behind closed doors. Did they also lack confidence? Why was that? Was it because they had been rejected earlier in their careers? Had someone else knocked it out of them? How can such a good player have no belief? It certainly made you think.

Grimes had been set to become a free agent at the end of the season but neither he, Cook or the club wanted him to leave. He had played every minute of every league game in the 2022/23 campaign, had started every league game since Cook had returned to the club and was on track for a remarkable 100 consecutive league starts. It was the most the defender had ever enjoyed his football. "To work with a manager like Paul Cook is fantastic," Grimes said. "I feel like if I had had that guidance when I was younger, I could have played at a higher level. He has shown such belief in me. He makes you feel 10-feet tall."

***

The first league game of December brought about a hard-fought, ugly at times, 1-0 away win at Hartlepool United in difficult, blustery conditions nine days before Christmas. Since the reverse fixture in August, the Spireites had gone marching on, but the Pools had dropped like a stone and were now looking over their shoulder at the relegation zone. Armando Dobra scored the winner on five minutes, his deflected volley from the edge of the area finding its way into the bottom corner.

It could have been a different story had former Spireite Mani Dierse-ruvwe not fluffed his lines in the first 30 seconds with the goal gaping. He had another glorious chance before half-time when he went through one-on-one but he rolled the ball wide. There had been a lot of slipping and sliding in the wind and rain and some Town players switched to longer studs at half-time. They kept the hosts at arm's length in the second 45, they didn't have a shot on target, while down the other end Cook's men had a Tom Naylor goal incorrectly ruled out. But thankfully, it did not matter.

Naylor also produced one of the last-ditch tackles of the season late on to prevent an undeserved equaliser and secure the first home and away double of the campaign. A ninth away win in the bag by the middle of December meant a club record 12, set in 1994/95, looked to be in danger.

It was another clean sheet, the sixth in the league and eight in the last 13 in all competitions. Webb had said the leaks would be plugged and he was right.

Second-placed Bromley won 2-1 at Southend United, but the Blues were still eight points in front with two games in hand. There were nearly 1,000 Chesterfield fans at Victoria Park and they were in good spirits, gleefully stretching their vocal cords. "Jingle bells, jingle bells, jingle all the way… Oh what fun it is to see the Spireites win away."

***

With Christmas just around the corner, Spireites supporters received early presents in in the form of two more contract extensions as Mike Jones and Tyrone Williams both signed new deals until summer 2015. Chesterfield's turnover of players was one of the things that had baffled Cook when he returned to the club in February 2022. Instead of developing players and trying to make them better, the club had just signed new ones. That wasn't Cook's style. He didn't believe in that. He was a builder. He enjoyed working with this group and seeing them improve and he was happy to take them along for the journey ahead. The aim was to always try to improve players first rather than recruit new ones. Cook is a big advocate for managers getting time and, quite often over a beer in his office post-match, he would tell opposition coaches about how it took him around 18 months to assemble this squad.

Williams was another one who had got better under Cook. He wasn't the finished article but he was far more consistent than when he first joined in November 2021. It didn't go unnoticed by those in the press pack how Williams, at this point 29 years of age, had come back to pre-season in tip-top shape. He was leaner, faster, stronger. He was like a racehorse in its prime. He was all shiny and new, ready to cruise to victory at the Grand National. And if ever a man had earned himself a new deal, it was Jones. He approached every game like his life depended on it. The midfield destroyer played like every fan in the stand would if they were playing in an FA Cup final for their team. He ran himself into the ground until his legs fell off.

He had started the season out of the side, but he was recalled after the defeat to Altrincham and started seven straight wins. After serving his suspension against Maidenhead United, he came back in again for another five league wins on the spin. He was on the bench in the defeat to Southend United — and how they missed him that day — before making another winning return against Woking. Chesterfield had won all 13 times he had started. He was 36 years old, but no wonder Cook had no problem with giving him another year.

Jones was grateful, too. He appreciated that Cook had allowed him to come in on trial the previous summer. Had that not worked out, he was thinking he would have had to call it a day. What a shame that would have been. He was thankful for being offered another year's security for him and his family. But he'd earned it. It wasn't a token gesture. He would run through a brick wall. "We've got Jonesy in the middle," as the song goes.

On December 20, Spireites fans woke up to the headline "Chesterfield boss Paul Cook in contention for Plymouth Argyle job" on one football website. *Football Insider* claimed Cook was one of "several candidates" under consideration following Steven Scumacher's departure to Stoke City. The local newspaper, the *Derbyshire Times*, checked it out but found nothing of substance. Cook had always joked that he would only leave if he was offered the Liverpool job. A month later, in January, Jurgen Klopp announced he would be leaving Anfield at the end of season — and Cook made the bookies list for his replacement!

Social media can be a funny place at times and this was one of them, with Town fans posting messages along the lines of "back off" alongside a picture of a machete. They weren't kidding, either.

***

He's a pesky one, Andy Woodman. A graduate of the school of dark arts. Heading into Christmas, his second-placed Bromley side were eight points adrift of the Spireites and had played two games more when he told the *BBC*: "Chesterfield have won the league — it's done. That's the narrative we like to keep using. The narrative from Chesterfield is that they have won the league, the narrative from everyone else in the country is that Chesterfield have won the league. It will have to take a real landslide of mishaps for them to fall away. So, we will go with that and just keep concentrating on ourselves and you never know. What I will say is that no title is ever won without a challenge and that's what I'm hanging on to a little bit."

Was it mind games? Was Woodman trying to lure Chesterfield into a false sense of security? Was he trying to take the pressure off his own players? Was it an attempt to put some fire in the belly of his side? Or was he simply stating the truth? It felt like he was trying to get in the heads of the Spireites players. But, when sitting around the local media at a game later in the season, he said it wasn't.

He was very complimentary about Chesterfield's style and, as a former goalkeeper and goalkeeping coach himself, was a fan of Harry Tyrer. What definitely wasn't true was the bit about Chesterfield thinking they had already secured the title. Nothing could be further from the truth. This was a hardworking, humble and honest group. No arrogance. No getting carried away. Woodman had got that wrong. But anyone who had been watching the Spireites all season would tell you this lot weren't going to throw it away. So, in a way, Woodman was right about it already being done.

Two days before Santa came down the chimney, Aldershot Town were the visitors to the SMH, which would mark the halfway stage of the season. They were a surprise package and were challenging for the play-offs. They had goals at the top end of the pitch in Josh Stokes, Lorent Tolaj and Jack Barham and they ran Town close in the reverse fixture. This was seen as a very tough encounter and many supporters were feeling nervous. If Chesterfield were going to lose a game, then this was seen as a strong contender.

Aldershot were seventh but a huge 20 points behind Chesterfield and had been conceding a lot of goals, including five the previous week against Eastleigh. Some of their matches were bonkers. Incredibly, they had led 7-0 away at League Two Swindon Town in the FA Cup first round after just 58 minutes, before conceding four themselves. In the next round, they showed they could defend properly, securing an impressive 1-0 away win at another League Two side in Stockport County.

Aldershot boss Tommy Widdrington didn't travel to Derbyshire due to illness and was forced to watch from home from bed. Mandeville also missed out for the same reason. There had been some jokes about it being just 24 hours after "Mad Friday" — the last Friday before Christmas which sees workers down their tools and log off from their computers for a night on the town. But Mandeville genuinely was poorly. He'd missed just two training sessions in three years, so there was a gasp of disbelief when he phoned in sick. Cook and Webb had him on loudspeaker to make sure he wasn't trying to pull the wool over their eyes, but their senses were that he was being honest.

The fixture was dubbed "Santa Hat Day" and Town fans responded in great numbers. By full-time they were jingling happily all the way home despite Stokes scoring after three minutes. But it was 1-1 just 120 seconds later when Darren Oldaker curled in a brilliant free-kick to become Chesterfield's 13th different scorer of the campaign. And the blistering Blues ran away with it in the second half, their dominance too much in the last 25 minutes as Ryan Colclough, Will Grigg and Dobra sent the majority of the 8,320 in attendance back to their cars in a festive mood. And they felt even more chirpy a couple of hours later when Bromley conceded a 92nd-minute equaliser to draw 2-2 against Altrincham. Chesterfield were now 10 points clear with two games in hand. Merry Christmas, Mr. Woodman.

Aldershot, meanwhile, must have been sick of the sight of the Spireites, after not beating them in 17 attempts. Chesterfield had now won 13 consecutive home matches and scored 71 goals in all competitions. It was 19 points gained from losing positions. They had notched in 23 consecutive games at the start of a season for the first time. They had responded to the defeat to Southend by winning six on the bounce. This team refused to lose two on the spin And they had three more points than eventual champions Wrexham had at this stage of the season a year before. It really was pinch-yourself time. The Baileys could be cracked open.

***

Bleedin' Solihull. Like Maidenhead, they had been a pain in the buttocks ever since Chesterfield had fallen into non-league. They were the 'housery kings. Pinching. Pulling. Prodding. Poking. Of course they would be the ones to turn the Spireites' festive cheer into misery. Moors, led by former Blues loanee Andy Whing, had been right up there with Town at the start of the season, going 14 games unbeaten from the opening day. But they lost 5-0 at Southend United in October and then 6-1 at Altrincham in November. After 14 matches, they were three points worse off than the Spireites. Before kick-off on Boxing Day, they were 19 points behind. It just showed once again how relentless Chesterfield had been.

Cook's men actually played really well on the day. It was the best they had looked in their trips to Damson Park, but they just couldn't score and ended up losing 2-0. It was the first time they had not found the net all season and in 31 matches going back to April. They were denied by great saves, last-ditch blocks, clearances off the line and the post twice. On another day, they could have scored six or seven.

A rare mistake from Jones allowed Mark Beck to open the scoring early on, the striker pouncing on a loose back pass before tucking in. Callum Maycock made it 2-0 on 15 minutes and they could have gone further in front. It was a crazy little spell that cost Chesterfield the game. The Achilles' heel that Cook had spoken about before. The visitors had started well, lost their way for a short period and then totally dominated again.

With the game gone, Grimes was shown a straight red card for an apparent headbutt in the 93rd minute. Cook was more disappointed at losing his captain for the next three matches than at losing the game. Apparently, he didn't speak to Grimes for about a week. It was an uncharacteristic moment of madness from the centre-back, who saw the red mist after being of the opinion that Jack Stephens had been diving about. Grimes went head-to-head with him, Stephens went down like a parachute with a hole in it and referee Gavin Ward gave him his marching orders. The dark arts. The 'housery kings. Bleedin' Solihull.

Grimes would later apologise. He would be suspended for the next three matches, including Watford away in the FA Cup and his hopes of making a staggering 100th consecutive starts were scuppered. "I was bitterly disappointed," Grimes said of his red card when reflecting back in the summer. "I should have been cleverer and not got drawn into it. And I paid the price. I am still kicking myself now."

16

IT'S NOT SUPPOSED TO BE LIKE THIS

Chesterfield were starting to feel a bit disrespected. The National League had long been described as one of, if not the, hardest division to get out of in English football. With just one automatic promotion spot up for grabs it was ruthless, brutal and unforgiving. The Spireites were flying. Reaching 100 points and a century of goals was a possibility. They were playing some of the best football the fifth tier had ever seen. But some outsiders were claiming that just because Wrexham and Notts County were no longer around, the league was weak. It was a doddle. It was a breeze. That Chesterfield were only doing what they should have been doing. Some would have you believe that they were up against groups of postmen and scaffolders each week, who were still drunk after a night on the lash. It was Sunday League, apparently. They had the biggest budget. That had a massive squad. It was all utter nonsense.

They didn't have the biggest budget. They didn't have a huge squad. Yes, there were two players for each position, but over the season Chesterfield would actually use the fewest number of players in the league. While other clubs were scrambling around for players to rescue their season, Chesterfield's last signing of the season, Miguel Freckleton, came on August 30. They had done their business early and got it spot on.

They were extremely well coached by Danny Webb, Gary Roberts, Paddy Byrne, Kieron Dyer and Dave O'Hare. And they were of course led by a top operator in Paul Cook. They had been building for this season for a couple of years. It wasn't a fluke.

You could turn the debate on its head. Instead of playing down Chesterfield's achievement, why not ask why everyone else was so far behind? Why were Oldham so far off the pace? How come Bromley couldn't keep it? Why weren't Rochdale and Hartlepool United, just relegated from the

Football League, up there challenging? It had started to irk Chesterfield. Not to the point where they were talking about it all the time and they even had a laugh about it. But there was a sense that they weren't getting as much credit as they deserved.

**

Revenge is best served sweet. It was the perfect script. Just six days after losing 2-0 at Solihull Moors, despite pummelling them, Chesterfield got their own back to kick off 2024 in style. The game had actually followed a similar pattern to the one at Damson Park in that the Spireites had created bundles of chances, but through some wasteful finishes and last-ditch defending, including more clearances off the line, they could not find the breakthrough in the first hour and they were two goals down again.

Given Solihull's stubbornness, when they go 1-0 up you could have been forgiven for thinking that that was it. So when they doubled their lead, you really did think it was game over. And for Chesterfield teams of the past, that would have been the case. But not this one. They knew they would keep knocking on the door. They fancied themselves to go into deep water and not sink. And the fans knew it, too. They had learnt their lesson from thinking the world was going to end after trailing 2-0 to Hartlepool after six minutes. They were more patient now. They knew they were more than capable of coming from two goals behind. And they were right.

Three goals in five minutes from Tom Naylor, Ryan Colclough and Will Grigg turned the scoreline around and there were still more than 20 minutes to play. Naylor had slammed in after arriving late in the box. That was a career-best seventh goal in the league and a career-best ninth in total. Cook clenched his right fist and Roberts slapped his hands together before spinning his right hand around in a motivational way. It was game on.

Colclough, although tall in stature for a winger, was an unlikely header of a ball, but he got across the near post to nod in Jeff King's corner. It was something they had been working on. They thought he could be a decent weapon in the air and would be someone who other teams might underrate. Bruising opposition centre-backs would concentrate on the likes of Jamie Grimes, Ash Palmer and Tyrone Williams, leaving Colclough to be picked up by someone smaller than him.

And then Grigg — who else? — scrambled home from a couple of yards out. The turnaround was complete. The noise was deafening. Flashbacks of Curtis Weston being sent off, Jamey Osborne's regular dark arts, a pitch invasion featuring Aston Villa shirts and a corner flag being lobbed like a javelin into crowds of people flooded the mind. The fans had been waiting for their Moors moment. They celebrated this one that little bit more. This was another match in which supporters would say they knew that nothing was going to stop this winning machine.

Grigg slid on his knees. Solihull had collapsed. They had crumbled. The Moors' players were on the floor. They had been flattened. As quick as a flash. *Bang. Bang. Bang.* Three more second half goals. Fifty goals in total at the SMH. Cook-ball was in full flow. The chasing pack, Bromley and Barnet, who had both played two days before and won, were gutted. Bromley had cut the gap to four points 48 hours earlier. Imagine their joy at checking the score on 60 minutes. And then picture their faces 10 minutes later. Ouch. Brilliant.

Cook, with his infectious laugh, gave a classic line afterwards: "It's not supposed to be like this, is it? But it is, isn't it?" What he meant was that this was not how they had planned to win games. They didn't want to keep having to perform miracles. But, in a way, it's exactly how they wanted to do it. In their style. Putting on a show. They were *The Entertainers.*

Oh and with the final whistle pending, Jack Stephens, the man responsible for getting Grimes sent off in the reverse fixture, was on the floor when Harry Tyrer offered to give him a helping hand back to his feet — only to withdraw it at the last second. Sweet revenge. It was beautiful. See ya.

Chesterfield had won the first of five upcoming home games in the league in January and if they could get a healthy points return from the next four, then they really would be in the driving seat. "We were fitter than every team in the league that season by a mile," Ollie Banks said. "Sometimes fans ask us to play forward a little bit quicker but we work how we play in training. We tire teams out. That is the way that we played and it has worked."

Reflecting back on the team spirit shown across the season, James Berry said: "That was one of the best things we had. We are teammates, yes, but we are also mates off the pitch as well. We all have this special bond. We are really tight-knit and I think the fans can see it as well. We are all a load of mates playing really good football. We respect each other and we really like each other. The coaching staff and the gaffer add to that; they bring a great vibe and it is just a really good place to play football."

***

It was one of those moments where you thought: "That can't be real." It had to be fake. It couldn't be true. But it was. It really was. Sir Elton John had been speaking about the Spireites to Gary Lineker in a *BBC* interview for *Football Focus*. Now there's a sentence we didn't think we would be writing. It was so random. And totally out of the blue. In it, Sir Elton was talking about the importance of momentum. He mentioned Leicester City, a 5,000/1 shot, miraculously winning the Premier League in 2016.

He spoke about Ipswich Town and their quest for successive promotions, which they achieved. And then, unexpectedly, out of nowhere, he said: "And then you see Chesterfield down there in the Conference and you see the momentum they have got. They lost out in one of the best matches ever. Notts County and Chesterfield, last year, in that play-off final, was incredible. And this year they are still there; they are top of the league."

Now, it would have made more sense had the interview happened in the build-up to Chesterfield's FA Cup third round tie against Watford, because Sir Elton is the honorary life-president at the club which he has supported all of his life. But it aired on November 25, six weeks before the third round clash. Town had not even got past Leyton Orient at that point. So it seemed like fate when the Blues were tasked with facing Sir Elton's beloved Hornets on January 6.

Two years previous, there had been an incredible 6,000 Spireites fans at Stamford Bridge for a third round clash against then European champions Chelsea and it had been hoped that they would be given close to that number again by Watford. The Vicarage Road Stand has a capacity of 5,800, but Chesterfield were only given an allocation of 3,500.

The Hornets initially said they would not be giving any more, but they ended up releasing another 450 to take the total close to 4,000. If you were to be sceptical, it made you wonder whether the ex-Premier League side feared being outnumbered by National League Chesterfield in their own backyard. Now that would be a little embarrassing.

In the end, they weren't, although it sounded like there were 40,000 Blues in the stadium such was the racket they made. Watford might not have been outnumbered, but they were definitely out sung. The Hornets were 10th in the Championship at the time and they showed respect by naming six players in the line-up who also started their last league game. Chesterfield made five changes themselves, which would have been unusual for an ordinary non-league outfit, but the Spireites were a different animal. Taking up his position in the dugout that day for the first time in the season was Kieron Dyer, who thankfully had recovered from his liver transplant.

In the first meeting between the two teams in 26 years, the Spireites started nervously and could have been a couple of goals down in the first 10 minutes. But they soon found their rhythm and took the lead just before the half-hour mark when Joe Quigley headed in Ryheem Sheckleford's delicious cross. And they were the better side for the rest of the half, playing some top football, with the hosts booed off by their fans. Just like against Portsmouth and Leyton Orient, Cook's men had no fear and fully believed they could win.

Banks went close to doubling Town's advantage early after the break but Watford were much-improved in the second half and they equalised when substitute Mileta Rajović headed in at the near post. Colclough had a great chance to put Chesterfield back ahead in the dying minutes but he nodded over from about five yards out. Liam Mandeville whipped in a deep corner, Grimes headed it back across goal and Colclough, who had been standing goalside of Francisco Sierralta, anticipated it well and jolted back the other side of the Chilean defender. The opportunity seemed to drop to him in slow motion.

"This is it," you thought. He'd just scored a smart header against Solihull. He'll bury this one. But it went over. He'd got good power on it, but he couldn't keep it down. The Spireites hordes behind the goal jumped up as high as the roof before flying back down into the seats. They couldn't believe it. Neither could Colclough, who rested both hands on the top of his head. That was the chance.

Moments later, Tom Dele-Bashiru drilled in a late winner in the 95th minute to save the Hornets' blushes.

Being truthful, it wasn't quite the same sickening feeling had it been an important league game. To be frank, Chesterfield weren't really that fussed. Of course they wanted to win. But a draw wasn't that appealing. They didn't really fancy adding a replay to their already-packed schedule, which included seven fixtures in January. They didn't want an eighth.

Had it been a once-in-a-lifetime ticket to take Manchester United or Liverpool back to the SMH, then emotions would have been very different. No offence to Watford, but it wouldn't have been a glamour tie. Besides, they got Southampton in the next round, drawing 1-1 at home before losing 3-0 on the south coast, so it wasn't a big loss in the end.

Chesterfield were alright with the result. They had done themselves proud. They had got to the third round for the third successive year and they had not looked out of place at all. There did not look three divisions and 63 places between the two sides. And there was another reason for them to have an extra spring in their step. Bromley had been held to a goalless draw by Maidenhead United and Barnet had lost 3-2 at Altrincham.

After a defeat, post-match interviews can be hard to navigate. You have to read the room. No laughing and joking. Ask the important questions, but respectfully. But the mood was more relaxed than normal. The media had noticed the other results. The backroom staff had glanced at them. Everyone could see the bigger picture. They were out of the cup, but one step closer to the bigger end goal.

During the second half at Vicarage Road, Watford showed a picture of their greatest-ever manager, Graham Taylor, on the big screen in the ground. He died aged 72, on January 12, 2017 and this was the nearest home game to the anniversary of his passing. In a classy touch, Watford also put up an image of legendary former Chesterfield boss John Duncan, who died aged 73 on October 8, 2022.

Spireites fans had joined in applause for both Taylor and Duncan and they also sang the name of Captain Tom Sawyer, of the 29 Commando Regiment Royal Artillery, who was from Watford and supported the club. He died in Afghanistan in 2009, aged just 26. His family were at the match and he was honoured on the pitch at half-time. In the days after, the parents of Captain Sawyer, Sue and Martyn, emailed Chesterfield. They wrote: "Dear Chesterfield FC. We are the proud parents of Captain

Tom Sawyer RA 29 Cdo KIA Afghanistan 14-1-2009 who was honoured at Watford FC on Saturday 6th January at half-time during their game with Chesterfield.

"Tom was Watford born and bred and an avid Watford supporter from childhood. We just wanted to thank your supporters for the respect and amazing support they showed during the photo montage and speeches – at one point even breaking into a rendition of 'There's only one Captain Sawyer,' which was such an emotional highlight for all Tom's family and friends present. Your supporters were an absolute credit to their team and their club throughout the game and especially for us as a family."

A member of Watford's operations team also got in touch, praising the Spireites fans. They wrote: "Your fans were impeccably behaved and are a credit to both Chesterfield FC and the National League. It was a pleasure to have your fans at our ground on Saturday. I am sure you are all disappointed about the result but from what we saw I am sure Chesterfield will be back in the EFL next season."

They clearly knew their football.

***

Had Chesterfield's game against Gateshead in October not been postponed due to the floods then it could have been a very different outcome to the one in the middle of January. Back then, Gateshead had been having a terrific season, although they had just lost manager Mike Williamson to MK Dons. They had been playing some fantastic football and striker Marcus Dinanga, who had managed one goal in 12 appearances for the Spireites during the 2020/21 season, had scored 12 goals in 13 outings by the end of September.

Gateshead were fifth come January 10, but their squad was threadbare and Dinanga had not netted in 12 matches. Several of their key players had either been recalled from their loans by their parent club, sold or were injured. In their previous match at York City, a 2-0 defeat, on New Year's Day, they had only been able to name four substitutes and one of those was a goalkeeper.

With ex-Newcastle United keeper Rob Elliot now in charge, they had scrambled to sign a handful of players to boost numbers, including 20-year-old stopper Eddie Beach, who was on loan from Chelsea and would get quite the introduction to senior men's football. And by that, we mean that he would concede four times in the first half, including a clanger and five in total, with Grigg scoring his first hat-trick for Chesterfield.

The writing was probably on the wall for the visitors when they arrived late to the stadium, which delayed the start of their warm-up and probably contributed to them being a goal down after just 12 minutes. It was Grigg's first of the night, assisted by Williams, who was back from injury after two-and-a-half months out. Naylor added a second from a tight angle and then two goals in two minutes in first half added time ensured there was no way back for Gateshead.

The third goal, Grigg's second, was poetry in motion. There was a delicate flick from Berry, a reverse pass by Michael Jacobs and a clinical finish from Grigg. It was a goal worthy of much higher than the fifth division. One that brings us as football fans so much joy. The club's media team had been creating a montage of potential goal-of-the-season contenders and that one gave them another piece of material to add to it.

The next goal might not have made Chesterfield's end-of-season reel, but it wouldn't look out of place on one of those football blooper DVDs that used to come out every Christmas. Remember those? The type that made former Aston Villa goalkeeper Peter Enckelman want to hide behind the sofa. Forever. To be fair, it was nowhere as bad as that. But it was quite comical. Straight from the kick-off, Gateshead worked the ball back to goalkeeper Beach, who seemingly forgot which team he was playing for. He passed the ball straight to Jacobs, who could not believe his luck, to slot home. It really was crackers.

Grigg completed his treble, his first since April 2021, from the penalty spot, taking him to a remarkable 10 goals in his last 11 appearances and rounding off a five-star performance which was the perfect way to celebrate Cook's 250th game as Chesterfield manager. The evening was dampened a little bit when it emerged that Colclough had gone to hospital for an X-ray on his ankle, which was like a balloon, after taking a whack by Kenton Richardson. It would end up keeping him out for two months. But Berry had come on in his place and had been electric, including winning the penalty for goal number five, so he wasn't a bad replacement to have.

The Spireites had ticked off one of their three games in hand and they were now nine points clear at the top. In the two previous seasons, FA Cup third round defeats to Chelsea and West Brom had resulted in a dip in form, but this result put any concerns of that happening again to bed. There was no hangover. In the background, Cook was keeping everyone calm. With three league titles already to his name, he knew there was a long way to go.

***

It's not often you go into a game thinking you'd be okay with a reasonably heavy defeat, as long as it didn't get too embarrassing before a ball had even been kicked. But that was the feeling behind the scenes as Chesterfield's academy lads were given the chance to represent the club against Welling United for the FA Trophy fourth round. That wasn't any disrespect to the youngsters. It was just that the average age of the starting line-up was younger than 20 and they were coming up against fully-grown men who were only playing one division below the Spireites' first-team.

Fair enough, Welling were struggling in the National League South but the Spireites youths were very raw and not used to facing this level of opponent. They were up against Anthony Grant, an experienced midfielder who had started his career at Chelsea and had spent most of his days in the Football League playing for the likes of Wycombe Wanderers, Southend United, Crewe Alexandra, Peterborough United and Swindon Town. And between the sticks they had Reice-Charles Cook, who had played for Bromley against Chesterfield in the play-off semi-final only a few months before.

With tired eyes but excitement in their bellies, the squad met at the SMH at 7am, travelled down on the day and had a pre-match meeting and meal at a nearby Holiday Inn. Even that was new to them. But the club wanted to give them a proper matchday experience. In the team meeting, academy manager Neil Cluxton outlined his masterplan. The aim had been to stay in the game as long as they could. They wanted to pinch possession and counter-attack at speed. In the early stages, it was all about hitting the channels and getting Liam Jessop and Thomas Marshall running at Welling. They had also been working on set-pieces, knowing that they might be their best chance of scoring.

In fairness, had the first-team been used, the players would have travelled down the day before. So to spend about eight hours on a coach for a 360-mile round trip made the performance they put in even more impressive. They ran themselves into the ground, pressed like their lives depended on it and gave every inch of what they had. A handful of them had cramp towards the end. No clear chances came their way but they held Welling for 50 minutes before eventually falling to a 2-0 defeat. They did the club proud. It was a moral victory.

Having departed in the early morning and not arriving back until late at night, it had been a long day, with many of the lads absolutely cream-crackered and in the land of nod on the coach home. Phone calls home to parents, grandparents and friends had been made. Pictures of their shirts with their names on the back uploaded to social media. Many had dozed off with headphones still in and iPads still playing. They'd stayed up well past their bedtime.

The FA Trophy perhaps could have been a competition that Chesterfield could have taken more seriously had they known what was around the corner. But while the youngsters had been grafting in Welling, the seniors had been back in Derbyshire working hard preparing for a tough fixture against play-off hopefuls Altrincham. On the Sunday before the Tuesday night encounter, Roberts had been plotting a particular pattern of play which he felt could open up the Robins down their left side.

A lot of time and effort went into it, a lot of attention to detail. If one person messed up, that was it. It had to be a slick machine. And much to his satisfaction, it came off in the 25th minute as Sheckleford, Jacobs and Naylor all linked-up down the right with some beautifully-timed passes and movement off the ball which ended with Banks sweeping home. The new training ground, alongside the hard work of the talented coaching team and the players' desire to execute it, had paid off again.

But the Robins themselves scored a fantastic counter-attack goal, labelled "first-class" by Webb, which got them level as much-coveted Chris Conn-Clarke fired in his 13th league strike of the season. And although the match itself was hard-fought, ugly and scrappy at times, Chesterfield's second goal was also a beauty. Grimes played a pass out wide left to Berry who was hogging the touchline. He fizzed a first-time ball into Banks, who returned it back with a clever flick, before

Berry opened up his body and curled the ball into the bottom corner with a finish that Thierry Henry would have been proud of. Berry was the last one off the training pitch every day practicing his finishing and it was showing.

Berry had been at Altrincham before signing for Macclesfield but he didn't make a single appearance for them. But that didn't stop their fans booing him on the night, which he found both amusing and bizarre. Parkinson's men made a big impression on everyone, with many fans being of the opinion that they were the best team to visit the SMH in the season. But victory made 16 consecutive home wins for Chesterfield in all competitions. Yes, sixteen. More importantly, they were 12 points clear at the top. They hadn't been at their best, but it was another game ticked off.

***

Thursday, January 18 was a busy day of announcements at the club. So, naturally, this author was off work and away from his laptop when he got word about what was to unfold. Being a journalist keeps you on your toes. Things happen when you least expect it. A rare Friday night tea down the pub? That is guaranteed to be interrupted. Sunday lunch with your family? Forget it. Just logged off for the day? Better get ready to sign back in again.

In the media industry, you need to have understanding people around you. But it's hard for them too. At the beginning, they can't get their head around it. Why have you brought your laptop on a night out? Can't it just wait until the morning? When will you finish? "How long is a piece of string?" is normally the answer.

It's not a nine-to-five job that once you log off, that's it for the day. Most things happen in football in the evenings as well. It's a side of the job that people don't see or give much thought to. And why would they? Most folk know what days and hours they are working. They have done the same schedule for the last 10 years. Once it hits 5pm on a Friday, they are out of the office and won't be back until Monday at nine.

But don't feel sorry for us. Being a football reporter is one of the best jobs in the world. And luckily, you can plan ahead when you get wind that something is brewing, write it in advance and just press send when the time is right. In the space of a couple of hours, the club announced that Armando Dobra and Sheckleford had signed new contracts until summer 2026, Bailey Clements and Bailey Hobson had been recalled from their loans at Eastleigh and Kidderminster Harriers respectively, while Laurence Maguire's loan at Crawley Town had been extended until the end of the season.

Dobra's deal was the big news. He had six months left on his contract and there were concerns he was not going to sign another one and walk away for free at the end of the season. There had been reports of a bid from Oxford United, which had nothing in them when the *Derbyshire Times* checked it out. The biggest pull for Chesterfield was that Dobra had a lot of respect for Cook and loved playing for him. Cook had given him his chance at Ipswich Town and now he was helping to develop him at the Spireites.

With Freckleton suffering a hamstring injury against Watford, a decision was made to bring back Clements, but they wanted to give him the chance to play in a potential dream FA Cup fourth-round tie against Manchester United. But, sadly for Clements, after holding Newport County to a 1-1 draw, they were beaten 3-1 at home in the replay. Just two days after that defeat, he was back at the Blues.

Hobson, meanwhile, had made a great impression at Kidderminster. He had been one of their better players as they fought against relegation. He'd been running an average of 13 kilometres a match, had got stuck in and had scored three goals. The Harriers had just appointed former Hull City boss Phil Brown until the end of the season and despite only working with Hobson for a couple of days, he had liked what he had. Brown was disappointed to lose him and was a little annoyed by the decision, believing that Hobson would be better off staying with his side and playing every week.

Maguire's extension was the writing on the wall for him. But everything turned out just fine as he won promotion to League One through the play-offs with Crawley. One year on from that heartache at Wembley, this time he left a winner — and just one week after his brother Harry had got his hands on the FA Cup with Manchester United after they beat rivals City. Cook spoke highly of Maguire, saying he loved his football and remained professional, but it was the end of the road for the academy graduate who was Chesterfield's longest-serving player.

Disappointingly, a much-anticipated top-of-the table clash at Barnet was postponed due to a frozen pitch. Chesterfield's players and coaching staff had delayed their journey down south on Friday afternoon and the longer and longer it went on, to hear back about what was going to happen, it was felt that it would be best if it was called off as their preparations for the game had been disrupted. For a start, they would not have arrived at their hotel until much later than they first planned, which would have knocked back their evening meal and sleep.

The Spireites had been due to take a large following to The Hive, despite the game being on TV, but many of them would still make the trip when it was rearranged a month later. The temperatures were actually above freezing and Barnet had got some injuries to key players. Only they will know whether they could have done more to get the game on. But, either way, it wouldn't matter a jot.

***

Liam Mandeville whipped in another free-kick delivery that was virtually impossible to defend. It was inswinging. It had plenty of pace. It was in an area that left Woking goalkeeper Alexis Andre Jr. — a part-time internet personality and reality TV star who has 4.6 million followers on TikTok — uncertain whether to stay on his line or come and try to get something on it. It was similar to the one against Portsmouth. And it had the same outcome. Goal.

Everyone called it as a Grimes goal. The commentators. The written press. The radio journalists. He'd stuck out a leg and got the final touch. The skipper clenched his right fist in the air and ran off to celebrate behind the net in front of the North Stand. Then he turned to his left and saw Grigg pointing at himself, to claim it was actually him who got the decisive flick. Grimes then threw his right arm up in Grigg's direction as if to say: "No chance." The pair then hugged and were embraced by their teammates. As the group broke away, Grimes turned back to the North Stand and squeezed his fist again, reiterating that it was his goal. And then Grigg stuck his right arm in the air to once again make sure everyone knew it was his. The fans started singing his song.

Stadium announcer Howard Borrell, a stickler for accuracy when it comes to pronouncing names and goalscorers, raced up and down the press box, gathering opinions on who got it. In the end, it went down as Grigg's. Of course it would. He would claim a goal was his even if he wasn't in the same postcode. It was hard to tell on the replay. But it had got to the point where the players were joking that whoever celebrated the most got it!

It was enough to secure another win. It wasn't particularly memorable and Woking — led by Michael Doyle, who had played under Cook at Portsmouth — almost grabbed a late point with a header cleared off the line and a one-on-one squandered. Back in the dressing room, the phones went back on. Bromley had only managed a draw at Aldershot Town and Barnet had lost 2-0 at Oldham Athletic. Chesterfield had created a 13-point lead with two games in hand. They had their foot to the floor while others were stalling. An amazing 71 points before the end of January and a 17 successive home wins in all competitions. It was unbelievable.

"We had a two or three game period where we didn't play great but we were picking up results," Grigg said. "It is a sign of a really good team. We were coming off the pitch having won 1-0, but still frustrated. It sounds crazy but they were the standards we set. Those narrow victories felt a bit disappointing in the changing room."

Cook had never been one for individual awards. His view had always been that it was a collective effort. Since coming back to Chesterfield he had not sought to be in the limelight, very much keeping himself to himself. So when a 3-0 win at home to Southend United secured him the National League manager of the month for January, with the Spireites having won all five league games, it wasn't much of interest to him. He didn't want to be seen as the one taking all the credit. He had his eyes on the bigger prize.

January would be the month that the coaching staff and players would later reflect on as the key period of the season. Five league matches all at home. Some of those were games in hand. The SMH pitch was looking worn. Seven fixtures in total meant the squad was stretched. Some of their performances had not hit the heights of other ones, but they had found a way to win.

Southend's future was looking brighter than it had been for a few years. Their takeover had still not gone through, but the consortium had advanced funds so that they could strengthen. They had not played for two weeks, but they had used that time to sign some new players and they had ambitions of still making the play-offs. This was another fixture which felt trickier than some of the others. Southend were a strong out-fit and the game was in the balance until the latter stages.

But by full-time, Chesterfield's media team had more material for the end-of-season goals reel, with Berry opening the scoring after just four minutes with a thunderbolt off the underside of the crossbar. He made it look like he did that every day in training, and he did. Quigley scored with his first touch after 35 seconds of coming on as a substitute to make it 2-0 with 17 minutes remaining and then Dobra added a sublime third which included a dummy from Mandeville and a perfectly-weighted set from Jacobs before the ball was smashed in.

Webb went down the tunnel. Got his phone out. Had a glance at the results. Bromley and Barnet had both lost. The lead at the top had been increased to 16 points by January 27. Secretly, they were obviously chuffed, but they had to keep a straight face in front of the media.

"We are certainly not getting carried away, but hopefully the fans are, because they have had some tough times and this season, so far, is go-ing to plan," Webb said. "A few years ago they were thinking about go-ing into the National League North, away at Chorley, so days like today should be enjoyed, while understanding there was a long way to go. We all want that common goal — we are getting closer."

It was the first time in the club's history that they had beaten 21 sepa-rate teams. No side could now do the double over them. A club record 18 home wins on the spin in all competitions had been secured. The bookies had stopped taking bets on Chesterfield to win the title. It was turning into a season for a record of club records.

"It just felt like we were going to win every week," Grimes said. "You don't even think about losing, you just think about what you can do bet-ter each week. Despite the points gap, nothing changed. It was all about how can we win the next game. As mad it sounds, you always thought you could be caught. I wasn't even looking at the table at that stage."

Jeff King remembered the "weird feeling" of the Spireites constantly getting told how good they were. "Every result was good and there was nothing going on that was negative. We were winning game after game after game and the gap was getting bigger and bigger and bigger. You are just starting to think that it is a matter of time."

Mandeville said: "I feel like we knew we were going to win it for a long time. I was probably more confident than anyone else. But the staff would never say anything like that. They would always be: "Next game, next game, next game." We didn't play that well in the last third of the season but it was like we had already done the work. At that point we were just desperate to get it over the line — probably due to what had happened the season before. I think sometimes it felt like other teams were a lot closer than they actually were. But when you actually looked at the league, no one was anywhere near really. You never expected to be that far in front in January time."

And Grigg added: "At the end of January, without saying it we were probably looking at each other thinking: 'We are not far off.' You hear a lot of talk about the 'next game' from managers and pundits but that was genuinely the mindset within the changing room. That is a big skill of the gaffer — he is never too high and never too down."

17

RUNAWAY TRAIN

I t was wet, windy and, quite frankly, pretty horrible. It was a Tuesday night and Chesterfield were 170 miles from home down in Essex. It reminded you of the saying: "Could they do it on a cold Tuesday night in Stoke?" It was always rolled out whenever a top Premier League side – usually someone like Arsenal, who got beat up there a few times under Arsene Wenger – had to go there. It sorted the men from the boys. Could they defend Rory Delap's cannon-like long throw? How would they cope with 6ft 7in Peter Crouch, with his gangly arms and legs everywhere? Would their strikers stand up to hardman Robert Huth, or would they shy away after taking an elbow to the face early on?

It had gone 10pm and Danny Webb was standing pitch side. The floodlights were flickering. A few Dagenham and Redbridge players had been sent out to cool down. Or warm-up, whichever way you look at it. Chesterfield's lads, washbags tucked under their arms, were trickling out of the dressing room and onto the coach. Every now and again, the smell of expensive aftershave filled your nostrils, or the crunching sound of boot studs on concrete would make you turn your head to see who it was.

Despite the blustery conditions, not a hair was out of place on Webb's immaculate slick back. That was until a big gust of wind forced him to wince a little bit and a few strands sprung up out and pointed to the sky. As the season went on, his barnet even got its own thread on the *Bob's Board* fan forum and deservedly so. It was a masterpiece.

Chesterfield had just gone a mighty 22 points clear at the top and Webb, with a camera in his face and with journalists shaking in the cold, was about to tell the media that the title race was not over. "We all still believe we have got a job to do," he said. "We know we are in a great position, we know we are in the driving seat. But until it's all done, it is not all done."

Webb would laugh about it later on. But, at the time, he had to stick to the party line. He had to keep rolling out the clichés. He could not say anything else or he could have been at risk of being left with egg on his face. Imagine if there had been a humongous collapse and Chesterfield didn't win any of their last 15 matches? Webb would have had to leave the country! But deep down he knew it was done. And so did everyone else. There was no chance this team was suddenly going to start getting pummelled every week – and you didn't fancy Barnet or Bromley to turn into the Arsenal Invincibles, either.

Jeff King, however, was not as soft with his words as Webb. "We want to be a team who is remembered," he openly admitted. "We want to break records and be the best team the National League has ever seen." When asked about King's comments, Webb took an intake of breath before smiling. "He loves a quote, does Kingy," he said, "where everyone goes: 'Oh dear!'"

In fairness to King, he wasn't the only one saying it. The noise about Chesterfield potentially breaking Wrexham's 111 points record, which had only been set 12 months previous, was getting louder. They were on 80 and, with another 45 available, it wasn't totally unrealistic. Ollie Banks said: "I had mates who play for other clubs ring me and say: 'It's done now' in like November and December. I was like: 'Woah, steady on.' It doesn't feel like that when you are in it. We never really took the foot off the gas. We just wanted it done as soon as possible. I think, deep down, we knew we weren't going to get caught, but nobody really wanted to admit it. And the staff and the gaffer wouldn't allow us to feel like that. If I was a manager I would have been exactly the same. There was no talk about winning the league or what we are going to do when we win the league, it was just like: 'Let's get the job done first and then see what happens.'"

The Spireites passed their Stoke City test. The conditions may have had similarities to a night at the Bet365 Stadium, but the Daggers were nothing like them in terms of playing style. James Berry had really stepped up to the mark following Ryan Colclough's injury and he bagged his fourth goal in five games to give Town the lead after goalkeeper Elliot Justham spilled a powerful drive from Banks.

"I was walking on the pitch feeling 10-feet tall," Berry said. "I was really settled with all the lads. I was that confident and felt so fit, so sharp, I knew I was going to score. I was going into every game thinking I am going to score today. One of my main attributes is to sniff out goals and get into positions where I can score goals."

Ryan Hill equalised early in the second half and then Banks smashed a penalty against the crossbar before Armando Dobra scrambled home the winner with 15 minutes remaining to secure a seventh consecutive win in the league. Just three days earlier, Town had beaten Eastleigh 3-1 at the Silverlake Stadium, with Berry, Liam Mandeville and Will Grigg on the scoresheet. It could have been a different game had Harry Tyrer not made an important one-on-one save in the opening minutes and if former Spireite Paul McCallum, who was still the division's top scorer, had not been sent off for two bookings before half-time.

It's not often you are trying to get a manager or a coach to admit that they have won the league by February 6, but there we were. Chesterfield were a runaway train, and nobody could stop them.

***

It is natural in football to ease off the gas when you are so far out in front. It doesn't matter whether you are Manchester City or Chesterfield; if you have a 22-point lead, complacency is going to creep in. And, do you know what? You can be forgiven for it, because you have earned the right to have an off day here and there. You can have the occasional bad day at the office, because you've been sensational for the most part.

Fans had been looking at all the permutations. Would it be won at home to AFC Fylde or Oxford City? What about at Oldham Athletic? It was a matter of when and not if. The next three games gave a feeling of foot being taken off the pedal, of gears being gone down. Of job being done. It wasn't that they weren't trying, but perhaps the Spireites had just lost their edge a little bit.

Ebbsfleet United were third from bottom but under the leadership of interim manager Danny Searle, presented themselves as a side who were much better than their league position suggested. They took the lead inside 45 seconds before Town came fighting back with two goals from Grigg and Dobra. But the visitors equalised just after the break and they came close to claiming all three points before full-time.

That draw halted Chesterfield's seven-game winning run and their incredible successive victories at the SMH came to an end at 18. Remarkably, it was their first time they had dropped points on home soil since that draw with Oldham Athletic, back on August 19. Bromley and Barnet were in FA Trophy action so despite not winning, the Spireites stretched their lead to a not-so-shabby 23 points.

A second-v-first clash with 14 fixtures remaining would normally make for a nervy belly but Chesterfield travelled to Hayes Lane to take on Bromley in a relaxed mood. There wasn't much riding on it in terms of the race for the title and that was probably why it ended up being a seven-goal blockbuster.

The Spireites controlled the first half and were 1-0 up at half-time thanks to Grigg's penalty after Darren Oldaker was bundled over in the area. Whereas the first 45 had been straightforward, the second half was anything but. It was absolute chaos. A brace from Michael Cheek turned the game on its head, before two goals in five minutes — including a screamer from Banks which was voted goal of the season — and a header from Tom Naylor flipped the game back in Chesterfield's favour.

But a hat-trick equaliser from Cheek, the first Ravens player to score a treble in nine years, with four minutes of normal time remaining made it 3-3, before Sam Woods struck in the 94th minute to win it for Bromley. Just moments earlier Tyrer had made a stunning reaction save that was beyond belief, one that he would later say was his best of the season. Cheek, meanwhile, must wish he could play against Chesterfield every week, his hat-trick taking his record to 10 goals in 13 appearances against them.

All the goals Chesterfield had conceded that day were very similar and were the type they had given up throughout the campaign. Possession lost in the opposition half had left them vulnerable to the counter-attack and with players out of position, Cheek was left to gobble up the crosses.

It was a third defeat in succession at Hayes Lane and, funnily enough, the last time Chesterfield had shipped four goals was also on the astroturf at the same ground. As the gates shut behind the media on the way out, they hoped it would be the last visit for a while. But it wasn't. Bromley would go on to win the play-offs, beating Solihull Moors on penalties in the final at Wembley and securing promotion to the Football League for the first time in their history.

Had the gap between the two teams been much closer, it would have been a real sickener to lose so late on. But those in the press that day remember reacting to it with nothing more than a shrug of the shoulders. One look at the league table, which showed Chesterfield were still 20 points in front, soon cheered everyone up.

Initially, it looked like Paul Cook had dragged his coaching staff out onto the plastic pitch at Hayes Lane for a public dressing down. It was later clarified they did so because the dressing rooms at Bromley are tight and they wanted to hold the post-match inquest in private.

Bromley, as they had done all season after a win, uploaded a celebratory team photo to social media with the caption: "Some club." Just like the James Norwood video, it would provide some fantastic material for Chesterfield fans and a lot sooner than they could ever have imagined. Just three days after that humdinger in Kent Andy Woodman's men threw away a two-goal lead to draw against Dagenham in the 94th minute and then lost 2-0 at Eastleigh in their next outing. "Show us the dressing room pic" and "some club" were among dozens of similar cheeky and brutal responses online from Chesterfield fans.

Just like Ebbsfleet, Rochdale proved to be a useful outfit on their day, battling back from two goals down to earn a point in Derbyshire a week later. Goals from Naylor and Grigg, the latter's 15th in his last 19 appearances, put the Spireites in a commanding position but Dale came roaring back through D'Mani Mellor and Devante Rodney. By now, it was clear that Chesterfield were not reaching the heights of previous months and other teams were most definitely raising their game against them. The SMH pitch was bobbly and rough and that was hindering Cook's men as well.

Such were the high standards that this team had set, three games without a win was their longest without a victory up to this point. Other managers had started using the words "blips" and "wobbles," which was ridiculous, but behind the scenes Chesterfield were not affected by any of that nonsense. Everyone continued to be calm and level-headed, led by Cook. And they soon silenced those people with a statement victory at second-placed Barnet. When reflecting on the season, many of the players and coaching staff would state this match as the moment when they really knew the title was done and dusted.

Had Barnet won, the gap would have been cut to 17. It would still have been insurmountable. But a 2-0 win for Chesterfield, with goals in each half from Michael Jacobs and Grigg, restored their advantage to 23 points again.

It was a proper champions' performance. They were solid at the back and clinical in front of goal. They didn't play their prettiest football, but it was a confident, mature display. They bossed it. They needed just 11 more points from their final 11 fixtures to officially seal it. As they got back on the bus, they knew they were almost there.

Grigg's goal was their 100th of the season in all competitions. A century of net-bulgers by February 27. This was also their 11th away win of the season, which equalled a club record. What a team.

Perhaps it was because they were the ones living it, but it was not until this victory that the majority of those inside the camp actually started to think they were going to win the title and get the club back in the Football League. Those on the outside, fans and media included, could tell they were going to be champions probably months before. Watching their performances week in, week out, they never looked like letting it slip from their grasp. But as Kobe Bryant famously said in 2009 as the Los Angeles Lakers went 2-0 up in the NBA finals: "The job's not finished."

Webb reflected: "When we got back on the coach at Barnet away, we sort of half-looked at each other and thought that it was going to take a massive cock-up not to win this. But cock-ups can happen, so that is what you have to try to be cautious of. You are hoping you are not going to be the case that everyone looks at and goes: 'Let's not do a Chesterfield.' It would have been the biggest one of all time. I think, deep down, we knew we would take some stopping, but the mathematics of it meant that it wasn't done. The year before, we had gone loads of games without a win. So why couldn't we do it again?"

Mike Jones said: "I feel like we knew we had won it once we had won at Barnet. Everyone came away from the game like: 'Let's be realistic, we have won it.'"

Grimes explained: "That was a really professional performance. The gaffer changed the set-up slightly. We had a really solid three-man midfield to respect them. Because when they came to our place, in the first half it was like the Alamo. They had lots of chances and we managed to stay in the game and then beat them. The gaffer was saying that he didn't want to go down to Barnet and offer ourselves up like that again. He said we were going to be solid and then have a slightly different approach when we were playing and it worked to a tee. We frustrated the life out of them and then we scored from two long balls forward and crosses in the box. That is how the gaffer said it was going to play out. We knew that they just wanted to jump all over us, so we just went in behind them with runners forward."

Berry added: "After that game we were so high on confidence. They were second in the league and we had just gone to their place and beat them. We thought we could start believing a bit now. We had killed them off after that game. But if we had stopped playing football and lost every game, then we wouldn't win the league. And that is how we looked at it."

18

CHAMPIONS ELECT, OLÉ OLÉ

Four blokes were dancing in the rain. They were well refreshed, shall we say. Sozzled, in fact. For a 12.30pm kick-off, they had given the ball a good kick from the moment their 5am alarm clocks had gone off. It was a tremendous effort. The only conclusion one could come to was that they had poured lager, not milk, on their morning cornflakes.

Having just entered Meadowbank, the home of Dorking Wanderers, they took up their standing position left of the halfway line and had formed a little circle. They were jigging. Clapping. Arms out wide. They were having the time of their lives. They were looking at each other with mischievous smiles. The type of grin that can't be held in. It's too powerful, too forceful. It's got you. It makes your cheeks hurt. They were looking around at others to get them to join in. The problem was that not everyone had drunk Dorking dry by lunchtime. A lot were still yawning and rubbing their eyes from the early start and long trip down.

Peering through the raindrops that were dripping down the glass window in the press box, it was hard to tell what the four fellas were singing. They would start, stop, move away and then come back. But then there was a moment where the ridiculously loud music coming through the Tannoy system quietened. And you could hear them. It was something about champions. It was a short, upbeat tune. "Champions … olé olé." It was difficult to make out the middle word. But then the Dorking four edged closer and it became clearer. "Champions elect, olé olé." It would be the smash hit for the month of March. Sadly, the performance at Meadowbank was not one befitting of champions. Chesterfield did not turn up and lost 4-1.

They got beaten up. Dorking, who had the worst home record in the league and would go on to get relegated, went man-for-man and ran all over them. They simply wanted it more. It was a display riddled with errors and Wanderers were clinical. It was the Spireites' heaviest defeat of the season and it could have been much worse. Four goals at Bromley and now another four here; it was fair to say plastic pitches were not the Blues' friend. Ash Palmer's header in first half injury-time had given them an undeserved lifeline but that was soon undone three minutes after the break when a loose pass across his own box by Jamie Grimes was punished.

Had it been right at the start of the season, or a different group of players who had not earned the right to chuck in a performance like this every now again, the anger at full-time could have got nasty. But there was none, really. There were not even any boos. Everyone kind of just trundled off back to their cars for the three-hour journey home.

Paul Cook, though, was fuming and said that the "paint would have been coming off the walls," had his side not had such a fantastic season. In his post-match interview he mentioned Chesterfield's softness, their vulnerability. Once again, their Achilles' heel. "Going forward, will you keep living with it? That is the problem," he added, which gave an indication he was already thinking about next season.

Cook had been looking forward to getting back on the coach with a 26-point lead and then watching his beloved Liverpool on TV against Nottingham Forest. Instead, Barnet and Bromley won so he had to settle for *just* a 20–point gap. His mood was lifted, though, when Darwin Nunez struck a 99th-minute winner for Liverpool at the City Ground.

With such a large points gap at the top, there were suggestions that Chesterfield had taken their foot off the gas. "That was not the case at all," said Grimes. When it gets closer, you get more desperate to win. By that time you had been going seven or eight months and you were starting to feel the fatigue mentally. We had gone really hard when other teams were slipping up left, right and centre. We started to feel a bit of fatigue and we were almost trying too hard. And we were on that pedestal for teams to beat us. Dorking went man-for-man and followed everyone around on an astroturf pitch that was incredibly sticky. We couldn't get the ball moving, we made error after error and they capitalised and scored. They didn't win a game after that. The way they celebrated it was like they had won the FA Cup."

***

Shooooot!

Everyone was desperate for Mike Jones to score. Just give us one goal, Mike. It can go in off your backside. We don't care. His last goal had been for Barrow against Bolton Wanderers, three-and-a-half years earlier in October 2020. Having previously been a tricky winger, he had gradually dropped deeper into a holding midfield role as his career had gone on. It wasn't his job to pop one in the onion bag. He was the destroyer. His job was to protect the back four, win the duels and to start attacks. He was Mike "The Machine" Jones.

Previous cries of "shooooot" from the stands had either been ignored or, when answered with a crack from distance, met with disgust by Cook. He wanted the ball to be popped about and for his side to remain patient. But when the ball fell nicely to Jones just inside the area, in the 55th minute of Chesterfield's game against AFC Fylde and with the Spireites already 1-0 up, there was only one thing on his mind.

Before he had connected with the half-volley, there was a split second where the decibel levels increased as people realised who was about to pull his right leg back. As shouts of "shooooot" and "hiiiiit itttttt" merged together, the ball flew through the air and high into the Fylde net before crashing back down into the floor. The high pitch in club commentator Steve Yorke's voice was one of surprise. But then came the line: "I think it was Naylor in the end."

Jones' rocket had indeed taken a deflection on its way in. Tom Naylor had tried to get out of the way by ducking down; in doing so, he had directed the ball in via his back. Naylor initially stuck his finger up in the air and ran off celebrating with Palmer. And then he realised whose goal he had just pinched. As Jones ran towards him, Naylor held out both his hands in an apologetic manner, before Jones jumped into his lap. Such is Jones' popularity in the squad, all 10 outfield players went to celebrate with him. They were really chuffed for him. Grimes, meanwhile, flung his arms up at Naylor in a humorous way that said: "What did you do that for?" Naylor responded by putting both his hands on top of his own head, before he and Jones embraced again. Never had a goal against AFC Fylde been cheered so loudly or celebrated so much.

On Naylor's goal-grabbing antics, Jones said: "I was thinking: 'What is he bloody doing there? Go away!' It was going top bins, he took the shine off it! I got close to scoring many times and it ended up dragging on a little bit. It became one of those things. Everyone else was scoring, we were such a free-scoring team and I was the only one not really chipping in, so I was starting to feel a bit guilty. But it was not really my job in the team."

Armando Dobra had slotted Chesterfield in front in the first half, before two more goals from Will Grigg and Palmer capped a 4-1 win, with Liam Mandeville grabbing three assists and Harry Tyrer saving a penalty at 3-1. In Cook's office afterwards, he and his staff were the happiest they had been after a win all season. After a couple of draws and defeats, some had started to harshly criticise and doubt the players, especially after losing 4-1 the week before. But they silenced them with this emphatic victory.

One man who was not happy, though, was Fylde manager Chris Beech, who gave a slightly bizarre interview featuring "furniture" and "curry." Despite his side being awarded a penalty on the day, he felt referee Michael Crusham had played a big part in the result. Or maybe his team conceded four times and were just well beaten.

That victory was a club record 28th of the season, putting Chesterfield 20 points clear with only 27 to play for. Oldham, meanwhile, could now no longer win the league. It was only March 9. Mr. Norwood's social media mentions were on fire that night.

***

Sometimes in life it's the little things that make you smile. With Chesterfield's home game against Oxford City coming to an end, "Champions elect, olé olé" was ringing around the SMH. Every time it died down a bit, it came back louder and louder, the "Champions" part emphasised more and more. People were clapping harder and harder. Six years of hurt. All that heartache and anger was coming out in one jolly little song. It was so catchy. Even this author was singing it around his house for days and weeks.

With the final whistle expected at any moment, Cook — usually engrossed in every kick, every action of the game — turned away from it just for a split second and joined in. He too had got caught up in it, allowing himself a few little fist bumps. It wasn't the first time he had slipped from manager to fan during a match in the season — he had clapped along with other songs before — but it was just a lovely, warm, nanosecond moment which made you smile.

But, in the dressing room, it was surprisingly a little flat. Sweat dripping off foreheads. The clanking of boots. Panting. Very little was said. A few murmurings here and there. The door would swung open every few seconds as the players made their way back in. It was very low-key. Had you had no idea where Chesterfield were in the league, you could have been forgiven for thinking they were languishing in mid-table and had just been comfortably beaten.

Instead, they had just seen off Oxford City 2-0 and they were now one win away from winning the league title and promotion. The part-timers, who would go on to get relegated, were rock-bottom and 14 points from safety but they had given a good account of themselves. They'd had some big chances, including seeing a penalty saved by Tyrer at 1-0 for his second spot-kick stop in a matter of days, but had failed to take them. That probably summed up why they were down there.

Chesterfield had scored inside a minute through Grigg and you wondered whether it might be a night where they got six or seven. But they had to wait until minute 55 for Naylor to add a second from a tight angle. They got the job done, but standards were so high that, even with the ridiculous lead at the top that they had, they were disappointed in how they had performed. And it was actually the coaching staff who had to pick them up a bit. Lads, you are one win away from being crowned champions.

Non-league football can throw up some rather out-of-the-ordinary tales at times and, on social media, Chesterfield were getting some stick over claims they had not been great hosts to the 26 Oxford City fans that had travelled. Because so few away supporters had made the journey to Chesterfield, the club had made the decision not to open the away concourse because it would not be financially viable. Instead, they were invited into a warm room, offered free tea and coffee and … some fairy cakes. I mean, what more do you want from an away day? It was all very random and quite funny, but you could also understand both points of view. The idea had actually been to give them some food from an event at the club earlier on in the day, but sadly there wasn't anything left and not much time to make other plans. It was a classic.

***

You couldn't write it. After all the talk about Chesterfield and Oldham being likely title rivals at the start of the season, the Norwood video, the pitch invasion, it seemed written in the stars that the Spireites could win the league against them. Or, to be specific, on the coach back from Boundary Park following the lunchtime kick-off, while waiting for Barnet to slip-up at Woking at 3pm.

On social media on the morning of the game, Town fans were giddy at the thought that their team could finally, officially, be promoted to the Football League in just a few hours. Some of the tweets were quite emotional. They made you well up a bit. Strong emotions came to the surface. Of Forest Green Rovers. Of Chorley. Loved ones no longer here. Miserable days of the past stuck in the fifth tier.

Legendary club volunteer Phil Tooley, the godfather of all things Spireites, uploaded an incredibly moving video to Twitter, or X as it is now known, outlining his confidence that no matter what would happen at Oldham, Chesterfield would win the title. That they had their club back. He signed off, with tears in his eye and a wobble in his throat, with: "There is absolutely no nerves, but there is lots of emotion. Boundary Park, we're back!"

You would have to have a heart made of stone not to have felt his emotion. "I wasn't expecting to be like that when I started recording it," he said. "We had all known since January that it was going to happen and then that was the weekend it could happen." Tooley was one of those who actually didn't want Chesterfield to clinch the title that day. He wanted it to be done on home soil, for the first time in almost 90 years. "It had not happened in any current fan's realistic lifetime," Tooley said. "It was just one of those that as a historian, as well as a fan, I just wanted to see it happen because nobody had seen it happen since 1936."

Tooley got his wish because the Blues could only manage a 2-2 draw, although they did fight back from 2-0 down. There were a few surprises in the starting line-up, with a tweak in formation to a 4-3-3 with Bailey Hobson and Michael Jacobs behind Joe Quigley. Chesterfield had seen a weakness in Oldham's midfield and they thought that if they could over-run and outnumber them, they had every chance of claiming the three points.

Chesterfield fans had got in the ground early and they were in full voice throughout the warm-up, waving their inflatable trophies around and making sure Oldham knew who was in town. Norwood, obviously, had his little moment, glaring into the eyes of those 1,700 in the away end as he tucked away an early penalty before former Spireite Dan Gardner finished off a counter-attack to make it 2-0. To his credit, he didn't celebrate.

Hobson, who was Chesterfield's best player on his first league start, got one back before half-time before winning a penalty which Quigley rolled in for his 10th of the season. Could they come back from 2-0 down to all but seal the title? It would have been very Chesterfield. It would have been very fitting. Armando Dobra hit the crossbar, as did Oldham, but the points were shared. Being honest, it was the most Town deserved that day. The Latics, who had clearly seen Dorking's approach, had been bang up for it and the home supporters in front of the press box said it was one of their best performances of the season. Typically, just like Dorking, it was a while until they won their next match. Teams had raised their levels against Cook's men; they wanted to take their scalp, but they couldn't keep it up afterwards. They didn't even make the play-offs.

Annoyingly, Barnet lost 1-0 at Woking. So had Chesterfield won, they would have been champions. But there were more opportunities to seal it in the coming days so they wouldn't have to wait long. The fans had brought blow-up trophies to Boundary Park, but the real McCoy would be in their hands shortly. Despite the champagne being on ice for a bit longer, Chesterfield chalked up two more club records for points (92) and away goals (37).

Three days later, on Tuesday night, the car park at the SMH Group Stadium was filling up. The lights were on and excitement was building. It was a sea of blue and white. Fans young and old had their shirts on, which were also young and old. One bloke had a retro jersey with Moss, 8 on the back and a Town scarf draped over the back of his seat. Pints were being poured and the atmosphere was cranking up. This was another chance for Chesterfield to win the league. At home.

The strange thing was that the Spireites weren't actually playing. Second-placed Barnet were hosting Eastleigh and if the Bees dropped points, then the Blues would be celebrating. Many supporters were torn on what they wanted the outcome to be. Some wanted Barnet to slip-up so the title could be done and dusted. They wanted it to be over as soon as possible. Chief executive John Croot was one of those, Danny Webb another.

But others wanted it to be won on the pitch and not in the SBK Spireites Restaurant while watching a stream of a match being played 140 miles away. You could understand both points of view. Interestingly, more people cheered when Chris Maguire pulled a goal back for Eastleigh than when Barnet netted twice in the first 38 minutes through Dale Gorman and Gatlin O'Donkor. And there was more noise whenever the Spitfires ventured forward in the second half than whenever Barnet did.

At The Hive that night were Tooley and some of his pals. In April 1985, he and the same group of friends went to watch Chester City come from behind to beat Hereford United, a result which meant The Bulls could no longer catch Chesterfield and so John Duncan's men were crowned Division Four champions. In 2011, Tooley and some mates watched on as promotion rivals Wycombe Wanderers failed to beat Torquay United, which secured Chesterfield's promotion. And so off Tooley went again, looking for his hat-trick.

What was rather amusing was that Tooley and his gang, as well as some other Spireites, made up a decent chunk of the attendance at The Hive because there were less than 2,000 there in a stadium that holds 6,500. In fact, it looked like there were more people in the lounge back at the SMH! In the end, Barnet held on for a 2-1 win.

"All the time I was secretly hoping that it wouldn't happen that day," Tooley said. "It would have been nice in one way, because that would have been three times that I had seen Chesterfield promoted without playing. But I drove back home from The Hive that night not disappointed at all."

For Tooley's wish to come true, Chesterfield would also need to lose at Halifax the following night. The rearranged clash at The Shay should never have gone ahead on what was a mud bath of a pitch. The Shaymen had had difficulties with the surface all season, with the main problem being drainage, as well as heavy and persistent rain during winter. The fact that local rugby league club Halifax Panthers also played on it didn't help. Calderdale Council were responsible for the upkeep of it and they came under-fire as fixtures were called off on a regular basis. Chesterfield had had a good record with injuries, but that night Grigg pulled his hamstring and would miss the rest of the season and Ryan Colclough would be out for a month with an ankle injury. The surface had a lot to answer for.

The situation got so dire that Halifax had to play their remaining "home" games at Accrington Stanley and even played Oldham Athletic at the SMH. That of course left the door open for more Latics-themed jokes about them being able to play at the home of the champions; some Chesterfield fans suggested they should parade the trophy around the pitch at half-time with a "here's what you could have won" sign.

When Grigg notched his 25th goal of the season it looked like being a special night but before journalists had even posted about it on social media and the heart rates of the 2,300 in the away end had had a chance to return to normal, Halifax had equalised instantly within a minute. Rob Harker, the scorer of the first, then grabbed his second six minutes later. In what was a cheeky celebration, Harker pretended to lift an imaginary trophy in front of the visiting fans. It was a light-hearted moment and decent 'housery but, like the Norwood video, it didn't age well. Quick-witted Ollie Banks would later reply with: "I prefer lifting the real thing."

Andrew Oluwabori added a third goal in first half stoppage time and Aaron Cosgrave grabbed a fourth after the break before James Berry pulled one back with 12 minutes remaining. But it was too late despite a late rally. All of Halifax's goals were similar, on the counter-attack and exploiting the high defensive line, which was nothing new. Cook called the three goals in 15 minutes before half-time "madness" and wasn't best pleased when asked by the *Derbyshire Times* if it had given him some food for thought for the next season. He said it was an "unfair" question and that he only wanted to concentrate on this campaign.

And so the wait to finally be crowned champions went on into a third game at home to Boreham Wood.

19

PUTTING ON A SHOW

Paul Cook ripped his bobble hat off his head. He turned away with the biggest smile on his face and clenched both of his hands into fists. He then turned back, looked up to the sky, kissed his hand and did a little fist bump. He high-fived his backroom staff before shaking both of his hands frantically in celebration. His dad Chris, who had a massive influence on his footballing life, sadly passed away in September 2021. On March 23, 2024, the day of his dad's birthday, Cook had just watched Chesterfield score their third goal against Boreham Wood to seal the National League title and promotion back to the Football League. Some things are just meant to be.

Hours before, when all was quiet, the Boreham Wood players had been getting off the coach one by one, their boot bags nestled under their arms. They filtered into the stadium through an entrance in the West Stand which is also used by the media on matchdays. When inside, they walked across the front of the stand before turning right to go down the tunnel. In came a few familiar faces who the Spireites have had tough battles against over the years. But there was no sign of former Spireite Kabongo Tshimanga. Chesterfield had sold him to Peterborough in January 2023, for a fee believed to be about £250,000 and he had returned to Boreham on loan. Was he injured? Had he already arrived? Had he snuck in through another entrance?

It was none of the above. He appeared sometime after and, with his headphones in, made his way to join his teammates in the dressing room, but not before being asked for a selfie by *Talksport's* Ian Abrahams. And it turned out Abrahams wasn't the only one. That was the reason why Tshimanga had been delayed. He had been mobbed by Town fans wanting a picture with him. And he obliged as many as possible before he ran the risk of being late. Later Tshimanga, who scored 32 goals in 51 appearances for Chesterfield, was being booed by some supporters. It's a weird old game.

In the press box, there was a feeling that this was the day. It was a chance to win a league title on home soil for the first time since 1936. Those sorts of statistics and records had been mentioned in interviews with players and coaching staff all season but, unlike journalists and re-porters, they didn't obsess over them. They left that to us. There were always some nerves going into a game, but the players weren't overly anxious. Their attitude was, what was there to be nervous about? They were unbeaten at home and had been the best team in the league all sea-son. They didn't need to stress; they just needed to do what they had done for the last nine months.

Preparing to do full match commentary for *BBC Radio Sheffield* that day was Paul Fisher, alongside former Chesterfield defender Mark Jules. As a lifelong fan, the opportunity to commentate on his club's return to the Football League had brought about some "nervous excitement" for Fisher, whilst he tried to stay as professional as possible. "I can detach from being a fan to do my job very easily," he said. "But it was harder that day because there was something bubbling up inside — I just wanted them to do it."

In the build-up to the game, there had been no Churchillian speech from Cook. There were no over-the-top, cringey lines that had been pre-planned so that the media team could capture it all on camera and plaster it on social media. That's not his style. Instead, the squad all sat in a room and watched all the goals they had scored throughout the season. The footage did all the talking. Nothing else needed to be said. Look how good you've been lads. Just go out there and finish the job.

As the two teams walked out to *Mr. Blue Sky*, the sun was shining, although the sky was grey rather than blue. This match was the hottest ticket in town and the club had done everything to make sure as many fans could be there as possible. Boreham were given a tiny section in the North Stand, but they couldn't even fill that. In a crowd of 9,907, Boreham were credited with bringing 81 supporters. Even some of those had local Derbyshire and Nottinghamshire postcodes, with one from ... Mansfield! The official home support of 9,826 was a record for Whit-tington Moor. Just four years before, Chesterfield had been getting at-tendances of around 3,000. The turnaround was amazing.

One lucky boy who got a great view of the SMH as the sides came out of the tunnel was young Zach Cooper, who — along with his teammates from Wingerworth Wolves under-10s — had been invited to be a flag-bearer on the day. His dad Chris, also the team's manager, said: "It was an honour for the boys to be flag-bearers on such a special day. It had been arranged for some time but we didn't think it would end up being for the day they won the title. They were all very excited and we even ran on the pitch at the end!"

Up in the TV gantry, *TNT Sports* commentator Adam Summerton set the scene, as blue and white balloons swirled in the wind and referee Steven Copeland signalled for the game to begin. "Chesterfield are hoping today is the day," Summerton said, "but Boreham Wood will be aiming to spoil the party and boost their hopes of survival. There is such a sense of anticipation here in Derbyshire."

The game got underway and the Spireites had the first chance when some patient play down the left channel led to Michael Jacobs bringing a save out of Nathan Ashmore with his legs. You hoped, prayed, that Ashmore wasn't going to have one of those days like he had done so many times against Chesterfield. As well as Tshimanga, relegation-threatened Boreham had another former Town man in their ranks in Tom Whelan and he forced Harry Tyrer to scramble behind his well-struck long-range free-kick just minutes later.

And then came the breakthrough that everyone had craved just before the half-hour mark. And it was fitting that it should be the skipper, captain fantastic Jamie Grimes, who should get it. And it came from a Liam Mandeville corner — a method they got so much reward from across the season. Those gruelling double sessions in Portugal. The painstaking work at Loughborough University. Nobody deserved that moment more than Grimes.

You wondered how a man of his stature had been allowed a free header in the six-yard box against a team who were well-known for their physicality. But replays showed that Armando Dobra had produced the subtlest of blocks on Jamal Fifield, who ended up sprawled out on his backside as he scrambled to stop Grimes in his tracks.

"That day, I was supposed to be going around the back," Grimes said. "A lot of the season I had been going around the back to head things back in. I am normally marked by the biggest player so the plan would be for me to go around the back to take him out. He [Fifield] must have watched the videos, he knew I was going around the back because he was looking to go to the back the whole time. So I faked to go around the back and ran across the front and I managed to get a free header at the near post. Dobs ran over to me and was like: 'I got a block, I got a block.'"

On the Kop, fans lifted their inflatable trophies into the air in celebration, but the real thing was in the house and the blue ribbons were being prepared. Tyrer turned around to face the jubilant supporters behind him — part one of the job was done. In the dressing room at half-time, the "W" word got spoken about. *Wembley*. Remember the pain, they said. Remember how much it hurt. If you're tired and struggling, just remember how you felt that day and dig deep.

Within 30 seconds of the restart, with some fans not back from their half-time refreshments and while a faint chant of "We're on our way..." was starting to get louder and louder, Chesterfield doubled their lead. Jacobs pounced on a heavy touch by Whelan, Dobra collected the loose ball and drove into the box before drilling in a low cross which Mandeville buried from six yards out. Just as they'd had so much success from corners that season, they had also been a second half team. And both of those qualities had knitted together when it mattered most.

While Branden Horton had Mandeville in a headlock, while the flags were waved and drum smacked, while it was utter chaos in the stands, Cook stood on the touchline, bobble hat on, freshly made cuppa in his hand. He turned to Kieron Dyer and nodded in agreement. He was calmness personified. "The party is just about beginning to start," said Spireites favourite Kevin Davies on commentary.

Dobra had been inconsolable after Wembley. He walked out of that stadium a broken man, his dad said he didn't talk to anyone for a long time and all his pain came out against Boreham as he put in a truly magnificent performance. He grabbed his second assist of the afternoon after rescuing a lost cause before gliding into the box and shooting across goal. Grimes made sure the ball crossed the line for his first-ever career double. That was Chesterfield's 100th league goal of the season, the one that meant the wait for the title was over and the skipper was on a hat-trick. Everything was just falling into place. Ashmore, meanwhile, booted the ball away into the West Stand in frustration. It was beautiful.

Over in the dugout, Cook kissed the sky and remembered his dad. In the distance, a rainbow appeared over the East Stand. It was a sign that it was Chesterfield's day. After six years of hurt, the club had healed. The pot of gold was waiting for them.

Chants of "We've got our club back" started to reverberate around the ground. In the director's box, Phil Kirk had been welling up. He struggled to hold it together. This is why he and his brother got involved. They knew they were never going to make any money from it. But they wanted to give something back to their club, their town, their people. "I had a tear in my eye at that point," Phil said.

Brother Ashley described it as one of the top days of his life. "It was very emotional," he said. "I had blokes my age and older come up to me in tears. They were shaking your hand and patting you on the back. You realise how important it is for everyone. It was all anyone was talking about for weeks. I am getting emotional thinking about it now."

There was a sense of calm in the final 20 minutes. Everyone could just relax and enjoy the moment. Chesterfield were waving goodbye to the National League after six long years. Town fans went through their repertoire of "Champions" songs. It was soothing. As the ball went out of play, James Berry remembered having a little moment as "We Are Sailing" was belted out from all four sides of the ground. Grimes also found himself singing along to it. "That is my favourite song. It is unbelievable," Berry said. "When we won the league it was probably one of the best feelings ever. I just can't tell you how good of a feeling and how good of a day that was. No matter what happens, you will never forget that day."

In the opposition dugout, Boreham boss Luke Garrard started whistling for his players to come over to the touchline so they could get down the tunnel quickly before the home fans invaded the pitch. When the celebrations were over, Garrard spent a lengthy time in Cook's office picking his brain about all things football; trying to obtain some little nuggets which might help him in the future. Later, Phil and Ashley went into Cook's office for a beer with him and his coaches. "That was a special moment," Ashley said. "From his point of view I think he had got his love for football back."

The referee blew his whistle and Summerton bellowed into his microphone over the noise around him. "A team that has thrilled its way to the National League title," he said. "Back to the Football League they go. It is a moment that means so much. The Spireites' six-year exile is over. It is a triumph for persistence."

Jeff King blasted the ball up into the air and the party started. Gary Roberts walked past a camera and screamed in ecstasy. Tyrer celebrated with his fellow goalkeepers Ryan Boot and Luke Chadwick just inside the tunnel. Grinning Ollie Banks rubbed his hands over his face; an expression that said: "We've done it." "It was a relief more than anything, especially after what had gone on the year before," Banks said. "It felt like we were waiting for an age to finally get it done. It was unbelievable. The first thing I wanted to do was get my kids, because I had been speaking to them about it. We knew we were going to win the league probably four or five games before we did."

Danny Webb gave two thumbs up as he walked past Banks and Tom Naylor having an extended hug. Cook was further down the tunnel area and he slapped hands with his players as they arrived. King reflected: "It was amazing. I had not had a great season personally, but I had a goal from day one of signing for the club of getting Chesterfield to the Football League. Even though I didn't have the greatest of seasons, I played in that game and people will always remember it as the day we got over the line. For me to play was really important.

"The emotion was unbelievable, probably a feeling I have not had in football. Everything was a big blur while everyone was running on the pitch, it was really crazy. I could not have asked for a better group of lads, staff or club to do it at than Chesterfield. It was a sense of relief as well after what had happened over the previous years. They are memories for life and hopefully in 25 years, or whatever when we have a get-together, it will be great to speak about all these things."

Stadium announcer Howard Borrell, in his 36th season on the mic, had the difficult task of asking people not to run on the pitch. It was met with laughter. There was no chance that wasn't going to happen. "It was pointless," he later admitted. "A little like King Canute telling the sea to go back. Nothing would stop or dilute the pure happiness that took over the stadium."

Within seconds, you couldn't see a blade of grass. All of the emotion of falling out of the Football League for the first time in almost 100 years, watching the club drift away, watching it die in front of their eyes, came out in that pitch invasion. All of the dark times put to bed. Grown men were crying. Strangers were hugging. Women were screaming with joy. People couldn't whip their phones out quick enough to film it and send it to mates who weren't there. Others stood back and took it all in. There is something quite satisfying about a pitch invasion, as long as it is peaceful — it's like a present for your eyes.

A blue smoke bomb billowed into the air. Mandeville was on a fan's shoulders, his arms stretched out above his head, singing: "Championes, championes, olé, olé, olé." Berry, Bailey Hobson and Dobra were soon lifted up. A struggle took place as someone tried to pick up Grimes' 6ft 2in frame, but they got there in the end. Berry had got hold of a selfie stick and was recording the crazy events. Darren Oldaker was wearing a turkey hat. Grimes and Joe Quigley shared a mid-air handshake.

Ryan Colclough and Mike Jones were the next two to be hoisted up. Bailey Clements made his way through the crowds and was met with a hug from Tyrer. Ash Palmer couldn't believe that someone had managed to haul him up. He looked back towards Chadwick, who was in the tunnel and the two giggled. A chorus of "We're all Town, aren't we?" was doing the rounds. Palmer then whacked Dobra over the head a couple of times with a blow-up trophy. Mandeville, now back on the ground, was bouncing up and down with fans on either side of him all holding each other. It was all going off.

While all of this was happening, *We Are Sailing* was filling the Tannoy, followed by *We Are the Champions*. "It was unbelievable," Mandeville said. "I was actually just relieved. We knew we had won it for the last few weeks, it was almost we couldn't get it over the line. It had been such a tough few years at the club, I was just so relieved to finally get it done and get back in the Football League where we belong. The support on the day was incredible. The football wasn't that great, to be honest, it was the most bog standard National League game you've ever seen. I was glad it was comfortable and not a nervy one. To get 3-0 up and be able to enjoy it was amazing.

"I feel like it was a good ending chapter to my time in the National League. I have had some really tough times, times where I thought: 'Is football really for me anymore?' Especially in the first couple of years.

I was really debating just going part-time and getting a job, because I wasn't enjoying it. It is like hell on earth, the National League. But now the whole place is only thinking upwards. The boost it has given us all is just incredible."

Berry said: "I've got all the pictures on my phone. When the fans hold you up like that, you just feel on top of the world. You are there with all your teammates and you are there together ... it is a really good feeling. You think about it every day and you just want more of those moments."

In the dressing room, as players started to make their way back inside, they wasted little time toasting their success with champagne and beer. King was swigging a bottle of Peroni. Jones screamed: "Come on!" and Oldaker stood on his seat while putting his champions T-shirt over his head. Roberts started a chant of "Champions elect, olé olé," and everyone joined in. In the middle of it all was club photographer Tina Jenner, who was snapping memories of a lifetime. It was glorious.

A topless Quigley stood with his arms out as *Freed From Desire* started to play through the speakers. Everyone started to look at a slightly embarrassed Will Grigg, who had a Spireites scarf draped around him, before he too was handed a champions top. As the chorus kicked in, Grigg gave it some welly and the whole room started to bounce.

Webb and Dave O'Hare peered through the crowd of bodies. Mandeville got his phone out. It was a good job he did, because he wouldn't remember a thing! Roberts beamed from ear to ear as he clapped his hands above his head. He was loving every second. Colclough, bottle of beer in hand, came dancing into the room with *Just Can't Get Enough* by Depeche Mode next on the playlist. King and Oldaker started a dance-off and the roof came off once again.

At one point, Mandeville started to throw some darts at a board and Dobra danced around while draped in an Albania flag. The Kirks entered and shook the hands of the players as Chadwick walked in with two big boxes of beers stacked on top of each other. Chants of "Super Harry Tyrer in goal" echoed to the tune of Status Quo's *Rockin' All Over The World*. What a time to be alive.

Drink it in, boys.

Up in the press box, someone was chopping opinions. Josh Marsh, a volunteer for the club's in-house 1866 Sport radio commentary team, was fighting back his emotions as Phil Tooley asked him for thoughts. He replied: "It's hard to sum up, isn't it, Phil? It's the scenes on the pitch. It's absolutely joyous. I can't believe it. We have been here for six years; six years of pain, six years of National League suffering. We are back where we belong as a football club. It is everything that we have just been dreaming about, praying for, for so long."

Months later, Tooley remembered: "I was absolutely fine until the final whistle, that was tough. The day was almost to script. When you think back to the success of home games that have elicited that type of emotion, probably number two on the list after Boreham Wood was Luton when we avoided going down in 2004. That is the only thing that comes close to it. In between that there had not been anything to compare. There had been nothing on the outburst of emotions at home like the Boreham Wood game."

Reflecting back, Marsh said that he woke up that morning with doubts about whether Chesterfield were going to do it, that maybe the wait was going to rumble on for a few more weeks. "There was a lot of trepidation, it felt like a lot of nervous energy," he explained. "And I was certainly holding all that in. That contributed to that moment at the end because I was so pent-up with nerves and anxiety. Luckily, the players were a lot more cool, calm and clinical than I was on the day and they got the job done. That nervous energy then turned into pure elation and emotion.

"I think we were all really choked up. If you can't get carried away in a moment like that, I suppose, then when can you? It was all that raw emotion from all the stuff we have had to endure as Chesterfield fans for eight or nine years. When you go six years in the National League, you feel like you are never going to escape. Even when the points were racking up throughout the season, there was still something in the back of my mind saying: 'Surely not.'

"When Jamie Grimes scored the third it was like: 'Flipping heck, we are actually going to do this.' It was hard to believe until the referee finally blew the full-time whistle. The six years of pain and heartache just lifted straight away. There have been times in the National League when you have been doing miles and miles up and down the motorway and you question your sanity, thinking: 'Why the hell am I doing this?' But I think most of the people who were doing those miles last season were thinking: 'Why wouldn't I do this?' because they were going to see a full-blooded performance and some good football."

Further along the press box was Fisher, who was scrambling around to get some instant post-match reaction. "It was a sense of relief that they had done it," he said. "I still couldn't believe there was a month of the season still to go." After the game, Fisher and his family went to see his dad David, who had sadly suffered a stroke in late February and was still in hospital.

David had gone to his first match in the 1950s and had followed them up and down the country, including that horrible day at Forest Green Rovers in 2018. They took him a non-alcoholic beer, which he had a sip of, before they draped a Chesterfield flag over his bed and let him know that the Spireites had returned to the Football League. "I was happy that he knew that we had done it," Fisher said.

Someone else who was emotional was Dyer. He had been sitting in the dugout crying. He had been thinking about his donor. Earlier in the season, Dyer had been on his deathbed. Now he had been given a second chance by a stranger so he could enjoy days like this. He said at the time: "The family of the donor has reached out to me. I have spoken to them. They know who I am. The family asked me to kind of continue the legacy of my donor. So that was for him today as well."

Dyer, with all of his England caps and Premier League appearances, said winning the National League was his best-ever achievement. It was some statement.

Down by the tunnel, once the pitch which now resembled the Glastonbury festival had been cleared, company secretary Peter Whiteley, who had been shaking the hands of the players, had quite an emotional moment. He said: "There were several of us, John Croot included, who were on that pitch holding back tears because we knew that we had done the job. Our four-year journey had gone to the next chapter."

With the fans now back in the stands, the players waited to come back out to collect their medals and for the trophy presentation. One by one the names were read out and the noise got progressively louder. Borrell said: "It felt as if the roof would lift. The tunnel was crazy. They were all buzzing. They were all pushing and shoving and jostling and when you told them they had to go out in order, they didn't like it. They all wanted to go! I don't think I've ever seen anything like all the players on the fans' shoulders. We've seen promotions before … but I don't think I've seen it mean so much to anybody before."

Quigley zoomed out like a maniac with a scarf raised above his head and raced towards the Kop, only to forget he had not picked up his medal. That got a lot of laughs. Cook looked absolutely chuffed when he was introduced. He threw his arms in the air as the fans sang his name and he even joined in! After his time at Ipswich Town, he had wanted to enjoy being a manager again and he looked like a man who was doing just that. Ten years on from winning the League Two title at Chesterfield, he had returned to take the club back into the Football League and become the first Spireites manager to win two league titles. It was a football romance story.

"And finally, your captain, Jamie Grimes," Borrell bellowed and up went the trophy. Grimes lifted it high and proud for all to see. Chesterfield were back. That coach journey out of Wembley was forgotten. The penalties were banished. These players would be remembered forever. Pictures of them would be hung on walls behind the scenes with other promotion teams. They would be invited back to the club in years to come for anniversaries.

They all took it in turns to have their moment with the trophy as it was paraded around the pitch. Miguel Freckleton danced with it. Tyrer drank from it. Harley Curtis poured more champagne into it. Mandeville had his own bottle of champers, obviously. Naylor swapped his traditional three fist bumps in front of the Kop with three lifts of the trophy. It was magical. They had put on a show.

Cook, meanwhile, vanished early from his TV interview for a "couple of bottles of Peroni." And who could blame him? It was probably more than a few, mind. "It was just the perfect day," Mike Jones said. "It was like it was meant to be. It just felt perfect. Everything on the day went perfect. I remember being on the way in with the kids and they just thought it was done. I was like: 'We still need to win a game of football, it's not as done as you might think.' But no one was having it. No one was losing that game. We weren't getting beat that day. Everyone had an unbelievable time and it made up for Wembley and all that heartache."

Grimes added: "It is the proudest moment of my career by a long way and it will stay in my mind for a long time. I will be telling my grandkids about that day. We were never going to lose that day. Everyone was on it. It was a great day for everyone."

Will Grigg missed out on playing in the game because of a hamstring he suffered on the bog of a pitch at Halifax, so he watched on from the stands. "It was an incredible day," he explained. "It was absolutely gutting for myself not to be on that pitch but on the flip side it was quite nice to have a different perspective. On the pitch it is hard to take it all in because you are concentrating on the game, so you don't necessarily see the surroundings or the atmosphere. I felt really proud to be a part of it. It is something I will never forget."

20

#WHERESMANDY

I t had started to die down in the SBK Spires Restaurant. Last orders had been called. It was only about 8pm. Most people had departed for town or gone back to their local, it seemed. No one had gone home, that was for sure. But across the corridor over in the 1866 Lounge, the party of the decade was in full swing. "You want to get yourselves in there," people kept saying. So they did. It was the place to be.

The door swung open and Harry Tyrer and Joe Quigley were standing on the bar and the whole room was bouncing to *Freed From Desire*. There were arms and legs everywhere. It was absolutely nuts. You didn't know where to look. There was a lot going on. If you could have bottled the atmosphere for future times, you'd never feel sad again. It was the happiest room in the world. It was like Christmas Day when you were a kid. Everyone was just laughing, joking, dancing and singing.

England were playing Brazil in a friendly at Wembley and it was on the TV in the background, but nobody was taking much notice. It was a free bar and everyone was much more interested in that. Like all parties, different people approached it in different ways. You've got the ones who sit in the corner with their family and have a laugh and a joke and steadily get merry. That was Danny Webb.

You've got the ones who are really chilled, relaxed and take it at their own pace. Like Tyrone Williams. And then you've got people who are dancing on a chair while wearing a bucket hat and drinking spirits as the play button is hit on Will Grigg's song once again. Hello, James Berry. "That is why people have to look after me," Berry, whose idol outside of football is Liam Gallagher, laughed. "I know it was a team effort but that was for me as well. Three years ago I was going to jack it in and then three years later after triple promotions, I am back in League Two. I just thought: 'I am going to have a really good time here.' That is just me.

When there is a really special occasion, I like to have a bit of a party and a dance. Everyone still mentions what I was like that day but I just had a good time and enjoyed myself."

As said tune burst into life, Tyrer was at the bar draped in a promotion flag. Quigley had a scarf around his neck while holding two drinks. Ryan Colclough, medal around neck, was chatting to Tom Naylor, while Luke Chadwick was singing his heart out. Meanwhile Grigg, perhaps not as well-oiled as some of the others, was once again looking a bit embarrassed. Almost pretending that he hadn't heard it. But he couldn't really ignore it when he had Liam Mandeville, Ryan Boot, academy players George Wilkinson and Archie White, sports scientist Jordan Hardy and analyst Jack Stephenson surrounding him in a circle while bouncing up and down.

Grigg laughed: "It is a little bit strange. When it stops getting sung, that is when I will be gutted! I genuinely don't like the attention. I don't like everyone looking at me, it makes me feel slightly uncomfortable. I like to go under the radar. I have never enjoyed the limelight — but don't worry, I had a great time!"

This was his sixth promotion, five of them from League One. Despite his sixth being from the National League, he still holds it in very high regard. Reflecting back, he said: "At the moment it feels like my favourite one. Maybe I didn't appreciate my early career at the time and maybe I was caught up in the bubble, rather than taking a step back and really appreciating how amazing it was and how lucky I have been as a player. To be part of the team that has got Chesterfield back to the EFL is a really special feeling."

Out of nowhere, Jamie Grimes appeared, pint of Madri in hand, wearing a smile as wide as the Thames, before throwing his arms up in the air. Normally quite a serious character, it was unusual, but great to see him enjoying himself. "I don't go out that often — so when you win the league, you have got an excuse haven't you?" Grimes laughed. "It was good because my friends had planned to come on that day for a while. They thought we would have won the league by then so it turned out nice for them. They were on the pitch! It was great to have so many people there. Everyone at the club was in that room and it was a release of all that pressure and all that expectation. To finally get it done was an amazing feeling."

Berry had now got the trophy tucked under his arm. He was taking great care of it. Almost like a little brother. He even gave it a kiss at one point. Williams walked by and had a little chuckle. The silverware was passed around and Mandeville, Armando Dobra, Ollie Banks, Quigley and Harley Curtis had their picture with it. Quigley was still clutching his two bottles of beer. Paddy Byrne was loosening up, Tyrer now had a scarf tied around his head and Kieron Dyer was grinning from ear to ear.

Sweet Caroline came on and Quigley gave it some oomph, as did Branden Horton and Darren Oldaker. Good times never felt so good. You just wished it could go on forever. It was like being in a room of people who had just found out that they had won the lottery. Club media volunteer Josh Marsh was one of the lucky ones to witness it with his own eyes.

He said: "What was so special was that you really saw them as human beings, with families and friends, celebrating their amazing achievement. I can't imagine the hard work and sacrifice it must take to even get into professional football. But to win a promotion as well, I can only imagine the emotion that must have been feeling. To see them as a bunch of lads, a bunch of mates, celebrating together was really, really special. Those are moments that I will cherish forever.

"With Paul Cook you can see it is not just about recruiting good footballers, it is about recruiting good people who are going to fit in with that group. You have seen squads before where they are a bit cliquey, they will hang around with their little group and keep themselves to themselves. But not this group. You can see they are all one and that's what makes it so special. I think it is that team spirit that got them over the line in a lot of games last season."

Fellow volunteer Phil Tooley also had the same impression. "It was incredible," he said. "You could just see from the players and the backroom staff that they were as one. They were celebrating something that they had done together and Paul Cook is very much of the opinion that everyone has an equal part to play."

Later that night, there was a queue forming outside Armisteads on Corporation Street in town. Word had got out that that was where the afterparty was taking place. It was one in, one out. And when you were in, there was no way you were going to leave. To be fair, even if you couldn't get in, you would still have had a belting time. With fans gathering outside but unable to enter, the players kept popping out with the trophy so people could have their photo taken with it.

Had you been in the queue to get in, you would also have witnessed something rather incredible. Something really memorable. It would have left you speechless. Something you would talk about for years to come. For you would have seen Mandeville — Chesterfield's number seven, the Spireites' set-piece specialist, the Blues' makeshift right-back — grab a traffic cone and use it as microphone to sing: "Champions elect, olé olé." It was like a scene out of *the Inbetweeners*. It was student behaviour. It was fantastic. "It was hard going actually, to keep that up," Mandeville laughed, as he reflected on his long weekend on the lash. "It was a slog. It was unbelievable. It needed to be done. Especially for myself, after all the tough years, it was just a big release for me."

As the evening progressed, there was concern for the safety of the trophy. Chief executive John Croot asked football secretary Chantelle Young to go down to Armisteads and rescue it. She came back with it and locked it in Croot's office. It had been put to bed for an early night until it was awoken by a burglar. The thief was a slightly tipsy Ashley Kirk, who decided that the trophy needed a few more hours on the ale. He fetched it and bundled it into the back of his wife Helen's car. Off to town they went, with three other randomers who had "dived in" for a free lift.

"She drove us down there, we all jumped out," Kirk remembered. "I was in the boot, there were people queuing to get in because the players were in and there were stewards everywhere. I pulled out the trophy, everything parted like the Red Sea and I ran in with it. The next day I got such a b********* from my wife because I'd left all the car doors open, boot included and just ran in. I was in the doghouse!"

The next morning, Ashley had breakfast with the trophy. "There were moments of panic where I thought John was right and I shouldn't have taken it down," he laughed, "but there you go!"

The celebrations just went on and on. You wanted someone to press pause and for time to stand still. You had to make the most of it. As night turned into morning and light broke through the clouds, King pulled his phone out of his pocket and opened the Twitter app. At 5.49am, as the milkman did his rounds and the paperboy got on his bike, King, who had not slept, posted: "Who's still out?" with the eyes and laughing face emojis.

At 6.33am, he tweeted again: "Wetherspoons 7am, who's up for it?" with a laughing face and beer emoji. People thought he was joking. He wasn't. They were back on it again. Reflecting back in the summer, he said: "Me and a few of the other lads stayed up drinking. We tried to get into Wetherspoons at 7am in the morning but they wouldn't serve us any ale.

"So we had to go down to the local garage to get some drinks until we could go back to Wetherspoons at 9am. They are memories for life. They are great moments that we will never forget. Hopefully in 25 years or whatever it might be and we have a little reunion to celebrate promotion back to the Football League, it will be great to speak about all these things and we will have a right laugh."

Later that day, Cook paid for everyone to go down to the Barrel Inn pub on Chatsworth Road and it's fair to say there were some sad and sorry faces. On the CCTV in the bar, the footage was flicking from room to room and apparently at one point an extremely tired Quigley appeared on screen, trying to take a nap on a pool table! "Memories to last a lifetime," Mike Jones said. "You would do anything to go back and live it all again. Incredible times."

"It was an unbelievable weekend," Banks added.

Throughout the weekend, King had been uploading pictures of him and Mandeville on social media. While King looked surprisingly fresh, Mandeville looked like he had just been dug up. As Sunday evening approached, with fans keen to see what state Mandeville was in, #WheresMandy started to trend on Twitter. It was probably the greatest hashtag of all time. People with no Chesterfield connection were left baffled at who it was and what it meant.

And then he appeared. Looking like someone who had been dragged backwards through a bush. Twice. Mandeville had not been at home. He had had 20 minutes of sleep. He still had his tracksuit on, his furry chest poking through it, with a pair of black sunglasses clinging on for dear life on the top of his head. No matter what else he would achieve in a Chesterfield shirt, he had earned legendary status.

Speaking about it later, Mandeville laughed: "Being all over Twitter wasn't ideal. Kingy was keeping me up to date with everything that was going on and I was aware that he was the instigator in most of it. So that is definitely something I need to take up with him, actually! I think I would like to say that I was out the longest in total hours. It was a good 24-36 hour stint with a 20-minute sleep. So it was a good go."

Remember that night out in Chesterfield the players had after losing Wembley? Well, they never forgot the kind reception they got and they made sure they repaid the faith people had in them. "When we lost in the final there was no 'Us and them,'" King explained. "And then when we won the league there was no 'us and them' either. Everyone was together. We were all in one big group. We all had a drink together and had pictures together. Everyone was smiling and happy. There are pictures with people you don't even remember getting taken. You see them the next day on Twitter and you are like: 'Great, this is what it is all about.' We had worked so hard and that was the reward at the end."

Reflecting back, Phil Kirk said: "It was a slightly crazy 48 hours. What touches me most is that I am a Chesterfield man, I am a Chesterfield boy and to see the pleasure on people's faces — young and old — is in some ways a relief but actually joy. To have the honour of being able to walk around town or even in shops and pubs and have people thank me and my brother … that has been tremendous. That has been so, so nice and I am very proud of it."

21

FAREWELL TOUR

It was strange. Very strange. Nobody knew what to do. No one had been in this position before. Nobody had experienced winning a title this early in March. There were still five games still to play, but first place had been secured, the trophy had been lifted and the hangovers from all the partying had come and gone. Chesterfield had the silverware in the cabinet but yet other teams were still scrambling around to sign players to rescue their season. It was all very odd.

What probably didn't help was that four of the last five opponents all had something to play for and three out of the five games were away from home. York City, Kidderminster Harriers and Wealdstone were all fighting for their lives down at the bottom and Gateshead had play-off ambitions. Only last day visitors Maidenhead United had nothing to play for but, with Chesterfield only having beaten them once in 10 attempts, they were never going to be pushovers either.

Once the town had been drunk dry, meetings were held and the Spireites set themselves a couple of targets. One was to finish the season unbeaten at home. With only Kidderminster and Maidenhead to come to the SMH, that seemed realistic. And the other was to reach 100 points. The title-clinching victory had put them on 95 and again, that was very achievable. However, Chesterfield now had a target on their back. They were the champions. And everyone wanted to beat them before they departed for the Football League. They wanted to take their scalp. They wanted the bragging rights of being able to say that they had knocked the champs off their perch.

Metaphorically, the Spireites were on the beach. They had gone through the departure lounge and were on their way to League Two. They had checked out. Some ex-pros said that it was totally natural. It didn't matter whether you were Chesterfield, Manchester City or Real

Madrid; if you've won the league with a month to go, it was natural to ease off the accelerator. So while other teams were playing out of their skin against them, playing the game of their lives, finding those extra percentages, the Blues had done their job.

It wasn't that they weren't trying. If that had been the case then they would have got spanked heavily. But their levels had just dropped slightly and, with other sides raising their game, it meant that results swung the other way. For some fans it was disappointing, but most didn't care. They understood it was mission accomplished. After six years in the National League, if someone had offered you the title by March but four straight defeats afterwards, you would have snapped their hand off. Plus, in years to come, nobody would remember those losses. But they would remember the thrilling football that came before it and the trophy being lifted into the air.

"It was really difficult," Ollie Banks said when reflecting back on that period. "The gaffer was probably harsher and tougher on us after we had won the league than he was before. I think he just wanted to keep driving standards and he didn't want us to let ourselves down. It was always going to be difficult after we had put so much into it physically and mentally. Once it is done it is like a sigh of relief. It was also going to be difficult to maintain those standards once the season was done."

Funnily enough, Liam Mandeville had been in a similar position before when he was at Doncaster Rovers. They won promotion from League Two in the first week of April and only needed eight more points to win the title. But they ended up taking their foot off the gas and eventually finished third. And who won the title that year? Paul Cook's Portsmouth, who were top of the table for just 32 minutes in the whole season. They pinched the crown on the final day after hammering Cheltenham Town 6-1.

Backing up Banks' point, Mandeville explained: "After we had won the league was the angriest I had seen the gaffer. It was the most on it that he was. It was a very weird period. We were still training and doing everything that we had been doing for all the other games." Danny Webb added: "The preparations didn't change at all, but there was an understanding that the mindset might change, with maybe a few less butterflies in your tummy. I can only speak for myself but I certainly felt a little bit less nervous because the mission had been accomplished."

On Good Friday, 2,100 Spireites made their way up to York to see the champions in action for the first time since they got over the line. Given the number of pints that were knocked back the previous week, many had joked that the team would be made up of those who were the most sober! And funnily enough, the players were put through a pre-season-like week to get them up to speed again. But that also meant their legs were quite heavy.

You couldn't throw the "they didn't turn up" criticism at them for this one, but they did fall to a 2-1 defeat. Joe Quigley bagged the opener after just six minutes and they could have been out of sight by half-time. Quigley should have done better with a close-range header, James Berry had two one-on-ones, the first of which should have been a penalty for a blatant handball, and Armando Dobra went close.

But in the second half they conceded two soft goals, which were copy and paste from throughout the whole season, and they couldn't find an equaliser to despite controlling the last 20. Cook was angry in the dressing room afterwards, expressing how important it was that they maintain their high standards. He didn't like losing matches, whether they were champions or not.

It was a big win for York and it was celebrated wildly by their fans, as it helped them avoid the drop. Three days later, another struggling side in Kidderminster Harriers came to the SMH. Those aware of Cook and Phil Brown's apparent not-so-friendly relationship spotted that there was no mention of the opposition manager in Cook's programme notes. In the end, the Harriers, who would be relegated, deservedly won 3-1, ending Chesterfield's unbeaten home record. They had been one week shy of going a year without a loss on their own turf. It was also the first time that they had suffered back-to-back defeats in the season. The Harriers scored twice from long throws, won more duels and were tough to break down.

For the first time in the season, the Spireites had never looked like getting back into a game after going 3-1 down on the hour. And in another first of the season at the SMH, Town fans headed for the exits early. There was a 12-day break until the next game at Wealdstone and, having had a number of postponements at their Grosvenor Vale ground due to the poor weather, this was the Stones' fourth fixture in a week, which made it an ideal opportunity for well-rested Chesterfield to return to winning ways. But those who made the effort to dig out their best fancy dress costumes and head down south recall it being rather flat and more like a pre-season friendly as the Spireites slipped to a 1-0 defeat to the part-timers, who were without a permanent manager. They managed to stay up by four points after winning three of their last four.

Once again Cook had not been happy and the chance to get 100 points was drifting away. "Those three teams that we lost to were dying for survival," Mandeville explained. "It is harder than you think to play those teams at that point in the season. It was actually probably the toughest set of fixtures we could have had in the circumstances. In that league it is so close between everyone."

Having had an extended break between Kidderminster and Wealdstone, Chesterfield were forced into playing Gateshead just 48 hours later on Monday night. It should have taken place on Tuesday, but the National League requested it be brought forward by 24 hours, so that Gateshead could play Aldershot Town on Wednesday evening and ensure all teams had played an equal number of matches heading into the final weekend of the season. They needed the play-offs to start on time the following week because they had booked Wembley out for the final.

Initially, the Spireites, understandably, politely turned down the request to play two games in three days and they thought that was the end of the matter. That was until the league came back and threatened to stop them being promoted under some small print rule in their handbook about "refusing to play." They said it was important for the "integrity of the league." Oh the irony. So Chesterfield's hand was forced, even though Gateshead didn't want to play it on Monday either! It was a complete farce. Another reason to be happy to be out of the National League.

To further compound matters, Chesterfield conceded two penalties, the second of which was a shambles of a decision, with Harry Tyrer clearly getting a touch on the ball. As the teams went down the tunnel at half-time, the Spireites were told by referee Aaron Bannister that they would see it was a stonewall penalty when they watched it back. Oh dear. A penny for Mr Bannister's thoughts when he saw the replay which showed Tyrer had made a good tackle.

It impacted the result, with Gateshead winning 2-1 and meant that Town definitely could not get 100 points or a club record 13 away wins. It had been an improved performance, though and their best since being crowned champions. Victory for Gateshead secured them a play-off place, before it emerged that they could not take part because they could not meet a tenancy agreement relating to their stadium if they were promoted to the Football League.

After four consecutive Chesterfield defeats, there were a few moans and groans about how the season was ending. But the majority of people could see the bigger picture. "It was really disappointing to lose those games," Jamie Grimes said. "It wasn't through a lack of effort. We were trying so hard. We were playing against teams fighting for their lives and they had that extra gear that we couldn't quite find. All the fatigue and all the mental stress of the season had come out of us and you could see it. We didn't want it to be like that."

The farewell tour finished at home to old foes Maidenhead United, which was fitting, because Chesterfield had managed to beat them just once in 10 attempts during their non-league journey. On the final day, the players walked out to a record crowd at the SMH of 10,108 to fans holding up blue and white cards, while pyrotechnics lit up the scene.

It made for an eye-catching display and there were fireworks on the pitch, too. Town looked back to their best in the first half, with some slick football giving them a two-goal lead. But it wouldn't be a game against Maidenhead had it been a simple, routine win. So of course they scored twice in 10 minutes after the break to dampen the mood. It was a mad period that Chesterfield had had in them all season. They had conceded 65 goals on their way to winning the title. Half the league had better defensive records than them. But just as it was fitting to sign off from the National League against Maidenhead and Alan Devonshire, it was apt that the Spireites should bag a late winner to make it 3-2 — a popular scoreline from the start of the season — with Banks coming off the bench to arrow a shot into the far corner.

"The lads after were like: 'Thank god for that,'" Banks said. "Because we didn't want to go into the celebrations having drawn at home. We wanted that win and it was just nice that I was able to do that."

Those who missed the trophy presentation against Boreham Wood got another opportunity to see Grimes do the honours as the players and staff were once again presented with their medals before they made their way around the pitch with their families. It was a lot calmer than against Boreham, but it was no less beautiful.

22

POSTSCRIPT

Even the sun came out for Chesterfield. It had been a miserable 2024 weather-wise, but even the climate was in the Spireites' favour on the day they headed to the town hall to parade the trophy in front of their adoring fans.

Making their way onto the open top bus ready to depart the SMH Group Stadium, the players slapped the hands of supporters, who had given them a guard of honour. Once on board, Paul Cook gave them a wave and said "thank you" as they sang his name, while Danny Webb — looking like a member of the Liverpool FA Cup final squad back in 1996 in his bright white suit jacket — raised his bottle of Peroni in the air.

As they slowly passed the Crown and Anchor pub on Sheffield Road, which was decorated in blue and white balloons and ribbons, Webb recognised a few familiar faces, while Liam Mandeville filmed the scenes and shouted to those below. Further down the road, a bunch of young lads, phones in hand, got a glimpse of Will Grigg and started to bounce around while singing his song. As the bus turned the corner, opening up a tremendous view of the 7,000 estimated crowd waiting for them, Joe Quigley lifted the trophy into the air.

People young and old were there. Some had seen it all before. Others had only just started supporting. It hadn't always been like this. And it wouldn't always be like this. But what a moment it was. Scarves were held above heads, flags were waved, applause was exchanged. As the bus came to a halt, it was Mandeville's turn to hoist the silverware above his head as the players made their way into the town hall building.

Once inside, the players and staff could not believe how many people had come out to see them lift the trophy for a third time. Yes, a third time. The huge turnout could have been expected had this been the first opportunity for the fans to celebrate promotion, but many had already seen Jamie Grimes grip the handles twice before against Boreham Wood and then Maidenhead United. The massive numbers just showed that no one was ever going to get bored of seeing that sight.

As more and more people gathered, every now and again someone would appear on the balcony and an enormous cheer would go up. Webb tiptoed outside and was stunned by the masses below him. Cook's appearance obviously got the biggest reaction, with a chorus of "Paul Cook's Barmy Army" sparked up. The players, meanwhile, could be seen peering out of the windows with their camera phones. When they were spotted, supporters pointed and chanted their names. On the ground, the anticipation was building, with youths jumping up and down and blue smoke bombs being let off.

"That was surreal," Mandeville said. "I could not believe how many people were there. It was incredible. I can't lie, when they said we were doing an open top bus parade, I wasn't sold on the idea. We are not a city, we don't have 60,000 fans. So I was thinking it could be a ghost town. And then when we got to the town hall, I could not believe how many people were there.

"The support in the last couple of years has been indescribable, really. When we were getting a few thousand it felt like non-league football. Now it feels like we are playing proper football. Everything about the club now is Football League — the fans, training ground, it is back to being a proper club."

Inside, Phil Tooley had the tough challenge of keeping people listening online on 1866 Sport interested and did so by interviewing pretty much everyone in the town. "That was probably the most bizarre hour and a half or so of broadcasting that I have ever done in my life," Tooley laughed. "It was lovely. I really, really enjoyed it. The players were relaxed and were milking it on the balcony. And quite rightly so. All you could see was blue and white. The whole community feel with the club has changed the landscape. You have now got kids dragging dads along as opposed to dads dragging kids along and that is the most crucial thing that has happened in the last two or three years."

Announcer Howard Borrell, up on the balcony, did a fantastic job of keeping everyone informed of what was happening and he was loving every second of being part of such a day, as he blasted out the names of the players with such gusto while wearing a smile of the happiest man in the world. "The town hall civic reception was a very different affair," he said. "More like a theatre afterparty. The players looked and felt relaxed, club officials were able to chat and nibble knowing that they were surrounded by people thrilled at the club's achievement. Being back in the Football League is not just what the club and the fans wanted, it's what the whole town wanted. It brings prestige and status to a town in a way that nothing else can.

"The fans turned up in their thousands and the weather couldn't have been kinder. Every name I read out was greeted loudly but that level was doubled when Paul Cook arrived on the balcony. The entire squad and management spent time freely with the fans, who had waited patiently for their heroes. It was a joyous occasion that perfectly rounded off the celebrations."

Harry Tyrer, with his sunglasses propped on the top of his head, gave it some welly as he was introduced. Tom Naylor was in good spirits as he raised his beer and both arms up to the sky, but the biggest laugh of all came when Will Grigg and Joe Quigley pretended to share a kiss as if it was a Royal wedding. Cook came out with his collar up like Eric Cantona, while Webb hung over the balcony and yelled like a man who had been waiting for that moment for a long, long time.

The players huddled together at the front of the balcony with their arms out in front of them, Quigley captured every moment with a selfie stick and up went the trophy once again as *We Are the Champions* blared out. Memories to last a lifetime.

"It was incredible, the amount of people that came out," Grimes said. "Having been at the club for a while, I knew how much it meant to everyone in the town. If you are from Chesterfield, then you support Chesterfield and you are very passionate about football. That is what makes it such a good club to play for. To lift the trophy at the town hall in front of that many people is something I never thought I would experience. It was amazing. It is a memory I will hold close to my heart for the rest of my life. That is why I came to the club in the first place — I wanted to win something."

Afterwards, the squad and coaches went downstairs and spent time having pictures with fans and signing autographs. They were such precious moments. On the steps, Naylor gave the crowd what they wanted

— three fist bumps, all without spilling a drop. Armando Dobra high-fived everyone on the front row and Cook did his best to get in as many selfies as possible.

It was a day to remember. It was a day that said Chesterfield were back. Not just on the pitch, but off it as well. It had a real community feel about it. For a lot of the squad, this was the day that made their achievement feel real. The players were genuinely shocked by it all. They didn't really know what to expect. Not many had done anything like it before. Players who have played at high levels had never got the chance to do anything like it, so this group were keen to soak it all in and not take it for granted. It was a special day and one they will never forget.

Driving away after the crowds had dispersed and the party atmosphere had died down, it made you think about the bigger picture. Chesterfield Football Club has probably never been in a better position. Of course it has played further up the football pyramid, but its potential has probably never been higher. Actually, right now, in 2024, it is probably one of the most aligned clubs in the English game. It has a clear plan and vision, with good, honest people at the heart of it.

In Cook they have a winner and a true leader. He is infectious and has a natural ability to bring everyone together. Standing on the balcony at the town hall, Cook said: "The football club means so much to the community and now and again we need each other. We should always be there for each other when times aren't so good. There will be dark days ahead and when those dark days come, make sure we stay together strong."

Cook is a builder of clubs and a proper football man. No one loves the game more than him. He is underrated as a manager, apart from by fans at the clubs he has been at. He should be operating in the Championship at a minimum. He maybe even deserves a shot at the Premier League. Who knows what his level is? Or what he is capable of achieving. Chesterfield are lucky to have him.

Behind the scenes, there are so many good people, not just those that you saw on the pitch. With Phil and Ashley Kirk, alongside the community trust, the club is in great, safe hands. They are ambitious and are not settling for League Two. So let's do this all over again very soon, yeah?

As for the players, they will go down in history as the ones who brought Chesterfield back to the Football League. They were the ones who effectively had the title sewn up by January. They were the ones who broke numerous records. They were the ones who put on a show. Nobody can take that away from them. They will go down in history. They are as humble and likeable off the pitch as they are talented on it. Some will go into coaching and management, others will go on to even greater things. Either way, if you see them around town, get them a pint.

ACKNOWLEDGEMENTS

I first approached Danny Hall, of Vertical Editions, about writing this book at Christmas 2023. Having reported on Chesterfield in the first half of the season I, like most of the fans, could see they were going to get promoted. They weren't going to chuck it away. You could smell it. You could feel it.

Nothing was going to stop them.

Writing a book was never on my bucket list but having lived and breathed everything Spireites for the last five years, it felt like a story that was definitely worth telling. One that I was really passionate about and one that I would enjoy writing, that wouldn't feel like a chore. When I first started my planning, the book was just going to be about the 2023/24 season.

That is still its main focus, but as I went along I realised there was so much more to it and that I needed to set the scene of relegation from the Football League, almost dropping down again to regional football, nearly going bust, the takeover by the community trust, the Kirk brothers, Wembley and Paul Cook returning home. There are so many more layers to this journey than just promotion.

When I think back to my childhood, I was probably always destined to be a football writer. My older brothers, Ryan and Dean, would always buy a newspaper and I would read every inch of the football pages. Then when I got my first paper round, I would read all the stories from all the different titles before posting it through the letterbox. No wonder people complained I was sometimes late!

I would like to say thanks to Danny, and to all my interviewees who were so generous with their time and opened up about things that they have never spoken about before. I must give a special mention to Paul Fisher, of *BBC Radio Sheffield*, legendary club volunteer Phil Tooley, whose interviews and niche stats came of great use and to Spireites press officer Nick Johnson for his help, too.

The biggest thanks of all must go to my soon-to-be wife, Elle, who, as I like to say, has a proper job, which allows me to mess around writing about football for a living. And to my mum, Janet, for her support, kindness and encouragement. This is my first ever attempt at writing a book, but I don't think it will be my last. Danny, I'll be in touch soon, pal.

Liam Norcliffe, 2024.

SUBSCRIBERS' ROLL OF HONOUR

Both the publisher and author would like to thank fans who pre-ordered Putting on a Show *via Vertical Editions, sealing their name in Spireites history forever more.*

Charlie Aldred
Lorraine Alton
Matt Atkins
Jackson Atkinson-Combe
Lucy Bacon
Richard Bacon
Dylan Baker-Stansfield
Ryan Baldwin
Neil Ball
Logan Bargh
Sam Barker-Sabido
Stuart Basson
Karl Bennett
Marcia Bigg
Andrew Bingham
Nicholas D Bingham
Alicia Blackham
Matthew Booth
Mick Booth
Howard Borrell
Richard Bradbury
Paul Brassington

Ian Brewerton
Kevin Brown
Lily Brownlow
Harvey Brownlow
Leah Burns
Carl Buxton
Nick Cannon
James Cannon
Paul Carline
Darryl Carpenter
Geoff Charlton
Gordon Chisnall
Dean Antony Clarke
Kimi Coleman
Jack Colledge
Adam Collins
Craig Collyer
Matt Constable
Craig Cook
Lee Cook
Lewis Cooper
Zach Cooper

Tom Coupland
Mike Cox
John Crawley
Philip Dannatt
Harrison Dawes
Paul Dean
Garry Dickinson
Ethan Dove
Dave Dove
Colin Drew
Ian Dyer
Jack Eales
David Ede
Clive Edwards
Jorge Elliott
Stephen Elvidge
Halima Essa
Ady Evans
Will Fairey
Chris Fairey
Greg Fearn
Fred Fennell

Gavin Fidler

Stephen Fidler

Duncan M Fletcher

Paul Fletcher

Noah Follon

Ken Foster

Steve Frobisher

Scott Fullwood

Paul Furniss

Lewis Gallagher

Tracey Garfitt

David Garratt

Melvin Gee

Bradley George

April Germany

Keith Gledhill

Harry Golding

Nigel Goodlad

Calum Goodwin

Carl Goucher

Matthew Gregory

Bradley Gubby

Millie Gunn

John Hadfield

Scott Halfpenny

Craig Hall

Simon Hampton

David Hardy

Sam Hardy

Ian Hardy-Knowles

John Harris

Caroline Harwood

Malcolm Hayes

Trevor Haynes

Mark Haynes

Simon Haynes

Joseph Heeley

Jack Heeley

Brian Henry

Max Hepworth

Richard Hewitt

Steve Hewitt

John Heywood

Mike Hirons

Darren Hirst

Daniel Holland

Jill Holling

Ashley Holmes

Dave Holmes

Jack Horton

Jamie Houghton

Alfie Howells

Tony Hudson

Matthew Jackson

Ray Jaggers

Andrew Jarvis

Dale Johnson

Bradley Jones

Malc Jones

John Jordan

Toby Jordan-Brown

Steven Joyce

Grace Kay

Mick Kay

John Kelcey

Mark Paul Kelly

Neil Kerry

Ian Knott

Steve Lee

Arthur Lee James

Matthew Lennon

Dave Lewis

Malcom Lilley

Chris Lindley

Jack Lindley

Conor Loftus

Demetri Loizou

Richard Longmore

Stefan Marceniuk

Ricky Marceniuk

Nick Marshall

Karl Marshall

Ben Marshall

Stephen Meades

Neil Mettam

Stu Middleton

Lee Miller

Jack Mitchell

Matty Money

Joshua Moody

Jon Morris

Dexter Morrissy

Louis Morrissy

Will Mosley

Lorraine Mullins

Colin Muncie

Tom Needham
Sarah Needham
Stuart Needham
Sam Needham
Callum Needham
Rachel Needham
John Needham
Izaiah Nelson
Shaun Michael Nicholls
Chris Noble
Richard Norman
Jason Owen
Tom Oxley
Ollie Pardo
Benjamin Parkin-Smith
Chris Payne
Lawrence Peachey
Dave Pell
Chris Perkins
Hannah Perkins
Jacob Perkins
Ashley Perrins
Rob Perrins
Philip Pickering
David Pitchford
Thomas Preece
Adrian Radford
Steven Rawlinson
Andy Rhodes
Harrison Richards
Max Riggott
Colin Rimington

Alan Roby
Oliver Rodgers
Alan Roe
Chris Rosling
David Saunders
Oliver Schofield
Sara Scott
Andy Sears
Andy Shaw
Ella Brummell Sheppard
Maddie Sherlock
Susan Shipp
Mark Shipp
Andrew C Slack
Rob Slater
Michael Robert Slater
Kevin Smith
Benjamin Smith
Paul Smith
Paul Snarski
Livvi Beth Snarski
Liam South
Thomas Spencer
Dale Spragg
Adrian Stanley
Paul Stanley Stanton
June Steele
Ray Stephenson
Pete Stirling
Philip Stocks
Paul Stone
Bill Stoppard

Koichiro Suzuki
Stevie Symonds
Scott Thompson
Nick Thorneycroft
Craig Tinsley
Martin Towle
Chris Turner
Cees Visser
Rob Wager
Kevin James Wagg
David A Wall
Luke Waller
Ian Walmsley
Katie Walton
Martin Ward
Alan Watson
Andrew Watson
Peter Watts
David Robert Watts
Cameron Watts
David Watts
Gerald Watts
David Wellman-Riggs
Tom Weston
Stuart Widdowson
Ollie Wilbourn
Alan Wilkinson
Mick Wragg
John Wragg
Podge Wyatt
Ellie Yates
Steve Yorke